Engines of Truth

Engines of Truth

Producing Veracity in the Victorian Courtroom

Wendie Ellen Schneider

Yale

UNIVERSITY PRESS

New Haven & London

Published with assistance from the Kingsley Trust Association Publication
Fund established by the Scroll and Key Society of Yale College.

Published with assistance from the foundation established in memory
of Calvin Chapin of the Class of 1788, Yale College.

Yale University Press books may be purchased in quantity for educational, business,
or promotional use. For information, please e-mail sales.press@yale.edu (U.S. office)
or sales@yaleup.co.uk (U.K. office).

Set in Bulmer type by Newgen North America.
Printed in the United States of America.

Library of Congress Control Number: 2015935095
ISBN 978-0-300-12566-5 (cloth : alk. paper)

A catalogue record for this book is available from the British Library.

This paper meets the requirements of ANSI/NISO z39.48-1992 (Permanence of Paper).

10 9 8 7 6 5 4 3 2 1

For Graham B. Hovey and Frank M. Turner

Contents

Acknowledgments

THIS BOOK INITIALLY TOOK SHAPE at Yale University, where I was fortunate to attend classes at the intersection of York and Wall Streets, the literal coming together of a world-class history department and a law school unique for its critical self-awareness and intellectual vibrancy. Without that happy coincidence and the community of scholars and visitors it attracted, this project could not have happened. I am very grateful for both the legal history program at the Yale Law School and the broad-minded approach of the Yale History Department. Law and history may seem to occupy two independent intellectual universes, but at Yale the physical distance between them was less than a stone's throw, and the conceptual distance shrank markedly as a result. This book is the product of the climate of broad-based intellectual curiosity and questioning this proximity fostered.

At Yale, I benefited from the instruction of Mirjan Damaška, George Fisher, Robert W. Gordon, Laura Kalman, John Langbein, Jerry Mashaw, Reva Siegel, and James Whitman at the Law School; and Linda Colley, Geoffrey Parker, Jonathan Spence, Frank M. Turner, and David Underdown in the History Department. Rogers Smith in the Political Science Department encouraged and mentored me as a teacher of legal history to undergraduates. Bob Gordon and Frank Turner also served as the co-advisors of my dissertation research. It is an enduring regret for me that I am not able to give Frank a copy of this book. He, and Graham Hovey, who encouraged me at a very early stage to write and to think about history on a global scale, both passed away before this book's publication. Each of them left a permanent mark on the text that follows, which is therefore dedicated to their memory.

One of the wonderful things about studying legal history at Yale was the cohort of students interested in that topic during my time there. We truly learned as much from each other as from our readings. There were many fine scholars, both in the joint program in law and history and also among my colleagues on the *Yale Law Journal* and the *Yale Journal of Law & the Humanities.* Late-night conversations with my fellow students, as we struggled to pin down references and citations, shaped the intellectual foundations of this book.

Financially, the research for this book was made possible by awards from the Truman Foundation, the Mellon Foundation, the Yale Graduate School, and a travel grant from Iowa State University. The law firm of Debevoise & Plimpton also supported my research indirectly, as did the Yale Law School's COAP repayment program. At the University of Iowa, I benefited from the research help of a number of wonderful student assistants and library employees.

Research on this topic would not have been possible without the superb collections and knowledgeable staff of the India Office Collection at the British Library, the British Library Newspapers at Colindale, and the Public Records Office materials held at the National Archives in Kew. I am also indebted to the marvelous collections of historical legal materials at the Yale Law School library, the University of Iowa Law School library, and the Institute of Advanced Legal Studies in London.

I am grateful to the editors and readers at the Yale University Press who have provided helpful suggestions over the course of the development of this manuscript. Chris Rogers, Erica Hanson, and Dan Heaton have been remarkably supportive of my work over this book's long development, and Jessie Dolch was a very effective copy editor.

Ultimately, however, family and an array of furry creatures have spent the most time with this book project. Mocha the rabbit and dogs Suley, Dervish, and Djinn have contributed nothing to the content of this book but have provided ample distraction and occasional note-stealing services. John Monroe, my husband and partner in crime, has been there through the thick and thin of this project. His assistance has been invaluable, and his ability to remain interested in the follies of an array of nineteenth-century characters has kept this endeavor going. I cannot overstate my debt of gratitude to him.

Engines of Truth

Introduction

CHARLES ALLEN WAS UNLUCKY. In 1850, he testified for a friend in a case that grew out of a road accident. A brougham driven by a man named Haynes allegedly ran up against a pony-chaise and caused two pounds, eighteen shillings in damage. The owners of the chaise sued for damages, and Allen testified that in fact no collision had occurred. Rather unconvincingly, he suggested that the damage had been caused by the pony-chaise having been backed into a water tub. The County Court judge hearing the case ignored Allen's testimony, awarded damages to the plaintiffs, and committed Allen, still a teenager, on perjury charges. At Allen's trial, the prosecution argued that Allen had lied in order to prevent Haynes, apparently a friend, from losing his job. The jury convicted Allen, and, despite his youth, the judge sentenced him to seven years' transportation.[1]

Harriet Ricketts fared little better. In 1885, she petitioned for divorce from her husband, William, citing his cruelty, adultery, and desertion. Although she was successful before the Divorce Court, Harriet did not receive a divorce because her case attracted the attention of the Queen's Proctor, a Victorian official charged with discovering falsity in divorce cases. In a separate proceeding, Harriet had to defend herself against William's accusation that she had committed adultery with Silas Beasly. If petitioners for divorce had themselves committed adultery, their petitions were automatically rejected. Harriet responded that since their separation, William had repeatedly sought her out and verbally abused her at her workplace. In order to hide from him, she claimed to be married to Beasly when she gave a statement to the police about an unrelated traffic accident. Harriet denied any relationship with Beasly and contended that she used his name only because she was afraid her husband would discover her whereabouts.

Her word was not deemed sound enough to outweigh the Queen's Proctor's charges. The court denied her divorce petition, leaving her married to William.[2]

Charles's and Harriet's ill luck was a matter of bad historical timing. Had they been caught lying in court half a century earlier or later, they likely would have gone unpunished. Late eighteenth- and early nineteenth-century courts did little to prosecute perjury, even though judges regularly complained about its prevalence in their courtrooms.[3] Similarly, by the end of the nineteenth century, an indifference to perjury had returned, and prosecution of it was effectively restricted to a narrow range of cases. By 1898, the Home Office described perjury by criminal defendants as a "not very serious matter."[4] But courts in the mid-nineteenth century approached the question of truth-telling with unprecedented seriousness and adopted an array of innovative strategies to guarantee veracity in trials. Both Charles and Harriet had the misfortune to testify in this unusual era of experimentation.

This book explores the novel strategies for the production of truth implemented in law courts during this period. Mid-nineteenth-century jurists refused to content themselves with the "incoherence" of earlier trial practice, which largely sought to avoid the problem of mendacity by prohibiting those witnesses thought most likely to lie from testifying and placing those who did testify under oaths considered to bind their consciences.[5] Instead, these Victorian jurists responded to parliamentary reforms that allowed the participation of an ever-growing number of witnesses by adopting new ways of controlling the veracity of testimony.

Initially, they attempted to deal with the problem of perjury by recourse to the criminal justice system. A brief period of vigorous prosecution of suspected perjurers like Charles Allen was then followed by a retrenchment and a turn to the legal profession as the best defense against perjury. Cross-examination, initially reviled for the way in which it seemed to depend on competitive word-twisting rather than a serious concern for the truth, came to supersede perjury prosecutions as the primary means of guaranteeing witness veracity; its triumph owed much to the way in which barristers successfully redefined it as a respectable forensic technique, characterized by gentlemanly restraint and subject to professional norms. The growing confidence in cross-examination that accompanied the steady rise of the legal profession's prestige helped set the stage for the ultimate lifting of the last major testimonial restriction in the 1898 Criminal Evidence Act, which allowed criminal defendants to testify. This last step, which itself emerged from a set of complicated factors, some legislative, some more broadly social, indicates just how reconciled Victorians eventually became to the possibility of witness deceit.

Nineteenth-century innovation in this area was even more pronounced outside of the traditional common-law courts. In new judicial contexts, such as courts in the colonies or the newly created Divorce Court in London, the pursuit of truth could take extreme forms. Perjury in British India, for instance, was punished by tattooing the sentence "I am a perjurer" on the offender's forehead, a practice thought to translate the British concern with veracity into indigenous terms. And as we saw with Harriet, an inquisitorial Queen's Proctor was grafted onto the common-law system in the Divorce Court. Both of these examples are notable for the willingness they reveal among jurists to break radically with established precedent. Innovation, here, was a telling mark of anxiety in the face of relations of power—man and woman, state and subject, colonizer and colonized—fraught with contradictions and awkward conflicts between the clear principles of the law and the messy realities of particular social interactions. It is worth noting, for instance, how ambivalent even the Queen's Proctor himself felt about forcing estranged couples to stay married, and how few judges in India had the stomach to order actual perjurers tattooed, even as they professed to accept the validity of the sanction.

Given these profound contradictions and ambivalences, it perhaps comes as no surprise that many of these attempts to curb perjury failed. Their failure, however, is itself an important chapter in the history of the common-law trial. The various experiments discussed in this book marked the outer boundaries of innovation in trial practice. As such, they reveal the extent to which the modern common-law trial is a product both of the compromises Victorian reformers struck and of the lessons they learned from failed experiments. The Victorian trial, therefore, should be seen as a product of contingent institutional solutions shaped not only by the internal dynamics of the law, but also by practical exigencies and contemporary attitudes. To this end, where necessary, my analysis ranges somewhat more widely than is typical of most works of legal history, considering newspaper accounts of cases, novels, and works of psychology, among other things; my goal in doing so is to reveal the complex connections between the law and the historical context in which it was taking shape. The law during the Victorian period, as we will see in the chapters that follow, was not a separate world developing in isolation from the rest of society, but it was also not a simple reflection of broader cultural trends; instead, it was to some degree both things, often in tension with one another.

Constructing Sincerity

The Victorians, as many scholars have noted—and as Oscar Wilde satirically observed—deeply valued earnestness. Samuel Smiles, author of best-selling advice manuals such as *Self-Help* and the most famous voice of Victorian earnestness, placed sincerity at the top of the list of virtues: "loyal adherence to veracity," he wrote, was the most prominent aspect of character.[6] But this earnestness, while universally recognized as important, is nonetheless little understood by historians. More than fifty years ago, Walter Houghton noted both the centrality of earnestness to Victorian culture and the paucity of scholarly research on the topic: "The one thing . . . which every schoolboy knows about the Victorians is that they were earnest. But what is meant and why they were is less easy to say."[7] For Houghton, Victorian earnestness was primarily a product of the Evangelical movement in the Church of England, and indeed Evangelicalism provided a kind of unstated moral baseline that shaped both the arguments legal reformers made and their sense of which problems were most urgent. Outside of Evangelicalism, many other nineteenth-century thinkers came to stress the importance of earnestness and sincerity, including John Henry Newman, Thomas Arnold, and Thomas Carlyle.[8] This emphasis on earnestness was a backlash against what many of these writers saw as eighteenth-century complacency—against the frivolity and inconsequentiality of "old leisure" and against the easy assumptions of what the Evangelicals attacked as "nominal religion."[9] Sincerity had a strong moral aspect: truth was often most highly valued as a sign of good character, rather than as an end in itself.[10] This conception was particularly marked in discussions of India, which made honesty into a veritable cornerstone of British national identity, despite what we will see were quite pronounced anxieties about metropolitan truthfulness in such matters as poaching, divorce, and sexual scandal.

As this contradiction between colonial self-image and pervasive doubt indicates, Victorian attitudes toward lying were more complex than they might seem at first glance.[11] This complexity was particularly clear in the courtroom. Lying in the courts was among the least ambiguous of transgressions: it violated the state's law, the religious imperative of the oath, and cultural strictures against dishonesty. Yet even in the context of juridical deceit, Victorians found ambiguities. Although Evangelicalism provided a clear statement of the culpability of all lies, Victorians still sought a more complicated relationship with truth-telling. Determining which sorts of lies were actually criminal in nature, and which could be dismissed as expected, albeit regrettable, deceit on the part of women and non-English and lower-class individuals, was an evolving project throughout the nineteenth century. Similarly, judges and juries vacillated in their evaluations of the underlying motives prompting deceit. Both the identity of the liar and the type of lie mattered. Such qualifications became increasingly important as the Victorian entente with lying—the tacit acceptance of a wide variety of courtroom lies—expanded over the course of the century. These accommodations, however—at least when viewed from the jurist's perspective—were not signs of a willingness to accept moral ambiguity or playful, Wildean irony.[12] Instead, they were conservative in nature and tended to reinscribe social and sexual boundaries, for instance, by redefining perjury as a lower-class offense or providing respectable defendants an opportunity to defend themselves against scandalous accusations.

This book, therefore, paints a fuller picture of Victorian earnestness by shifting the focus to the social sphere of the courtroom and the legal system. Victorian earnestness, it argues, was negotiated and manufactured in the courtroom as much as it was in the catechism. Truth-telling in the courts was an active area of concern, and its boundaries were constantly disputed and redrawn. The courts participated in the nineteenth-century process of accommodating sweeping religious interdictions to the complex reality of social interaction. At the same time, the courts also provided leadership in the rhetorical condemnation of falsity in all its forms, even when the activist Evangelical beliefs underlying the condemnation had faded from public view in other contexts. Looking at the Victorian experiments with producing juridical truth, then, supplies a dual perspective: courts reflected social beliefs in their determination of the relative culpability of lies and liars while at the same time creating an internally consistent institutional backdrop for those beliefs.

The Law's Muscular Moralism

Cultural anxieties about sincerity emerged at a time when the legal system was increasingly attentive to the question of truth-telling. Several developments brought the issue of lying in the courtroom to the fore, including increased public interest in trial narratives and controversies regarding the role of defense counsel. Victorian experimentation with techniques for eliciting the truth in the courtroom therefore depended on the coincidence of a pervasive extralegal reverence for sincerity, changes in trial practice, and the law's newfound "muscular moralism." Just as muscular Christianity became a Victorian ideal, active enforcement of moral duties in the courtroom also became an important ambition for legal reformers.[13]

To understand how these factors came together, it is important to remember that the early nineteenth century saw a shift in the public face of the law, which was reflected in newspaper accounts of real trials and literary accounts of fictional ones. With the reduction of the number of hanging offenses and the movement of the site of execution out of the public eye, the public's main exposure to the legal system now came from reports of trials rather than from the spectacle of the hanging tree. Newspapers and the novel replaced the older genre of criminal broadsheets and biography.[14] At the same time, procedural changes, including the lengthening of previously lightning-fast criminal trials and increased participation by counsel, restructured the trial as a competition between multiple narratives.[15] The result of these changes was to inculcate new habits of reading for both fictional and real trial narratives. Popular accounts of real trials and the growing genre of "Newgate" novels, which centered on the trial as the climactic moment in a fictional criminal biography, invited audiences to judge the truthfulness of competing narratives.[16] Assessing credibility became both a public issue and a popular pastime.

Other changes in the law also served to heighten concern about truth in the courtroom. The 1836 Prisoners' Counsel Act allowed counsel to address the jury directly and make opening statements. This expanded role that barristers thus played triggered fears that they would abuse their role and use their command of rhetoric to deceive. Albany Fonblanque, a journalist for the radical weekly the *Examiner,* was among the most strident critics of the new law.[17] Fonblanque saw the ethics of advocacy as at best indifferent to the discovery of truth and often actively opposed to it: "we have been told, on high authority," he wrote, "that the advocate belongs, body and soul, to his client; that he is bound to make truth appear untruth, and untruth appear truth."[18] In this case, the barrister's growing role in the construction of narrative in the courtroom threatened to undermine the very cause of truth that lawmakers sought to advance, a problem it would take commentators and jurists the rest of the century to resolve — or at least to accept as unresolvable.

The mid-Victorian period also saw a dramatically increased willingness to use the courts to extend legal discipline to moral issues previously thought to be outside the scope of the law.[19] W. L. Burn first pointed to the mid-Victorian phenomenon of "increased readiness on the part of the State to apply sanctions against certain errant types of 'individual.'"[20] Martin Wiener explores one such expansion: the Victorian campaign against violence directed at women. In prosecuting wife-beaters, rapists, and murderers, Victorians used the state's power to promote and impose religiously derived ideals of self-discipline, orderliness, and nonviolence.[21] The imperial context provided additional motivation for these efforts. If the British were to justify their imperial dominion through a discourse of pacification and civilization, it behooved them to be exemplars of nonviolence at home.[22]

This judicial activity against masculine violence was part of a larger trend that Wiener has chronicled extensively. Law reform served to promote a program of moral reform.[23] In particular, it seemed to bolster notions of personal responsibility: "A crucial supposition underlying early Victorian law reform," Wiener writes, "was that the most urgent need was to make people self-governing and that the best way to do so was to hold them sternly and unblinkingly responsible for the consequences of their actions."[24] Legal prohibitions, Victorian jurists believed, should track moral distinctions precisely in order to form the public character.[25] Reformers—many of whom were motivated by religious concerns—thereby showed a surprising willingness to use state power to enforce the dictates of the conscience.

A similar optimism about the state's ability to discriminate between truth-telling and deceit, and innocent debtors and criminals, was apparent in the bankruptcy reforms of the same period.[26] Legislation in 1849 instituted a three-tiered system designed to differentiate between those who were unfortunate victims of circumstances beyond their control, those who were improvident, and those who were dishonest. Bankrupts deemed to be dishonest received third-class certificates in order to alert any future business associates to their history.[27] Markham Lester attributes this fervor for moral distinctions to the influence of Evangelicalism, noting that the 1849 act established a system by which distinctions could be made between moral and immoral businessmen. Law reformers were able to draw on Evangelical sentiment in legislation that also satisfied utilitarian goals.[28] This recourse to Evangelical ideas was combined, moreover, with an increased confidence in the fact-finding capacities of tribunals.

The attempts to bring the power of the state to bear upon false testimony described here, particularly in its early stages, reflected many of the same concerns. The influence of Evangelical ideas about the culpability of all lies—great and small—and the importance of punishment is clearly visible in these various attempts to resolve the problem of deceitful testimony. As with bankruptcy, however, mid-nineteenth-century law reformers were not content to leave the deterrence and punishment of the violation of a judicial oath to an individual's conscience; instead, they sought to enlist the state—through vigorous prosecution of perjury—in the enforcement of a moralized law. The legal innovations undertaken in India and with the Queen's Proctor in England show a similar conception of law as a means of inculcating moral norms. With the failure of these experiments, and the comparative success of cross-examination, reformers turned to other strategies, setting the stage for the emergence of present-day trial practice.

Engines of Truth

The title of this book is borrowed, with a twist, from one of the most famous phrases in American jurisprudence. Writing in 1904, Northwestern University Law School dean John Henry Wigmore declared that cross-examination was "beyond any doubt the greatest legal engine ever invented for the discovery of truth." Cross-examination was, to Wigmore's mind, even more important than trial by jury and represented Anglo-American law's "great and permanent contribution" to trial procedure.[29] It was a characteristic Wigmore declaration. William Twining notes that he was "apparently untroubled by doubt or the elusiveness of reality" and therefore "said what he had to say clearly, systematically and forcefully."[30] Wigmore's reputation as a scholar and the emphatic nature of his language contributed to its importance and longevity in U.S. law. His description of cross-examination as the "greatest legal engine" for truth continued to appear in Supreme Court analyses of cross-examination throughout the twentieth century.[31]

Wigmore's uncritical enthusiasm for cross-examination reveals the close connections between British legal thought of the nineteenth century and contemporary American evidence law. Born in 1863 and well-schooled in nineteenth-century British legal scholarship, Wigmore was affectionately referred to by colleagues as "the last mid-Victorian."[32] Trained by James Bradley Thayer at the Harvard Law School, Wigmore was familiar with English commentators on the law of evidence, including Thomas Starkie and Jeremy Bentham. In his *Treatise,* Wigmore provided extensive quotations from both Bentham and Starkie, including Starkie's 1824 description of cross-examination as "one of the principal tests which the law has devised for the ascertainment of truth."[33] Wigmore, therefore, provides a bridge between the period of this study and contemporary U.S. law as well as a parallel example of the progression from viewing cross-examination as one test among several to seeing it as "the greatest" test. The evolution from Starkie's 1824 statement to Wigmore's 1904 one also reflects a key theme of this book: the story of the burgeoning importance of cross-examination.

But this is not just a story of deepening emphasis on a single test for truth. The twist in the title—"engines" of truth rather than a single engine—represents one of this book's major points. During the Victorian era, there was a period of experimentation with a *variety* of engines for the production of truth. Cross-examination may have won out in the end, but it was not the only candidate under consideration. For Victorians, learning to live with the lie involved an evolution from religious and statist to professional solutions to the moral problem of deceit. Early and mid-Victorian reformers turned to the state to police perjury in England, while searching for a religious sanction against perjury in India; but by the end of the century, responsibility for detecting lies rested largely with the legal profession—a power that its members zealously guarded against infringements by the government in the person of the judge. Somewhat paradoxically, as we have seen, the Victorian period also saw an episode of relying on a continental-style inquisitorial judge to police perjury in the Divorce Court. In short, many "engines" were being experimented with during the nineteenth century, and various methods of managing mendacity in the courtroom helped to develop a clearer sense of the complex interaction of law and practice that shaped the Victorian legal system.

The first part of this book is devoted to experiments made to ensure or police veracity within the context of the common-law trial. Chapter 1 investigates the midcentury turn to perjury prosecutions as the main guarantor of testimonial veracity and the prosecution of perjurers over the ensuing decades, revealing how a ubiquitous offense came to be thought of as a lower-class crime and how prosecution came to be limited to offenders in a narrow range of cases. The chapter surveys perjury prosecutions in England and Wales from 1835 through 1900, using a systematic sampling of otherwise unrecorded accounts of trials in local newspapers to determine what types of lies and what types of liars were punished. It also looks at the law reformers' high hopes for perjury prosecutions and the institutional limitations that ultimately dashed those hopes, transforming perjury prosecution into a marginal phenomenon. Chapter 2 looks at the steady augmentation of the barrister's role as guarantor of accuracy. Developments in the law of evidence, shifts in power between barristers and trial judges, and the growing importance of cross-examination all contributed to this process. This chapter follows the rise of cross-examination by investigating the controversies regarding its role and nature that periodically erupted in the popular and legal presses. By the end of the century, cross-examination had assumed its contemporary place as the main protection against testimonial duplicity, a change driven in large part by the professional self-interest of the bar.

The second part of this book looks at experimentation outside the boundaries of the traditional common-law trial in two contexts in which it was thought that witnesses would inevitably lie. Chapter 3 explores the first context—the colonial courts of British India, where British administrators wrestled with their suspicions that they had no ability to discriminate between false and true testimony. Here our story backtracks chronologically to colonial practice in the early nineteenth century and continues through the aftermath of the Indian Rebellion of 1857–58 (also called the Indian Mutiny or Sepoy Mutiny). British administrators went through a variety of expedients, including tattooing on the forehead of the guilty, in a vain attempt to elicit popular indignation against lying. The extensive colonial records preserved in the India Office Library provide the source material for this chapter. Chapter 4 turns to a second context in which lying was thought to be inevitable: the new Divorce Court. Concerns about perjury regarding matters as delicate as adultery prompted the reinvention of the Queen's Proctor's role in 1860. Individuals found upon investigation to have lied, like the unfortunate Harriet Ricketts, would be denied their divorces. This chapter relies on the records kept by the Queen's Proctor's office during its first twenty-five years, revealing the ways in which cases were selected for scrutiny. It also suggests some reasons for the institution's ultimate failure, which derived both from moral scruples about the double standard in divorce law and from conflicts generated by the incompatibility of inquisitorial and common-law models.

Chapter 5 draws the two parts of the book together by looking at the passage of the Criminal Evidence Act of 1898, which allowed defendants in criminal cases to testify. The gap of nearly fifty years between its passage and that of the Evidence Amendment Act of 1851 allowing parties in civil cases to testify was, I argue, in large part a byproduct of the reform and experimentation that characterized the Victorian legal system's approach to the possibility of witness deceit. As such, it brings the process of change charted in the previous four chapters to a close. This final step in the elimination of witness exclusions marked the triumph of cross-examination as the guarantor of veracity in the courtroom, opting for a single engine of truth over multiple ones. Like the various experiments described in the preceding chapters, however, the history of the Criminal Evidence Act also provides an opportunity to investigate the intersection of social factors and legal reform. Accepting the idea that allowing defendants to testify would do something other than open a Pandora's box of rampant perjury required a set of counterexamples for reformers to find compelling. These came from a few highly publicized cases in which respectable men were accused of crimes so scandalous that the norms of gentlemanly fair play demanded the defendant be given a chance to respond—and created a situation in which legislators and legal professionals could imagine themselves in the place of those accused. The desire of respectable jurists to protect the rights of respectability, therefore, trumped the previously dominant concern that lower-status, uneducated defendants might be tricked into false self-incrimination, preparing the ground for the last major step in the elimination of the old exclusionary system of evidence.

We know much less about the Victorian trial than we do about other facets of Victorian life, a lacuna this research seeks to fill. Earlier periods, in contrast, have been more thoroughly studied. John Langbein's work has demonstrated the epochal importance of the "lawyerization" of the criminal trial, as rules of evidence and increased participation by counsel transformed the "accused speaks" trial of the seventeenth and early eighteenth centuries.[34] Allyson May, David Cairns, and Thomas Gallanis have analyzed the evolution of the barrister's role in the late eighteenth and early nineteenth centuries.[35] Christopher Allen has explored the factors underlying reforms in the law of evidence during the nineteenth century, with particular attention to the effect of ideas other than Benthamite utilitarian philosophy.[36] With the exception of Allen's work, however, most of these stories conclude in the 1830s, with the passage of the Prisoners' Counsel Act, or the 1850s, when major changes in the law of evidence in civil cases were made. The recently completed nineteenth-century volumes of *The Oxford History of the Law of England* add considerably to our understanding of the period, but the monograph literature is still less well-developed than it is for the eighteenth and early nineteenth centuries.[37]

What happened during the second half of the nineteenth century, both in the role of counsel and in the law of evidence, has not yet been comprehensively studied. This book, therefore, contributes to the history of the trial by exploring the process of restructuring and accommodation that followed these midcentury changes. Reforms driven by theory must be enacted in practice, and it is in practice that they take on their ultimate shape, under pressure not only from the internal dynamics of the law, but also from such factors as ideas about morality, assumptions about the nature of respectability, ideas of what makes a "good story," notions of civility, and so on. This story of theory meeting practice is crucial to our understanding of the development of the common-law trial, the history of the legal profession, and the history of the Victorian period as a whole.

One caveat is in order, however. Many of the historical processes described here have roots that reach back into the eighteenth century and earlier. Assessment of credibility, for example, was a topic of concern for Geoffrey Gilbert in his evidence treatise written as early as 1726.[38] Similarly, the rise of the barrister, and the consequent limitation of the judge's powers in the courtroom, dates back to at least the mid-eighteenth century. Nevertheless, a combination of factors accelerated these changes in the nineteenth century. As we have seen, the scope of potential credibility conflicts was greatly expanded by changes in the law of evidence at the same time that increased cultural sensitivity to sincerity made the problem appear more critical. Barristers, likewise, continued to see their courtroom roles evolve during the 1860s and beyond, as jurists and the public wrestled with the question of the proper scope of cross-examination. While many elements of the modern trial were already in place by the early nineteenth century, then, the succeeding decades were a time of adaptation and continued change that played an important role both in determining the outlines of the common-law trial and in the history of the legal profession.

Legal history has been slow to adopt trends within the broader historical community. The story of experimentation with truth that I tell here attempts to remedy this isolation by relating the history of the trial both to British colonial history and to metropolitan Victorian culture. Historians of modern Britain have increasingly recognized the "imperative of placing colony and metropole in one analytic frame,"[39] but legal historians have only just begun the process of drawing connections between British experiences abroad and changes at home.[40] By including the use of the rhetoric of empire at home and the experience of British courts in India, this book attempts to relate the two histories and point out previously unsuspected connections. Similarly, it seeks to expand the cultural context for changes of the common-law trial beyond the customary references to utilitarian philosophy.[41] I argue that the nineteenth-century changes in the common-law trial need to be understood within the context of evangelically inflected and largely middle-class ideas about the importance of sincerity and accountability. The evolution of the trial both reinforced and drew upon contemporary beliefs and practices. Law does not exist in a vacuum, however much jurists may sometimes wish the contrary. A full historical understanding of the modern trial must acknowledge its embeddedness in a larger social, cultural, and political context and the complex, sometime elusive ways that external forces shape the seemingly hermetic world of the law.

PART ONE

From Crime to Cross-examination

CHAPTER ONE

The Rise and Fall of Perjury Prosecutions

AS RECENTLY AS 160 YEARS AGO, most common-law trials were conducted without the benefit of testimony from those who were most likely to know the facts of the matter: the parties, their spouses, and all witnesses who had any pecuniary interest in the question, no matter how slight. Fear of perjury had provided one of the principal rationales for this system of disqualification; it was not only thought to protect excluded witnesses by denying them the opportunity to commit perjury—considered both a temporal crime and a spiritual sin—but also to guard the legal system against testimony considered most likely to be false. The abolition of these disqualifications began in England and Wales in the 1840s and 1850s, and contemporaries saw the change as nothing short of revolutionary.[1] Like most revolutions, however, the practical consequences of this one were unexpected. This chapter explores these consequences by describing the ways in which the English legal system attempted to guard against deceit in the courtroom after the reforms.

During the course of debate, reformers had supported prosecution of perjurers as an alternative to disqualification, and after the 1851 Evidence Amendment Act allowing parties to testify in civil cases passed, this suggestion began to affect trial practice.[2] As this chapter shows with a systematic sampling of perjury cases in civil courts between 1835 and 1900, the number of prosecutions rose dramatically at midcentury, so much so that judges worried whether perjury prosecutions would become the inevitable sequel to virtually every trial. Where prosecutions had formerly been extremely infrequent, they were now a regular feature of assizes throughout England and Wales. This surge was part of a search for alternative means of regulating witnesses in the absence of a system of disqualification.

Perjury's prominence was fairly short-lived. By the 1870s, perjury prosecutions had leveled off overall and had declined in civil cases. The pages that follow chart this rise and fall, tracing the crime's curious progress from fulcrum of anxieties about testimony, to viable weapon against forensic deceit, and finally to odd and infrequently employed appendix to the criminal law. I argue that perjury's return to comparative obscurity was contingent on a number of problems — including the slow development of criminal appeals, the lack of a public prosecutor, and the continued disqualification of criminal defendants. The decline of perjury also depended on the development of norms of prosecution that increasingly restricted perjury cases to a narrow range of offenses involving primarily lower-class defendants. By the end of the century, these norms had become so entrenched that even dramatic changes, such as the creation of a public prosecutor or the admission of sworn testimony from criminal defendants, did little to alter the increasingly marginal role of perjury prosecutions.

Perjury has often been neglected in the scholarly literature, but its history can provide a critical perspective on the dynamics of the modern trial.[3] Understanding what happened to the use of perjury prosecutions as a regular method for enforcing truthfulness, for example, can help account for the current importance accorded to cross-examination. As we will see in the course of this chapter, cross-examination's predominance was not always unrivaled. At the time of the reforms abolishing disqualification for interest, perjury prosecutions and cross-examination were both presented as guarantors of veracity. Cross-examination, as chapter 2 investigates in more detail, steadily grew in significance as perjury prosecutions became increasingly marginal. In addition to setting the stage for the next chapter, the nineteenth-century history of perjury also allows us to see how this offense came to assume such a peculiar place in Anglo-American criminal jurisprudence: often thought to be prevalent, it is nonetheless rarely prosecuted. The pages that follow show that selective prosecution of perjury cases is by no means a new phenomenon. Measures to encourage more systematic punishment of offenders have long been met with suspicion by both bench and bar, for reasons that these failed nineteenth-century attempts to use perjury prosecutions as a lie detector help us understand more clearly.

Perjury and the Reform of the Law of Evidence

In the early nineteenth century, there was wide-ranging support for reforms of the law of evidence that would remove the traditional disqualifications. The most radical program for evidence reform was set out by Jeremy Bentham in *Rationale of Judicial Evidence.* Bentham opposed all exclusionary rules and sought an inclusionary system of "natural procedure," in which all evidence would be admitted, subject to examination and commonsense evaluation. At the same time, he remained acutely aware of the need to ensure veracity in the courtroom. Using the terminology developed throughout his jurisprudence, he argued that the sanctions which prevented perjury included the physical sanction (lying produced a revulsion that was a physical pain), the moral or popular sanction (social disapprobation of lying and liars), the political or legal sanction (criminal punishments), and the religious sanction (the oath). For Bentham, none of these sanctions was currently effective. He listed a series of sanctions that could be used, including the oath or other form of ceremony, infamy, interrogation, orality, notation (recording), publicity, counterevidence, and investigation. But in his view, "At the head of the factitious securities for the trustworthiness of testimony, punishment, punishment by appointment of law, must stand without dispute." The criminal sanction, however, needed to be recast in order to be made effective. To begin with, Bentham insisted that perjury should be renamed mendacity, to reflect its independence from the oath. He also suggested a set of principles: first, that punishment should be applied in proportion to the extent of mischief caused by the deceit; second, that the punishment should be sufficient to achieve its ends without reliance on either popular or religious sanctions; and third, that punishment should extend to all false statements in a judicial context, including declarations and affidavits.[4]

Reform of the system of disqualification came piecemeal, however. The first two steps toward achieving Bentham's goal of dismantling the system of incompetence from interest took place in the 1840s. First, in 1843, Lord Denman's Evidence Act, which allowed nonparty interested witnesses to testify, was passed after an abortive attempt the previous year.[5]

Three years later, there was another decisive moment in the evolving Victorian rapprochement with the threat of perjury in civil trials. In 1846, after a long battle, the County Courts Act passed, establishing a system of County Courts in which parties, as well as nonparty interested witnesses, would be allowed to testify.[6] The passage of these two acts did not mean that concern about perjury had been vanquished by the mid-1840s. On the contrary, as reformers attempted to extend the reform to parties themselves, opponents began to invoke the threat of perjury more frequently. The prominence of this critique is reflected by the energy devoted to refuting it. Lord Henry Brougham, for example, began his discussion of the evidence reforms by moving straight to what he called "the main ground of the objection"—the problem of perjury.[7] Brougham went on to argue against the fear of perjury for three reasons. First, prohibiting testimony by parties merely prompted the silenced parties to suborn perjury from others—such as friends, relatives, and employees. Nonparty witnesses, for their part, would be more likely to commit perjury because of the popular idea that perjury on behalf of another was less culpable than perjury prompted by self-interest. Second, perjury by a party would be easier to detect than perjury by a nonparty witness, because a party witness would be expected to give a longer and more complete rendition of events, which would be more vulnerable to cross-examination. Third, not allowing parties to testify would necessitate testimony by a greater number of witnesses and therefore create a correspondingly greater risk of perjury: "The chances of perjury are increased with the total number of witnesses."[8] Brougham also contrasted the extreme solicitude manifested in the common-law courts with the relative indifference to perjury elsewhere in the English legal system, including Chancery suits.

To advance his case, Brougham drew on responses to a survey of the County Court judges regarding their assessment of the threat of party-witness perjury.[9] After citing statements from a number of judges who minimized the danger of perjury, Brougham summarized: "It is admitted then—it is a fact in the cause and beyond all dispute—that in the County Courts the principle has worked well; that without such evidence thousands, many hundreds of thousands, of causes could not have been tried;

that no encouragement has been given by it to perjury."[10] Brougham might charitably be said to have been acting more as an advocate than as an analyst. If one returns to the County Court judges' reports, one finds that they coupled support for ending testimonial disqualification with rueful acknowledgment of widespread perjury in the County Courts. One of the judges queried, for example, responded, "That the amount of perjury in the County Courts is very great cannot, I fear, be doubted."[11]

Brougham optimistically offered a prediction that perjury in the higher courts would be even less of a threat than in the County Courts because the parties "are more likely to be of a high station" and the judges more intimidating.[12] In the House of Commons, Attorney General Alexander Cockburn led debate in the same direction Brougham had. He stressed that excluding party testimony scarcely excluded perjury as long as unscrupulous parties suborned others to perjure themselves. He echoed Brougham's interpretation of the results from the County Court survey.[13] Interestingly, the response of members of Parliament to both Brougham and the Attorney General concentrated almost exclusively on whether to preserve an exclusion for spousal testimony, rather than the threat of perjury.[14] Once the reformers compromised by allowing for exclusion of spousal testimony, the Evidence Amendment bill quickly passed through Parliament.

One facet of the 1851 reform that legal historians have little noticed was the almost simultaneous passage of Lord Campbell's Administration of Criminal Justice Improvement Act.[15] In fact, the two bills proceeded almost in tandem through Parliament, often being debated immediately after one another. Campbell himself, although a supporter of Lord Denman's act, had reservations about allowing party testimony; the act, he argued did not provide adequate protections against deception.[16] Campbell's 1851 bill responded in part to the limitation under the Georgian Perjury Act that restricted the power to commit suspected perjurers to judges on the high courts. It also provided for a system whereby private prosecutors could be compensated for their expenses, as long as they received a certificate from a judge.[17] The bench felt this need keenly, so much so that Campbell told Parliament on its passage through the House of Lords that "the judges were so anxious to carry the measure into effect, that they had met for the purpose of taking the necessary preliminary steps."[18] In the House of Commons, the need for "rendering more easy and certain prosecutions" for perjury was attributed to the growing frequency of perjury "in part owing to the facilities of late years provided for the recovery of small debts," that is, the County Courts.[19]

Viewing the two bills together changes our interpretation of the role of the perjury argument in the 1851 reforms. Rather than discounting the risk of perjury, reformers, driven in large part by the reservations of lukewarm innovators like Campbell, emphasized strengthening provisions for enforcing perjury laws as they expanded testimony. But Campbell's act tended to be overshadowed by the dramatic extension of competency to parties. As the *Times* plaintively informed its readership shortly after the act's passage: "It is not generally known that there is an act in force called Lord Campbell's Act, under which all courts can order an indictment for perjury, including the Courts of Bankruptcy and Insolvency and County Courts. It is important that this provision should be known, now that parties and their wives can be examined in civil causes."[20] When these two acts are considered together, the reformers' project in 1851 comes to seem closer to Bentham's original conception of a reformed evidence system, encompassing both inclusion and punishment, than examination of the Evidence Amendment Act alone would suggest.

How this new system was to work in practice, however, remained to be seen. Edward Cox, a legal journalist and supporter of the reform, saluted the 1851 abolition of party-witness disqualification as "the greatest measure of law reform that has been effected in my memory."[21] Samuel Warren, a previous critic of the measure, was even more effusive: "this Act has thrown a sudden and vivid flood of light upon the whole administration of justice. . . . It is operating a silent but vast & rapid alteration and amelioration of our whole system of jurisprudence & is almost as great an Act as has ever found its way into the Statute book."[22] Amidst this celebration, however, there were also surprises. While the passage of Campbell's act indicates that the reformers foresaw more frequent prosecutions for perjury, it is unclear whether they understood just *how* much more frequent those prosecutions would be. In earlier parliamentary debates, Lord Brougham had concluded, albeit on the basis of a highly selective reading of the evidence, that no encouragement at all had been given to perjury by allowing parties to testify in County Courts. But rather than the trouble-free prospect described by Brougham, perjury was suddenly discovered on a daily basis in late 1851 and 1852. As Charles Phillips, an Irish barrister and confidante of Brougham, described the situation in a letter in late 1851:

> The evidence bill is in full activity and Newgate is becoming populous. It is becoming a *system* now where Plff & Defn are examined politely to detain them till the verdict and then immediately to *bag* one or the other, as the case may be! Scarcely a nisi prius day passes without a victim. Tom Platt brought down a plaintiff yesterday. This may be all right & in perfect good faith too—but if this is the result of so short an experience in the superior courts what are we to say to the certificates of all but one of the County Court men that in their experience the examination of the parties did not induce perjury? Martin & Erle & Platt must have been very unlucky in three weeks or the C.C. judges extremely fortunate in three years.[23]

Phillips's comments were echoed by John Singleton Copley, Lord Lyndhurst: "The Evidence Bill has now come into operation. Two indictments for perjury have been already directed by the Court, the Plaintiff is contradicted by the defendant, and the evidence of the Defendant is supported by another witness. The jury finds for the Defendant, upon this the judge orders a prosecution."[24]

Law reformers saw the enthusiasm of the judges for perjury prosecutions as another tactic for sabotaging the Evidence Act. One supporter of the act wrote in the *Law Review,* "the language of the Act being too clear and unambiguous to admit of repeal by way of construction, the next device resorted to was, to get up a reign of terror which might deter parties from having recourse to its provisions." The author tartly observed, "Judges, who had been in the habit of observing for years those flat gross contradictions

so constantly found between the testimony of witnesses apparently indifferent . . . were suddenly seized with horror and indignation when they
found the same discrepancies existing between the statements of plaintiff
and defendant." The *Law Review* author described a procedure identical
to that detailed by Phillips: judges would detain both parties until the verdict was delivered, then immediately commit the losing party for perjury.
This sudden mania for perjury prosecutions was explained by the author
as a demonstration of "how completely the Judge abandoned the discretion he ought to have exercised."[25] The enthusiasm for perjury prosecutions was not limited to high court judges, however: County Court judges
in particular also contributed to the upswing in the number of cases.

While reformers contemplated more active enforcement of the laws
against perjury, perjury prosecutions were not the sole guarantor of veracity in the new testimonial system. Where previously the oath and testimonial incompetencies were thought to protect accuracy in the judicial
process, now the burden was placed on a combination of the oath, cross-
examination, and perjury prosecutions. One way to think of the postreform
development of trial practice in the nineteenth century, therefore, is to see
it as a period when the weight allocated to each of these guarantors shifted.
The oath continued its decline; perjury prosecutions enjoyed a period of
relative prominence in the aftermath of reform and then subsided in importance. This was followed by a shift to cross-examination as the main guarantor of veracity in the courtroom, a development we explore at greater
length in the next chapter.

Increasingly, cross-examination came to dominate the reformers' arguments about safeguards against perjury. As the *Times* reported, Brougham
himself informed the House of Commons in 1858 that "he trusted so much
to the power of cross-examination by the counsel for the prosecution that
he had no fear of the march of justice being impeded by the talents of the
criminal."[26] Into the 1860s and 1870s, this idea was increasingly picked up
by barristers. Frank Safford, speaking about cross-examination, noted that
"upon it, rather than the efficiency of the ceremony of an oath, depend to
a great extent the verdict of juries."[27] By advocating cross-examination as
the main safeguard of veracity, barristers could advance their own profes-

sional interests as well, as they came to embrace cross-examination as their defining professional "art."

Before cross-examination triumphed definitively, however, perjury prosecutions struck reformers as a powerful means of enforcing veracity in the courts. We now turn to the dramatic growth in perjury prosecutions that followed the reforms of the 1840s and 1850s and suggest reasons why such prosecutions came to be relegated to a peripheral role by the late Victorian period.

Overview of Perjury Prosecutions

Parliamentary statistics reveal an initial surge, followed by a leveling off over time of the absolute number of perjury prosecutions. One of the immediate consequences of the 1851 reform was a dramatic spike in the number of perjury prosecutions and convictions in 1852, both of which tripled from two years earlier (see Figure 1).

Moreover, the 1850 figure already represented an increase from traditional levels as a consequence of the establishment of the County Courts in 1847. While still not a widely prosecuted crime, perjury had gone from being a comparative anomaly, with approximately ten to twenty convictions per year, to a regular feature of the assize docket, with each assize town likely to have at least one case yearly. There is a decline in the early 1860s, perhaps as a result of legislation adopted to make vexatious suits more difficult to bring; a slight increase in the 1870s; and a fairly steady absolute number of prosecutions for the remainder of the century.

Parliamentary statistics also reveal another significant trend. Over time, the length of incarceration assigned to convicted perjurers decreased markedly. As Figure 2 demonstrates, the maximum penalty of seven years' transportation or imprisonment was rarely employed by the end of the century, while the minimum sentence of less than three months' imprisonment, nearly unheard of during the early Victorian period, came to dominate punishment. This comports with a general trend during the late Victorian period of decreasing sentences in criminal cases. As Martin Wiener observes, after the early 1870s, "one index of a lower emotional temperature

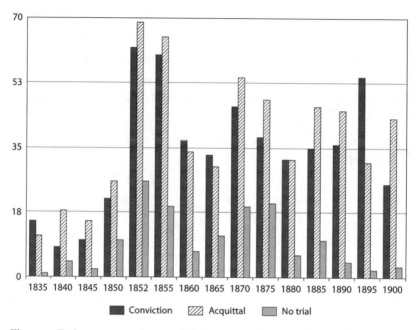

Figure 1. Perjury prosecutions and their results. Sources: House of Commons, "Number of Criminal Offenders in England and Wales," Parliamentary Papers, 1836, XLI, 11; 1841, XVIII, 255; 1846, XXXIV, 1; 1851, XLVI, 23; 1852–53, LXXXI, 1; 1856, XLIX, 1; "Judicial Statistics of England and Wales," Parliamentary Papers, 1861, LX, 477; 1866, LXVIII, 485; 1871, LXIV, 1; 1876, LXXIX, 1; 1881, XCV, 1; 1886, LXXII, 1; 1890–91, XCIII, 1; 1897, C, 1.

[regarding crime] was the gradual mitigation of sentences. The average length of sentences fell, and fines replaced many short jail sentences."[28]

These parliamentary figures have been supplemented by examination of case records—in both published law reports and local newspapers. Case records offer a sense of what types of individuals were being prosecuted, and in what sorts of underlying cases, without which it would be impossible to gauge the typicality of any case examined in detail. They also point to changing trends in prosecution over time, although they fall short of demonstrating them definitively. This chapter's conclusions are based on a systematic examination of case records of perjury prosecutions in England and Wales, sampling every fifth year from 1835 to 1900, with the addition of 1852, the year after parties were allowed to testify in civil proceedings. Because there are no official records, and few of these cases made it into the law reports, this chapter supplements the rare published law report with accounts drawn from newspapers in each assize county. Local papers were far more likely to present close-to-verbatim reports of trials and to include charges and summations by the judge, as well as popular reaction to the case.

An examination of perjury prosecutions during the prereform years, 1835–45, reveals that the earlier cases are noticeably distinct in two ways. First, perjury prosecutions arising from civil cases were very unlikely to result in a conviction. The low percentage of convictions in civil cases suggests that prosecutions may have been motivated more by revenge or a desire to use litigation to inconvenience the opposing party in civil litigation. Anecdotal evidence tends to confirm this.[29] Second, police informers and alibi conspirators were prominent among those convicted of perjury committed in criminal cases. Charles Mumford and John Brown, for example, were both convicted for their roles as informers in two separate licensing

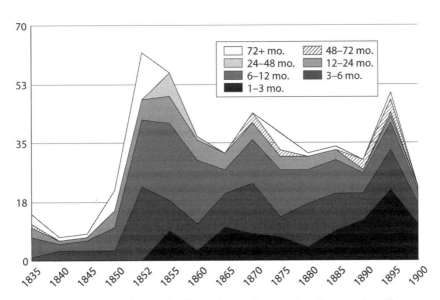

Figure 2. Decline in the length of punishment (in months). Sources: See Figure 1 caption.

cases in 1835.[30] Licensing offenses were a particular topic of suspicion because they were easily developed in order to extort money from helpless publicans. So widespread was this problem that London's victuallers banded together to bring perjury prosecutions against informers.[31] Just as informers threatened to undermine criminal justice, so too did organized attempts to evade prosecution, which were similarly singled out for conviction. Joseph Allison Sr., Joseph Allison Jr., and Hannah Ostle, for example, received sentences of seven years' transportation for their roles in orchestrating an alibi in a murder case.[32]

One rough postreform trend that can be discerned is an immediate increase in the percentage of perjury prosecutions deriving from civil cases, which subsided by the end of the 1850s. In the late 1840s, the number and composition of perjury cases began to change. The County Courts had allowed party testimony on oath beginning in 1847. The early 1850s saw a marked upswing in the total number of perjury cases. As in 1850, perjury prosecutions arising from civil cases continued to make up a significant percentage. After the mid-1850s the composition of the perjury cases shifted again, with a decline in the number of perjury prosecutions growing out of civil cases.

In the 1860s and later, a narrowing of the types of causes likely to give rise to perjury prosecutions occurred. Among the cases that continued to generate perjury prosecutions, three were particularly common: affiliation, game law, and licensing cases. Sociologists have argued that some forms of lying respond to disparities in power and constitute a type of resistance by subordinates.[33] The Victorian experience, with perjury cases increasingly restricted to a narrow range of underlying types of cases, seems to confirm this insight. These cases were among the types of Victorian legal proceedings most likely to have generated popular resentment. It is not clear, however, whether the predominance of these types of cases in generating perjury prosecutions reflects anything more than their simple numerical predominance as a percentage of all cases heard. But it would seem that judges and prosecutors were reacting to a perceived challenge to the law, manifested in "bold-faced" or brazen defiance of the court through obvious lying.

The laws of bastardy had been substantially revised under the new Poor Laws of 1834, in part to lessen the threat of false accusations.[34] As one modern scholar notes: "the [old] system was an incitement to perjury. Loose women would swear not to the real father of the child, but to the wealthiest man against whom the charge would stick."[35] The revised system, however, led to additional dissatisfaction by too tightly restricting a woman's ability to filiate a child and by denying her the child support paid by the father. Finally, in 1844, another revision passed that provided for a procedure whereby a woman could apply for an affiliation hearing before the magistrates.[36] She was required to provide some corroborative evidence of paternity; the alleged father, meanwhile, could defend himself before the magistrates on oath.[37] As the *Law Times* noted during the debate on party testimony, affiliation suits were one of the few types of actions in which the defendant could testify under oath.[38] This apparent anomaly was justified because the proceedings were officially considered civil in nature.[39] Affiliation proceedings were numerous: in 1848, the *Law Times* pointed out that there were more than thirty thousand per year.[40] By the end of the century, perjury in bastardy cases was widely noted. The *Law Times* acknowledged in 1895 that "more prosecutions for perjury arise in connection with bastardy proceedings, than out of any other class of disputes."[41]

The crime of poaching, although historians may be more familiar with the controversies surrounding it in the eighteenth century, remained an area of contention in English society well into the nineteenth.[42] Poaching constituted a significant part of the docket of rural magistrates; in Suffolk, for example, as many as one in four convictions was for offenses against the game laws. Game offenses occurred in waves: in the late 1840s and early 1850s, the late 1850s, the late 1860s, and several other periods.[43] High levels of game offense convictions tended to precede periods of agricultural unrest. With the exception of the early 1850s, however, prosecutions for perjury growing out of game law cases do not coincide with the general trends in game law convictions. This may be because perjury cases could follow up to several years after the original conviction. In general, however, the disparity is probably attributable to the small absolute number of perjury cases in comparison with the thousands of game law cases heard each

year. Nonetheless, some of these perjury cases took on a Robin Hoodesque
flavor of popular rebellion. In one case, a judge described Devon Forest as
a well-known "alibi resort."[44]

Like game law offenses, many of the perjury prosecutions growing
out of licensing laws were characterized by popular resentment against official interference.[45] Perjury cases growing out of licensing laws tended to
fall into two types. The first, as mentioned above, saw informers punished
for their roles in enforcing such laws, at times corruptly. The second type
involved defense witnesses who sought to protect publicans accused of
selling alcohol outside of the regulated hours or allowing gaming in their
establishments. Licensing cases also resembled affiliation cases in that, after 1872, the law allowed defendants to give testimony under oath. Reformers debating the extension of competency to all defendants referred to the
experience of these types of cases, noting, "it was unfortunately true that
there was a great deal of perjury, but the offence of perjury was not confined
to those who were defendants in cases under the Intoxicating Liquors Acts
and affiliation cases."[46]

This concentration on a limited range of offenses had consequences
for both the level of court generating the cases and the class status of defendants in most perjury cases. The bias toward lower courts was overwhelming. Few perjury cases came from the assizes or the high courts after 1860.
In an 1865 case, Baron Arthur Channell noted that perjury cases seemed
to come exclusively from the lower courts. Perjury, he commented while
sentencing a defendant for lying before local magistrates, "had fearfully increased in this country of late years, but it was seldom that charges for that
crime came from the higher courts."[47] This selection of cases had the effect
of distancing the judges hearing perjury cases at the assizes from those who
often referred the cases from the County Courts and petty sessions.

The focus on affiliation, poaching, and licensing questions also resulted in a pronounced correlation between class status and perjury prosecutions. Participants—prosecutors, defendants, and witnesses—in these
cases were not necessarily lower class, but in practice, middle- and upper-
class involvement was vanishingly rare. Respectable perjurers had always
been rare birds, but by the end of the century they were effectively extinct.

While it is difficult to determine the class status of criminal defendants from newspaper accounts, it is possible to identify a number of respectable defendants from either their occupation, when it was given, or from the newspaper's own description of them as "respectable" or "respectable-looking." Inevitably, this method is both overinclusive, in that it counts lower-class defendants who merely appeared respectable, and underinclusive, in that it misses respectable defendants who were not described in the newspaper accounts, as was true for many brief reports of cases in which no true bill was found or in which no one appeared for the prosecution. Even with these limitations, the paucity of respectable defendants is striking nonetheless, as is the decline in their numbers over the course of the century. Nearly 10 percent of defendants were described as "respectable" in 1852; this was the highest total of any year. In 1870 there was only one respectable defendant, and in 1895 there were none.

This de facto limitation of perjury to lower-class offenders did not reflect a desire to overlook middle- and upper-class deceit. On the contrary, one of the reasons behind this shift was the development of alternative institutions to ensure veracity without recourse to perjury prosecutions. In both bankruptcy and divorce cases, two topics of keen interest to middle- and upper-class Victorians, liars were subject to new forms of control. In bankruptcy, new laws penalized fraudulent insolvents under a simpler procedure that made conviction and punishment more certain than in perjury prosecutions.[48] In the newly created Divorce Court, meanwhile, as we will see in chapter 4, the office of the Queen's Proctor was charged with ferreting out suspected cases of collusion. When collusion was proved, however, the sanction was that the sought-after divorce was denied, and as a result, liars in the Divorce Court rarely faced perjury prosecutions.

A final pattern does not change much over time, but is striking nonetheless. While contemporaries remarked on the difficulty of obtaining convictions in perjury prosecutions, examination of the case records reveals that the most significant obstacle to conviction was not lenient juries intent on acquittals, but rather the judge himself. Directed verdicts are concealed in the parliamentary statistics, which simply count them as acquittals. Newspaper accounts, moreover, probably also undercounted directed verdicts, because reporters were likely to describe them as acquittals. But even with this limitation, the number of recorded cases of directed verdicts in the newspaper accounts is striking. In 1852, the peak year for this as for all perjury statistics, judges directed verdicts in nearly 25 percent of all cases. In some of these cases, the judge was responding to an objection raised by defense counsel, but in many of them, the judge acted to stop a case by directing a verdict before the prosecution had rested. A perjury defendant, therefore, was more likely to encounter leniency from the judge than from the jury.

Limitations on the Prosecution of Perjury

A number of different factors led Victorians to prefer the selective and infrequent prosecution of perjury under the existing law to any more easily employed and reliably enforced alternatives. Problems specific to the Victorian period prevented systematic prosecution of perjury, including incomplete reforms in other areas of the law, such as criminal appeals and testimony by defendants, and the limitations of private prosecution. Limitations such as these, in turn, encouraged judges to minimize the problem of perjury by avoiding prosecutions.

Once the fear of encouraging perjury was overcome and the reforms in the law of evidence passed, reformers were content to discount evidence that perjury had increased. John Pitt Taylor, a prominent law reformer and author of the Evidence Amendment Act of 1851, showed a typical nonchalance toward the threat of perjury in an 1861 address to the Law Amendment Society: "Some plaintiffs and defendants have of course committed perjury and possibly that crime may have increased to a slight degree; but assuming such to be the case, the evil arising from the increase cannot be regarded as very alarming, since only thirty-five persons were convicted of perjury last year; and it really sinks into insignificance when contrasted with the benefits that have resulted to the cause of truth."[49] Such statements were more than a little disingenuous, given law reformers' eagerness to avoid evidence that perjury had in fact increased. Seven years later Pitt Taylor, in his capacity as judge of the Lambeth County Court, dodged a request to commit a suspected perjurer for trial. According to the *Solicitors' Journal,* "Mr. Taylor said he was very chary of exercising that power, for he had observed that where such prosecutions had been ordered the delinquents generally escaped through the inefficiency of the prosecution in laying the evidence before a jury."[50] Pitt Taylor never publicly acknowledged the contradiction between his dismissal of the threat of perjury on the basis of conviction statistics and his pragmatic recognition as a sitting judge that such figures were artificially low because of the limitations of private prosecutions.

Explaining the reformers' behavior is fairly simple: they had bigger fish to fry. In particular, their desire to press on for the right of the criminal defendant to testify under oath gave them little motivation to explore the shortcomings of existing measures to combat perjury. By using low conviction rates in perjury cases as an indicator of the success of evidence reforms, however, the reformers effectively blinded themselves to problems in the enforcement of perjury laws. Instead of asking how the undeniably widespread deceit practiced in courts could be ameliorated, they committed themselves to a policy of denial.

Reformers sought to change both the continuing prohibition preventing criminal defendants from testifying on oath and the absence of a criminal appeals structure. Despite legislative proposals dating back to 1844, a criminal court of appeals was not created in England until 1907. Similarly, despite legislative initiatives from the 1850s on, defendants could not testify on oath until 1898.[51] Perjury prosecutions were inextricably linked to both problems and came to be eclipsed by them. Their conjunction created an opportunity to use perjury prosecutions as a crude substitute for criminal appeals.

In civil cases, perjury had long been held to be grounds for a new trial.[52] Yet in criminal cases, there was no such assumption. Nonetheless, individuals continued to pursue perjury cases in the hopes of strengthening their appeals to the Home Secretary. Prosecution for perjury was left mainly to private individuals, who often employed their power to take revenge on the other side after losing a case. The main advantage of a perjury indictment to a private prosecutor seeking revenge was that it effectively silenced the opposing party by making that party a new defendant who, under the rules of criminal evidence, was prohibited from testifying.[53] As the *Law Times* complained, recent cases "afford further illustrations of the growing practice by which the defeated party in any proceeding, whether civil or criminal, attempts to obtain a new trial under advantageous circumstances, by indicting his successful adversary for perjury."[54]

In the early 1860s, two dramatic cases made the problem abundantly clear. First, 1860 saw the lurid Hatch case. The Reverend Henry Hatch, a country vicar and part-time schoolmaster, was convicted of indecent assault after one of his pupils, an eleven-year-old girl named Eugenia Plummer, accused him of fondling her at school. Desperate to salvage his reputation, Hatch responded by prosecuting Plummer for perjury. She was then convicted herself, although immediately after her sentencing she received a pardon from Queen Victoria.[55] The Hatch case left a deep impression on peoples' thinking about perjury and testimony by criminal defendants, particularly when a respectable defendant's reputation and livelihood depended on the testimony of a young girl. Then, in an 1865 disputed will case between Jean Lafourcade and Louise Valentin (both were French nationals, but the case was heard in England because the inherited shares in question were located in London), first Lafourcade and then Valentin were charged with and convicted of perjury. The *Law Times* commented, "she has been convicted, and now we have the extraordinary spectacle of two persons convicted and punished for perjury in a transaction in which it is quite certain that both cannot be guilty."[56]

While the Lafourcade and Hatch cases were distinctive for the notoriety and the amount of attention they generated, they revealed a widespread problem. Because no court of appeals existed for criminal cases in England until the twentieth century, convicted defendants sought to demonstrate the invalidity of their convictions by other means, including prosecutions for perjury. In the absence of a formal appeal process, the temptation was strong to overturn verdicts by discrediting the testimony of prosecutors. The trial of Edward Neville in 1852, for example, demonstrated the hazards faced by prosecution witnesses. Neville, barely a teenager, had testified for the prosecution in an arson case that resulted in four men being transported. The convicts' relatives sought to lay the groundwork for a clemency request by persuading the witnesses against them to change their stories. Several of the witnesses did so, and the main prosecutor left the country, leaving Neville the sole hold-out. Neville was then prosecuted by the relatives for perjury and narrowly escaped conviction largely on the basis of his counsel's eloquence.[57]

As we will see in chapter 5, the Hatch case became a symbol of the need for a criminal appeal and the need to allow prisoners to testify on oath.[58] Yet, decades after the Hatch case, the problem still persisted. In 1881, one correspondent wrote to the *Solicitors' Journal* complaining, "It is surprising that attention has not been called to the astonishing nature of the proceedings which attend the prosecutions for perjury which so frequently follow some notorious case at the Central Criminal Court or assizes."[59] J. R. Hall went on to describe the process: "An appeal is made to the Home Secretary to review the sentence, and release a man from the horrors of perhaps undeserved slavery in penal servitude. What does the Home Secretary do? He cannot direct a new trial, and he declines to take on himself the reversal of the sentence in the conflict of evidence, but he offers, if the principal witnesses for the prosecution are convicted of perjury, to advise the Crown to grant a free pardon."[60] Not much had changed since Neville's experience nearly thirty years earlier.

The slow development of a public office responsible for overseeing prosecutions, like the delays in establishing a court of appeals, significantly affected the development of prosecutions for perjury.[61] Legislation establishing the office of a Public Prosecutor was not passed until 1879, even though a similar measure had been proposed as early as 1854. In 1884, the office of the Director of Public Prosecutions was formally put under the control of the Treasury Solicitor, which had previously been responsible for prosecuting its cases.[62] Until then, however, abuses by private prosecutors had led to the imposition of limitations on perjury prosecutions, rather than efforts for more effective prosecution.

The limitations of private prosecution led both to overenforcement of dubious cases and to underenforcement of possibly meritorious cases. As one barrister described the situation in 1855, private prosecution was responsible for a litany of evils: "escape of criminals for want of prosecution;

deliberate mismanagement of prosecutions; improper compromise and abandonment of prosecutions; the securing of prosecutions by 'low attorneys'; . . . the high cost of private prosecutions; and the failure properly to instruct grand juries."[63] Perjury prosecutions motivated by revenge or the desire to inconvenience an opponent could be added to that list. Perjury prosecutions, in particular, were also singled out by the Attorney General as too frequently settled by the parties in exchange for compensation, rather than proceeding to adjudication.[64]

Private prosecutors' ability to abuse the grand jury system was a frequent topic of complaint by judges. In Thomas Hewlett's case, at the Somersetshire Assizes in 1852, the judge complained that "this case afforded an example of the injustice which may be inflicted by means of the grand jury system."[65] Hewlett had sued a relative for recovery of a debt of six pounds in June 1851. The suit clearly arose out of a family feud; the newspaper noted that "it also appeared that the prosecutor and prisoner had been on bad terms, and that they had quarreled and fought since the [County Court] trial took place," and that the prosecutor was jealous of the prisoner.[66] Some nine months after the original trial, the prosecutor preferred a bill against the grand jury, following the fight between the two. After hearing this testimony, the judge directed the jury to acquit.[67]

Hewlett's experiences were not unusual. A large number of perjury prosecutions appear to have been motivated by spite or revenge, or even blatant extortion. As the *Law Times* put it, "Private prosecutions are, it is feared, sometimes conducted with extreme acrimony, this usually occurring in cases where the prosecution is, in fact, secretly aimed at gaining some personal object, and is not solely dictated by a desire for the attainment of public justice."[68] Some of these disputes had a bewildering complexity, with suit and countersuit and successive prosecutions for perjury. Judges occasionally argued for the dismissal of perjury cases that were clearly vindictive, or when the prosecution had been brought in order to extort money from a wealthy defendant.[69]

In response to these problems, and to a prominent case in which a solicitor was charged with perjury by a disgruntled client, Parliament passed the Vexatious Indictments Act of 1859, which applied to prosecutions for perjury, conspiracy, indecent assault, and other selected misdemeanors.[70] This act prevented presentments to the grand jury unless the accused had been committed for trial or the prosecution had been preferred with the direction of a judge of the superior courts, or if the prosecutor had been bound over to prosecute. Prosecutors willing to forgo the twenty pounds' bond put up to ensure their attendance, however, could still abuse the process. Although the act may have been limited in its ability to stop vexatious prosecutions by those who were truly determined to harass their opponents, it does reflect a suspicion on the part of the government and judges toward perjury prosecutions that would persist well past 1859.

Judges, in turn, played a crucial role in shaping the contours of perjury prosecutions. Because of their legal complexity, perjury cases were tried only at the assizes, even though they were technically considered misdemeanors. This meant that all of the judges hearing perjury cases were superior court judges from London on circuit, rather than local magistrates and justices of the peace who heard cases at quarter sessions. One consequence of this limitation is that the judges who heard perjury cases were distanced from the judges who committed perjury defendants for trial. Most perjury cases were based on testimony before County Court judges or local magistrates. Perhaps because of this distance, the judges who heard perjury cases at the assizes were often surprisingly cavalier about the prospect of convicting perjurers, despite their frequent protestations of the danger posed by perjury.

Judges had tremendous influence over most perjury proceedings. Case records frequently record the judge telling the grand jury whether he thought a true bill should be granted in a perjury case, or interrupting the testimony during a trial to ask the jury whether they had heard enough and directing an acquittal.[71] Juries also used their power to interrupt the presentation of cases, although less frequently, and would tell the judge unbidden that they had heard enough and were ready to acquit. Occasions in which the jury openly defied the judge are recorded, but they are rare.[72]

Judges at times used this power to impose ordering systems on perjury cases that had no basis in the law. In addition to expansive and highly variable use of motive and the two witness rule, judges also redefined perjury in original ways. One leading practitioner of redefinition was none other than Justice James Fitzjames Stephen. In his published writing, Stephen had taken a particularly hard line on perjury:

> Perjury is one of the few crimes for which the punishment appointed by law appears in many cases totally inadequate. It may be the instrument of the foulest kinds of murder and robbery, or the means of inflicting loss of liberty, character, and property in any degree, and yet the utmost penalty that can be inflicted is four years' penal servitude. It would not be too severe to provide that perjury, with intent to procure the conviction of any person (guilty or not) for any crime should be punishable for life. The offence, no doubt, is a rare one, but circumstances might arise in which no punishment short of death could be too severe.[73]

It comes as something of a shock, therefore, to read case after case in which Stephen cajoles and berates the jury into acquitting perjury defendants.[74] There was a method to his madness, however. Stephen wanted to reserve the criminal sanction of perjury for cases of criminal inculpation; the rest he was willing to dismiss as "hard swearing." As he told one jury, "there was considerable difference between what was called hard swearing by a partisan and deliberate perjury."[75]

Other judges attempted to introduce a similar modification in the law under the rubric of "degrees" of perjury. Justice James Hannen made such an appeal on behalf of George Drake:

> Of course the crime of perjury is one which is various in its depth—from the lowest to the highest degree. It has been my lot on one occasion to try a policeman on the charge of endeavouring to fix upon an innocent man the charge of having murdered an individual who had undoubtedly come to his death by the negligent act of the policeman. The amount of criminality in that case could hardly be exceeded; it approached in char-

acter murder itself. Probably the present case may be taken as standing very near the opposite pole. It is a case in which a man is alleged to have stated falsely that someone bearing a certain name had not been in a public-house on a certain evening.[76]

But the attempt to distinguish perjury by degrees was by no means a uniform trend. Ten years after Hannen's charge, in an era of increasing leniency, Justice Robert Lush angrily rejected the idea that different levels of culpability should play into an assessment of guilt: "The prisoner had committed perjury in order to save a friend from being punished. People seemed to think this a very light matter now-a-days, but they were very much mistaken — it was really a very serious offence against the law."[77]

Why were judges so willing to direct acquittals in perjury prosecutions? Part of the answer appears to have been the superior court judges' desire to discipline the lower courts. Judges used directed verdicts to draw attention to what they saw as flaws in lower court practice, ranging from incomprehension of the requirements of the law of perjury to inadequate documentation and incorrect courtroom conduct. In 1895, for example, Justice Alfred Wills excoriated the conduct of a County Court judge, saying, as a local paper reported, that "no policeman would have been allowed to cross-examine in that way. He [Wills] hoped the learned judge of the County Court would take what he had said in a friendly spirit, that it was wise to allow someone else to step in in such matters."[78] Judges in the County Courts, meanwhile, protested the dismissive treatment. W. T. S. Daniel, judge of the Derby County Court, blamed the higher court judges for the increase of perjury in the County Courts, saying, "the judges of the superior Courts discourage all prosecutions for perjury in the inferior Courts, and as this fact is well known, the offence can be (and often is) committed with absolute immunity."[79]

One suspects that an unacknowledged motivation was that the superior court judges did not want to be overwhelmed by perjury cases. In 1855, at the March assizes in York, Sir Cresswell Cresswell confronted six indictments for perjury. The 1852 Leicester Assizes offered five different cases of perjury from affiliation suits alone. Nor were these numbers just for the height of perjury prosecutions in the early 1850s; in 1865 there were six cases of perjury at one assize, five of which stemmed from affiliation cases.[80] For busy central court judges eager to finish their assize circuits and return to London, the temptation to deal summarily with perjury cases must have been strong.

Finally, judges could also limit systematic prosecution through their refusal to commit offenders for trial. Director of Public Prosecutions Augustus Stephenson criticized the judges for this in 1894, attributing "no small part of the evil to the omission of judges to exercise the summary power of committal which was conferred upon them in 1851."[81] The *Law Journal* earlier explained that "the real reason why the statutory procedure is not more frequently resorted to is the dislike of the judges to try cases of perjury without the assistance of the deposition, with which they would be furnished if the charge were preferred in the ordinary way."[82] Whatever the cause, refusal to commit must have been widespread in order to explain the almost complete absence of prosecutions for perjury arising from cases heard in the higher courts.

These problems limiting prosecutions for perjury, including unreliable private prosecutions and the interaction of the absence of formal criminal appeals and prohibitions on testimony by criminal defendants, undoubtedly influenced both judges and law reformers. These individuals, as a result, exhibited a striking hesitancy in dealing with the problem of perjury. Under such conditions, it is unsurprising that selective prosecution emerged. Given the significant problems involved in mounting a perjury prosecution, only the most egregious cases were likely to be pursued.

Perjury, the Public Prosecutor, and the Criminal Evidence Act

Toward the end of the nineteenth century, two important changes restructured the institutional context within which perjury prosecutions occurred: first, the establishment of a public official responsible for overseeing prosecutions, and second, the extension to criminal defendants of the right to testify under oath. The norms of selective prosecution, and the concomitant unwillingness of judges to actively prosecute perjury, persisted almost entirely unchanged despite these significant transformations.

The Board of Trade assumed control over government prosecutions in a merger of the Director of Public Prosecutions and the Treasury Solicitor in 1884, shortly after the office was established in 1879. The Board of Trade included perjury among its priorities, albeit in a position distinctly subordinate to the enforcement of bankruptcy law violations. While the Director had little discretion to turn down bankruptcy cases, he could and frequently did refuse to prosecute perjury cases referred to him. As a result, demands for the Director to bring perjury cases always exceeded the number of cases brought. The Director received as many as eighty applications per year, while never bringing more than forty cases (Figures 3 and 4). In

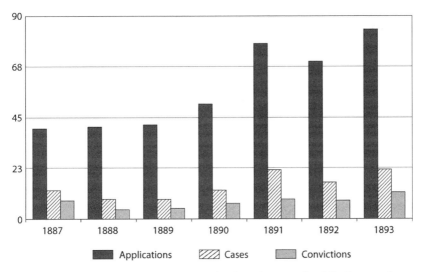

Figure 3. Interventions in perjury cases by the Director of Public Prosecutions. "Applications" are cases referred to the Director for possible prosecution; "cases" are those actually prosecuted by the Director. Both can include more than one defendant per case, but the conviction figure refers to individual defendants. As a result, this figure overstates the Director's ratio of success. For a clearer indication of that ratio, see Figure 4. Sources: "Prosecutions of Offences Acts, 1879 and 1884," Parliamentary Papers, 1888, LXXXII, 475; 1889, LXI, 137; 1890, LIX, 203; 1890–91, LXIV, 509; 1892, LXV, 163; 1893–94, LXXIV, Pt. 1, 559.

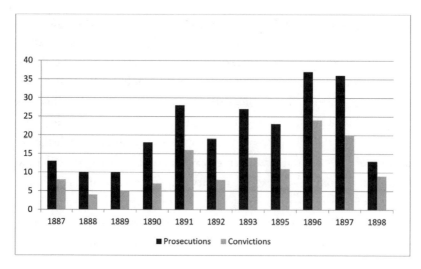

Figure 4. Success of the Director of Public Prosecutions in perjury cases. Sources: See Figure 3 caption, and 1894, LXXI, 231; 1895, LXXXI, 467; 1896, LXIX, 259; 1897, LXXII, 33; 1898, LXXIII, 441; 1899, LXXIX, 279.

1895, for example, the Director pursued prosecutions in only twenty-three perjury cases out of a total of sixty-six referred to him. By contrast, the Director prosecuted nearly all bankruptcy cases.[83] He enjoyed greater success with the perjury cases he brought than did most private prosecutors. In 1895, again, the Director obtained only eleven convictions in the twenty-three cases he brought.[84]

Though perjury cases were only a small part of the Director's activities, they loomed large in the public imagination. Perjury cases formed the bulk of complaints against the Director, who was also repeatedly summoned to Parliament to respond to members' concerns about inactivity in selected perjury cases.[85] One paper, the *Globe,* editorialized bitterly: "There is, we believe, an official known as the Public Prosecutor. He is certainly not over occupied; and official leisure could not be better bestowed than in a systematic crusade against the terrible growth of perjury, which has become the scandal of every Court in the country, and menaces the whole social system with poisonous corruption."[86]

In particular, perjury in divorce cases dominated public complaints against the Director.[87] The *Law Journal* commented on the Director's annual report, "It is in the Divorce Court, perhaps, that the most wilful perjury is committed, and yet the cases in which any action is taken to punish the offenders are very rare."[88] The *Globe*, meanwhile, saw the Divorce Court as the fount of all perjury: "the Divorce Court ought to receive especial attention, as being almost the point of origin of the offence which poisons the stream of justice at its source."[89] As we will see in chapter 4, concerns about perjury in divorce cases led Victorian legislators to develop the Queen's Proctor as an investigative official, rooting out deceit and collusion in the Divorce Court.

Complaints of perjury in divorce cases are not surprising. In Victorian England women were thought to lie without reservation when accused of adultery, while men were expected (even obligated) to lie to protect their mistresses.[90] Hence, the Divorce Court was called the "Supreme Court of Lies" and the "playground of perjurers."[91] As the *Law Times* put it, "In the Divorce Court, the issue is between husband and wife and another party, on a subject of such extreme delicacy that the truth could not be expected."[92] Why demands for the Director of Public Prosecutions to bring perjury prosecutions against witnesses in divorce cases would rise dramatically in the 1890s is unclear, however. As Barbara Leckie has demonstrated, levels of public interest in the Divorce Court had been high since its foundation in 1857. It is possible that the notorious Campbell divorce of the late 1880s, and the Russell divorce of the 1890s, stirred outrage.[93] In 1888 Mr. Charles Darling, a Queen's Counsel and member of Parliament, offered a bill that would enable either the judge or the jury in Divorce Court to immediately consider whether a co-respondent had been guilty of perjury and pass sentence upon him or her as if he or she had been indicted and convicted through the regular process.[94] Darling's bill was never passed, but it reflected a heightened state of anxiety about perjury in the Divorce Court.

In his annual reports, the Director attempted to respond to the complaints by explaining the reasons for the difficulty in attaining convictions.

He did so by describing his policy of selective prosecution and suggesting changes in the substantive law of perjury. Even when "the strongest cases have been selected, and the cases carefully and efficiently put before the court and jury," he noted, "it is certainly remarkable that in so large a proportion of such cases juries should have refused to convict." Additional prosecutions, he concluded, only would have elevated the acquittal rate further by including weaker cases. He defended his rejection of many applications by pointing out that many of them came from unsuccessful parties who sought to continue litigation by other means.[95] In divorce cases, the Director noted that perjury was often effectively taken care of through the intervention of the Queen's Proctor, which was often followed by the parties abandoning the case.[96] As for the cases brought by the Director that resulted in acquittals, he reminded his critics that the requirement of materiality often proved insurmountable.

The Director followed a stringent policy of screening perjury cases. In addition to evidence of contradiction, he demanded "an amount of corroborative evidence forthcoming which will give at least a reasonable presumption that a conviction for perjury will be the result of such prosecution."[97] Perjury cases would be brought against Divorce Court witnesses, meanwhile, only if "*further* and *independent* and *reliable* evidence is procurable, in addition to the evidence *on the balance* of which the Court and jury have decided in the original proceedings" (emphasis in original). Otherwise, the same factors that promoted perjury in the Divorce Court would guarantee an acquittal — the tendency for juries "to find excuses for, at all events to look with indulgence upon, such perjuries."[98] The Director defended his standards by publishing a letter from the former President of the Probate Division (the chief judge of the Divorce Court) saluting Stephenson's policy of selective prosecutions: "I entirely concur with your views as to the objections to multiplying indictments for perjury by the Director of Public Prosecutions, especially in the case of witnesses in divorce suits."[99]

The Director also had several suggestions for improving prosecution of perjury. First, he encouraged judges to make more vigorous use of the powers of committal under Lord Campbell's act. He noted that judges of the superior courts rarely exercised the power, even though County Court judges and police magistrates showed less hesitation. Second, as a way of encouraging judges to commit suspected perjurers, he urged consideration of a modified power to commit to a magistrate for investigation, rather than the existing power to commit for trial. Third, he proposed the creation of a lesser crime of "lying" or "wilful false swearing," which would differ from perjury by not requiring materiality and could be punished as a contempt of court by the judge hearing the original case.[100] The reaction to the Director's suggestions was mixed. The *Law Journal* approved of treating prevarication as a form of contempt, but others feared giving too much power to judges.[101] The Manchester *Guardian* supported a combination of measures, noting that "a case of serious perjury might require independent magisterial investigation, while a case of mere equivocation might appropriately be punished as a contempt."[102] Despite interest expressed in the Director's proposals, however, none of them was adopted. Selective prosecution remained the government's response to the problem of perjury.

The institutional context was altered still more by the Criminal Evidence Act of 1898, which allowed criminal defendants to testify on oath.[103] Many factors were behind the timing of the act, including opposition by Irish members of Parliament, as well as the effect of other laws that permitted testimony by defendants charged with selected criminal offenses, often those with dire potential reputational consequences. The debate on the act will be discussed in chapter 5; however, one element of that debate bears mentioning here. Christopher Allen observes that perjury had "declined" as an argument against reform by the 1870s.[104] That decline was made possible by the selectivity discussed in this chapter. The sting of perjury's prevalence had been diminished by a habit of categorizing only some forms of the offense as particularly dangerous. Through the creation of norms, therefore, perjury had been made to appear manageable, although this appearance concealed a failure to develop any sort of infrastructure that would have made possible the reliable and proportionate punishment envisioned by Bentham. Instead, perjury was seen as largely the province of hardened offenders and best managed through cross-examination, not systematic prosecution.

During the debate on the Criminal Evidence bill, Justice Henry Hawkins was one of the only opponents who evoked the specter of an epidemic of perjury similar to that described by opponents of the 1851 act. Hawkins opposed the Criminal Evidence Act in sweeping terms: "Prisoners who are guilty will recognise that their only chance of escape lies in swearing that they are innocent. The criminal Courts will thus be flooded with perjury, the sanctity of the oath will be destroyed, and juries will cease to attach more importance to a statement that is sworn than one that is not. Hence the very object with which the bill is promoted will be defeated."[105] Few joined Hawkins in his prediction of widespread perjury. More common was the fear that hardened criminals would abuse the privilege of testifying by successfully convincing juries of their innocence. Justice William Grantham testified to the danger posed by such individuals: "I have known scores of cases where clever old hands would have escaped conviction and innocent prosecutors would have been sent forth from Court as perjured witnesses or even branded as blackmailers."[106] Supporters of the bill, however, tended to dismiss the problem. If hardened criminals wanted to add perjury to their list of crimes committed and suffer the consequences, then so be it. As the *Solicitors' Journal* concluded, there was "truth in the objection . . . that the Bill tends to the increase of perjury, but this is a matter which persons who are guilty must settle for themselves."[107] Worry about adding perjury to other crimes was seen as misplaced solicitude for the guilty. The *Solicitors' Journal* commented, "if it *is* a hard thing, it is hard only upon the guilty person."[108]

Following the act's passage, there was controversy about whether criminal defendants could be prosecuted for perjury. Before the act, several options had been proposed. The *Law Times,* for example, suggested that criminal defendants be protected from private prosecutions for perjury for their testimony, prompting an abortive attempt to alter the bill to prohibit perjury prosecutions against criminal defendants.[109] The question reemerged immediately after passage of the reform. In one case, Justice Walter Phillimore opted to increase the sentence on a convicted robber rather than ordering a perjury prosecution, saying that he might "inflict one punishment for two crimes."[110] Other judges were quick to order prosecutions of convicted prisoners for perjury. The *Law Journal* frowned on this, noting it was "a course, obviously to be deprecated save in extreme cases."[111] The opposite course—refusing to bring any prosecution against a convicted defendant—was also seen as problematic. It was suggested that this would amount to double jeopardy by retrying the same facts.[112]

Instead, a general consensus emerged to reserve prosecution for troublesome cases. As the *Solicitors' Journal* suggested: "it is submitted, some sort of leniency might be in most cases shown to this class of perjurer. Of course, in some cases, when the prisoner tries by sworn evidence to lay his guilt on some innocent person . . . no punishment is too severe."[113] The same periodical criticized judges who made "wholesale threats against prisoners of prosecution for perjury" and quoted with approbation Justice Thomas Bucknill's suggestion that perjury prosecutions be reserved for "extreme cases."[114] In short, the selective prosecution of perjurers by the Director of Public Prosecutions would be echoed by selective actions by judges against suspected perjurers among criminal defendants.

By the end of the nineteenth century, the English trial had taken on a modern form that would be easily recognizable to early twenty-first-century Americans. Parties in civil trials and defendants in criminal ones could testify on oath and were subject to the hazards of cross-examination. Judges still frequently bemoaned the prevalence of perjury in their courtrooms. As one County Court judge put it poetically: "Truth and honesty are like some of those rich colours which we cannot now produce."[115] At the same time, however, they participated in an informal system of prosecutorial norms that meant that little would be done to combat perjury. Rather than relying on the threat of perjury prosecutions, or contempt of court sanctions, it was hoped that cross-examination would expose the liar's tale, leaving the jury to draw the appropriate conclusion.

CHAPTER TWO

The Gentlemanly Art of Cross-examination

CROSS-EXAMINATION IN THE VICTORIAN era was both deeply resented and indispensable to the functioning of the legal system. Anthony Trollope compared tolerance of the abuses of cross-examination to the widespread practice of skinning eels while they were still alive to guarantee their freshness: both were tortures "allowed even among humane people."[1] James Fitzjames Stephen, for his part, asserted that cross-examination had been "more severely censured by the unprofessional community" than any other aspect of legal practice.[2] At the same time, cross-examination increasingly came to be the primary defense against perjury in the courtroom. This tension between public disapproval and utility provoked periodic controversies about the practice —both its manner and the extent of its subject matter. This chapter explores the progress of these debates between the admission of evidence by parties in 1851 and the Criminal Evidence Act at the end of the nineteenth century. Different aspects of cross-examination had tellingly different fates during this period. These disparate results stemmed from the Victorian bar's effort to impose limits on abusive cross-examination while preserving counsel's unfettered discretion in posing questions. By undertaking this careful balancing act, the bar successfully claimed cross-examination as its distinctive "gentlemanly art" while distancing itself from the technique's most infamous practitioners— criminal defense counsel.

One caveat is in order, however. This is a history of *controversies* regarding cross-examination, not an empirical study of its practice. Because even the few surviving Victorian trial transcripts frequently omit or paraphrase cross-examining counsel's questions, the methodological challenges posed by any empirical study are so daunting as to be practically insurmountable. Nor, given the highly fluid definitions of professional etiquette regarding in-court conduct, do I claim that even prominent scandals resulted in sweeping changes on the ground. Accusatory cross-examinations, for example, still occurred after their condemnation in the 1870s. What I hope to reveal instead is the shifting ideology of practice: the ways in which the bar explained to itself both the distinctive nature of its professional identity and the boundaries on advocacy that it chose to police, albeit very episodically.

These Victorian debates reveal not only the shifting fortunes of cross-examination, but also important developments in the histories of the adversarial trial and the emergence of legal ethics. Until now, most scholarly attention has been focused on an earlier stage in the history of the common-law trial. Many writers have devoted their attention to the period from the 1780s to the 1840s. By the latter date, according to the standard account, the adversarial trial had fully emerged as a gladiatorial contest between opposing counsel overseen by a judge acting as a neutral umpire.[3] Historians have seen this rise of adversarialism reflected in a variety of forms. Defense counsel appeared with increasing frequency in criminal trials, for example, culminating in what Stephan Landsman calls the "full-flowering of cross-examination" in the last decades of the eighteenth century.[4] Then, in 1836, the Prisoners' Counsel Act expanded the role of defense counsel by allowing them to address the jury directly. And finally in the 1840s, debates prompted by the trial of François Courvoisier, a Swiss manservant, for the murder of his employer, Lord Russell, helped solidify the principle that lawyers should defend even individuals whom they knew to be guilty.[5]

It would be a mistake, however, to assume that the evolution of the criminal trial stopped in the 1840s. As Ray Cocks notes, the late Victorian trial was very different from its early Victorian predecessors. The triumph of adversarialism was by no means clear-cut: controversies regarding advocacy continued into the closing years of Victoria's reign, and the popular press frequently took the bar to task for what it saw as the bar's abuse of the "license of counsel."[6] The bar itself, meanwhile, continued to wrestle with the acceptable boundaries of legal advocacy. Few barristers wholeheartedly embraced Brougham's famous exhortation to use "all expedient means" on their clients' behalf.[7] At the same time, however, the bar lacked a formal system of legal ethics or even a comprehensive institutional structure that would make possible systematic professional discipline. Standards for legal ethics emerged only in vague outline, and as late as the early twentieth century, commentators lamented the fact that lawyers' ethics were largely dependent on the dictates of their individual consciences. This conundrum emerges clearly in late Victorian controversies over cross-examination, which highlighted the tensions between the bar's desire for respectability and its vigorous maintenance of professional autonomy.

Cross-examination, therefore, was a particular bone of contention in the Victorian "license of counsel" debates regarding emerging norms of legal advocacy after the 1840s. In the criminal courts, it had been a target of criticism as early as the mid-eighteenth century, and these criticisms continued despite the "flowering" of adversarialism. The limits of cross-examination were thus well-known. As John Langbein observes, it is a "puzzle" why contemporaries could accept cross-examination as the main guarantor of truth in the courtroom when they were well aware of its potential abuses—though the previous chapter moves us a bit closer to an explanation.[8] As we have seen, part of the solution to this puzzle is a recognition of the limitations of perjury prosecutions as a means of ensuring veracity. Another key element, this chapter argues, derives from the way in which the bar went about shedding some of the most criticized aspects of cross-examination while defending the individual barrister's control over its scope. In particular, the bar condemned accusatory cross-examination designed to suggest that a witness was perjured or corrupt while allowing almost entirely unfettered discretion with regard to so-called cross-examination to character. The barrister, here, was to be limited by his own sense of propriety and fair play, rather than by explicit rules. This solution achieved a twofold result, expanding the bar's control over cross-examination at the expense of the bench, while nominally tailoring it to comport with the sentiments of civilized society.

This emphasis on the tempering role of "civilized" manners made the question of the barrister's status as a gentleman an important theme throughout the debates. In Stephen's description, the barrister had the discretion to "act like a gentleman or like a blackguard," the assumption being that his innate honor, as an educated professional man, would guarantee that he chose the former.[9] The Victorians saw cross-examination as a distinctively masculine pursuit, but one that required the barrister to place limits on his manly urge to dominate. Instead of drawing analogies to the battlefield or boxing ring, they presented cross-examination as a professional technique controlled by the norms of gentility. In 1892, the *Law Times* decried abusive cross-examination as "a species of forensic attack." Should the practice "become universally prevalent . . . we bid farewell to the glory of the English Bar, which would cease to be a profession for gentlemen."[10] For cross-examination to be transformed from a disreputable practice into a legitimate facet of the lawyer's "art," in other words, it needed to be reinterpreted and systematized in ways that seemed to evoke masculine honor.

Critically, gentility also entailed independence—in this case, independence from the client's control or from the client's solicitor. Manly independence required the barrister to distance himself from—and if necessary, to constrain—the untempered passions of his client. This contrasted with an earlier period characterized by lawyers' deference to their elite clients.[11] This ideal of professional autonomy was developed during the same period that the prohibition of contact between barristers and their clients was moving from an ambiguous and erratically obeyed guideline to a firm rule established by the newly founded Bar Council.[12] Even as they distanced themselves from their clients, however, barristers also placed the blame on clients and solicitors for abusive cross-examinations. Barristers argued that their duty was to avoid becoming a weapon wielded in the service of a client's desire for revenge or humiliation. Baron Farrer Herschell's 1890 formulation of the duties of an advocate included, for example, "never yield[ing] to the solicitations of a client, however pressing, to blacken the character of an adverse witness."[13] To understand the history of the ideal of zealous advocacy, therefore, we need to recognize that nineteenth-century barristers demanded the freedom to pursue their clients' causes without interference from the judge at the same time as they accepted personal responsibility for policing the techniques used on their clients' behalf. The triumph of adversarialism was made palatable by the bar's assurances that it would be pursued within the boundaries of gentlemanly honor.

These controversies, and the redefinition of cross-examination they provoked, were driven in part by professional challenges to the barristers' monopoly on courtroom practice. Cross-examination's emergence as the profession's defining skill distinguished common-law barristers from Chancery barristers and also from solicitors who had little experience with courtroom practice before the creation of the County Courts. For most of the Victorian period, the bar's monopoly was threatened on a variety of fronts—from economic pressures caused by increased numbers of barristers, to legal educational reforms pioneered by solicitors, to the prospect of competition from the equity bar in a newly unified court system. Elevating cross-examination as the barrister's "art," an "art" not shared by solicitors or equity barristers, served to demarcate professional boundaries that appeared in danger of blurring.

For those familiar with the rhetoric of nineteenth-century professionalization, it is striking that barristers relied on the trope of "art" rather than "science" in differentiating their particular abilities. Cross-examination, as they presented it, was a form of practical knowledge best learned through observation or apprenticeship, rather than in the lecture hall. It was, therefore, different from the body of specialized, standardized, and perhaps even scientific knowledge that, along with exclusive access to a vital arena (for example, courtrooms or hospitals) and control over entry, constitutes a crucial ingredient of most theories of professionalization.[14] Thus, paradoxically, while English barristers were among the prototypical professions, their claim to exclusivity rested not so much on a specific body of knowledge as on practical skill and personal judgment.[15] That personal judgment, in turn, was presented as inseparable from the gentility of the barrister. Evolving professionalism depended on older norms of aristocratic conduct. As Mark Osiel has commented, English barristers confound the traditional narrative of professionalization with their persistent interest in donning "aristocratic garb" even at the expense of economic success.[16]

Finally, shifting norms of cross-examination brought with them various and sometimes self-contradictory concepts of how the truth of a witness's testimony should be assessed. Barristers' new standards of cross-examination were rooted in contemporary associationist psychological theory and ideas about circumstantial evidence. These standards placed a new onus on barristers to carefully review the evidence before the trial and to skillfully apply their knowledge of human nature during the trial. In part, this shift was made possible by the lengthening duration of many trials. Rather than the brief contests that typified eighteenth-century criminal proceedings, both criminal and civil trials now commonly occupied days and, as a result, required barristers to be well-acquainted with the record. The new style of cross-examination closely reflected this emphasis on pre-trial preparation: it sought unheralded contradictory admissions from witnesses that could later be deployed in an argument to the jury, rather than dramatic confrontation and confession on the stand.

The Case against Cross-examination

To understand why cross-examination was so contentious we must turn to the Old Bailey bar. It was at the Old Bailey—the criminal court for the City of London—that advocates began to develop a reputation for devastating cross-examinations. In part, they had no choice. Restrictions on advocacy before the 1836 Prisoners' Counsel Act, which finally lifted the prohibition on speeches to judge and jury, forced defense counsel to present much of his case in the guise of cross-examination.[17] William Garrow, the celebrated Old Bailey cross-examiner, described the limitations of this situation: "all that is permitted to us who stand as counsel for prisoners is to endeavor, by such questions as may occur to us, to impress on the minds of the Jury observations tending to excite distrust of the evidence."[18] Because of this, the frequency of cross-examination grew apace with the appearance of defense counsel. Landsman, for example, notes that as the presence of defense counsel became more common during the decades between 1740 and 1780, the importance of cross-examination increased

markedly.[19] This trend then accelerated dramatically during the last decades of the eighteenth century, as Langbein has pointed out by identifying
William Garrow's aggressive cross-examinations of the 1780s as a turning
point in the history of Old Bailey adversarialism.[20]

The new assertiveness of defense counsel was widely condemned.
Though the Old Bailey bar had been a target of raillery from the eighteenth century, opinions of it slid still further in the nineteenth century.
The growth of the legal periodical press, which provided a regular forum
for the airing of critiques within the professional community, did much to
accelerate this decline. Old Bailey barristers were frequently accused of being both ignorant of the law and innocent of manners.[21] Looking back from
the safety of the late Victorian period, barristers recalled a sharp divide between Old Bailey practitioners and the rest of the common-law bar. William
Ballantine, for example, had been refused membership at the Reform Club,
which led a wag to remark, "An Old Bailey Barrister would be blackballed
even if he were Jesus Christ."[22] Henry Hawkins recalled the Old Bailey in
the 1840s as "a den of infamy in those days not conceivable now. . . . Its as-
sociations were enough to strike a chill of horror into you. It was the very
cesspool for the offscourings of humanity."[23]

Critics attributed the Old Bailey's lack of decorum in part to the absence of the social controls over behavior that existed in the circuit messes
outside of London. On each of the judicial circuits, judges and barristers
traveled as they held assizes. All the barristers, therefore, belonged to a circuit mess, a largely social group, but one that could and did impose fines,
social sanctions, and even expulsion from the mess for breaches of professional etiquette.[24] The metropolitan courts of London, however, were not
part of a circuit and therefore lacked even this form of rudimentary and
informal discipline.

For its critics, the contemptible amorality of the Old Bailey emerged
most clearly in the practice of cross-examination. Barristers had taken over
the role played by judges in an earlier period—that of sarcastic interro-
gator. Old Bailey barristers' cross-examinations were criticized on several
grounds: they confused the honest witness; they resorted to browbeating
accusations of perjury and tainted testimony inspired by reward money;

they failed to respect the rank of witnesses; and they often resorted to cruel ridicule of witnesses that may have been entertaining to the courtroom but was at best irrelevant to the matter at the bar.[25]

The history of thief-taking provided an important backdrop to the scope granted to defense counsel in their cross-examination. Notorious scandals during the 1720s and 1730s established the image of the prosecutor as a perjurer out for blood money at the expense of an innocent defendant. Garrow, for example, demanded of one prosecution witness, "Upon your oath, do not you prosecute this young man for the reward?"[26] As Allyson May's important research has demonstrated, defense counsel's role was justified by the threat of perjury, especially perjury motivated by reward money.[27] Accusing witnesses of perjury, however, became an easy rhetorical last resort for counsel; the refrain "upon your oath" suggested as much without requiring any well-founded suspicion of perjury.

To the ire of their more deferential critics, Old Bailey counsel deployed these rhetorical tactics without regard for the social status of the witness whose credibility was being undermined. Propertied and penniless witnesses alike could expect no mercy from cross-examining counsel. Garrow's treatment of one titled witness, Baron Hompesch, provoked an irate pamphlet from a solicitor named Thomas Hague, who chose the pointed title "A Letter to William Garrow, Esq., in which the Conduct of Counsel in the Cross-Examination of Witnesses, and Commenting on Their Testimony, is Fully Discussed, and the Licentiousness of the Bar Exposed." Hague excoriated the bar for "brutal insolence and wanton scurillity" and labeled their cross-examination exercises in "prolixity, howling violence, frothy extraneous matter and nauseous ribaldry."[28] For Hague, Garrow's cross-examination of Hompesch exemplified the threat to decent reputations that cross-examining barristers posed. In his cross-examination, Garrow implied that Hompesch, a landowner who sought monetary damages from a man convicted of poaching on his property, had designs on the poacher's wife. Moreover, Garrow asserted that given a choice between the baron and his dog, at least the dog was an honest witness. Hague repeatedly contrasted Garrow's insolence with Hompesch's status as a gentleman and an officer. The conflict between aristocratic notions of honor and the norms of courtroom combat had been made clear by Garrow's refusal to take up Hompesch's invitation to a duel. According to Hompesch, Garrow "meanly sheltered himself under the shield of the law."[29]

Garrow's frequent deployment of two of the types of cross-examination that would feature prominently in late-Victorian debates—accusations of corrupt perjury and irrelevant attacks on witnesses' characters—no doubt was driven in part by the exigencies of contemporary trial practice. Defense counsel typically had little time to prepare, and having a brief presented to them in the courtroom itself was not unheard of. In one case cited by Landsman, the defendant was unable to find his counsel, and another barrister volunteered to handle the cross-examination with no apparent preparation other than having listened to the prosecution's case.[30] But by making these sorts of attacks hallmarks of an aggressive cross-examining style, Garrow left the bar in the uncomfortable position of relying on tactics that ran contrary to notions of gentility: gentlemen did not accuse other gentlemen of fraud.

Ridicule was not uncommon: Garrow famously asked one witness whether he pulled off his false curls when he went to bed.[31] Even Thomas Erskine, universally celebrated as being the courtliest of the Old Bailey barristers, was not above using cross-examination to score unfair points at witnesses' expense. In an action for payment of a tailor's bill, Erskine cross-examined a witness who swore that a dress coat had been badly made with one sleeve longer than the other. Erskine haltingly queried the witness, "You will swear that one of the sleeves was—longer—than the other?" The witness responded that he did so swear. Having lulled the witness into a false sense of security, Erskine then followed quickly with an angry, "Then, Sir, I am to understand that you positively deny that one of the sleeves was shorter than the other?" Startled, the witness declared, "I do deny it."[32]

Criticisms directed at the Old Bailey bar inspired novelists, who saw the literary potential of the duplicitous wit attributed to its barristers. The prolific author Anthony Trollope frequently included scenes of abusive and misleading cross-examinations in his novels. While Trollope was not alone among Victorian novelists in deploring cross-examinations, he was probably the Victorian era's most prominent critic of their abuse.[33] As we have seen, he once compared the beleaguered witness to an eel being skinned alive by a fishmonger. Despite the extravagance of both creatures' gratuitous suffering, he wrote, "no one's blood curdled at the sight, no soft heart is sickened at the cruelty"—though, as we will see, in the case of eels this was not entirely accurate by midcentury.[34] Elsewhere he compared evidence extracted through cross-examination to that produced "by means of torture—thumb-screw and such-like,—[that] we have for many years past abandoned as barbarous."[35] Trollope's father was a Chancery barrister, and Trollope seems to have inherited an equity barrister's disdain for the common-law bar. His hostility to cross-examination appears to have been a lifelong preoccupation; one contemporary records him as "raging and roaring" against the system of cross-examination at an 1877 dinner with Henry James, a prominent criminal barrister who subsequently served as Solicitor and Attorney General.[36]

Trollope himself had firsthand experience of cross-examination. During the 1840s he worked for the Irish Post Office, where he had a reputation as an aggressive and active supervisor. In order to trap a suspected mail thief in Tralee, he sent a marked coin in a letter that would pass through the Tralee post office. When the letter did not arrive, Trollope hurried to Tralee, where he found the coin in the pocket of Mary O'Reilly, a young postmaster's assistant. Trollope's testimony as a prosecution witness was central in the ensuing two criminal trials (the first ended in a mistrial).[37] In the first trial, O'Reilly's counsel asked Trollope whether he had drawn his plan from the same source as the novels he had "dabbled in." At the second trial, O'Reilly was represented by the famous Irish barrister Isaac Butt. Butt asked Trollope whether he "deal[t] in fictional characters" and recited an antibarrister passage from Trollope's recent novel *The Macdermots of Ballycloran,* asking him whether he still felt the same animosity.[38]

Trollope's aversion to partisan cross-examination appears to have stemmed from his conviction that barristers actively sought to conceal the truth: "it is not that [our lawyer] fails to look on the truth as excellent; it is not that he is less averse to murder than another; it is not that he would have crime escape unpunished; but the habits of his education, of his trade, and his life will not allow him to see clearly."[39] One contemporary reviewer

described Trollope's novel *Orley Farm* as "an attack upon the whole system of advocacy—not upon its misuse, but upon its use."[40] The novel
centers on a perjury trial in which the defendant, Lady Mason, is patently
guilty. It abounds with antilawyer barbs, such as: "There were five lawyers
concerned, not one of whom gave to the course of justice credit it would
ascertain the truth, and not one of whom wished that the truth should be
ascertained. Surely had they been honest-minded in their profession they
would all have so wished . . . I cannot understand how any gentleman can
be willing to use his intellect for the propagation of untruth."[41] Barristers,
in Trollope's view, were not only willing to overlook evidence of guilt when
it suited their professional interests, they were also unscrupulous about
casting false aspersions on other individuals whom they knew to be innocent. In the *New Zealander,* Trollope describes the fate of the witness:
"The poor wretch, who has come there to tell, as best he may, what truth
he knows on the matter, is exposed first to the ridicule, and then to the
ignominy of the whole court. Nay, may it be possible that he himself did the
deed? It is clear, so says Mr. Allwinde, that this man is a liar, why not also
a murderer?"[42]

Trollope subsequently personified his complaints about common-
law barristers in the memorable character of Mr. Chaffanbrass—modeled,
as we will see, on a famed Old Bailey counsel—who appears in several of
his novels. In *Phineas Redux,* Lord Fawn, a potential witness, contemplates
with horror the prospect of association with Chaffanbrass, "hating the little man, despising him because he was dirty, and nothing better than an
Old Bailey barrister."[43] In *Orley Farm,* Trollope covers his stereotyping
bases by comparing Chaffanbrass to both an Irish assassin and a "dirty old
Jew."[44] Chaffanbrass delights in the chase; he "bullies when it is quite unnecessary that he should bully; it is a labour of love."[45]

Trollope's eel analogy resonated with contemporary concerns. In
striking contrast to an eighteenth-century indifference to animal suffering,
the nineteenth century saw the foundation of the Society for the Prevention
of Cruelty to Animals in 1824 (less than two decades later, in 1840, Queen
Victoria permitted the addition of "Royal" to the name), the initiation of
private prosecutions of animal abusers on a widespread basis, and legisla-

tive interest in the question of animal suffering.[46] Indeed, by the time Trollope made his comparison, cookbooks and household manuals already deplored the "horrid barbarity" of killing eels by skinning them alive, instead recommending a quick blow to the base of the skull "with a sharp pointed knife or skewer."[47] In the nineteenth century, interest in animal welfare was part of a broader fascination with suffering and pain. Pain became an object of dread, not merely an inevitable fact of life. But the impulse to protect animals was not simply humanitarian; the language of cruelty was closely intertwined with visions of class. An accusation of cruelty implied that the abuser was both a revanchist throwback to less civilized times and, very clearly, *not* a gentleman. Trollope's description of Chaffanbrass in *The Three Clerks* includes both an indictment of Chaffanbrass's delight in inflicting pain—"it may be said of him that the labour he delighted in physicked pain"—and lack of civility—"Mankind in general take pleasure in cruelty, though those who are civilized abstain from it on principle."[48]

Despite the heated rhetoric of critics like Trollope, the bar's response tended to either dismiss the question entirely or skirt the issue of whether some form of control should be imposed. One frequent theme in the legal literature of the 1830s and 1840s was that abusive cross-examination was not really a problem because it tended to alienate the jury. "But this is dangerous ground," cautioned William Forsyth in his work on advocacy. "The feelings of the jury revolt at such an assumption, and in their sympathy with the witness whose character is thus causelessly assailed, they are apt to conceive prejudice against [the opposing party]."[49] Counsel, it was implied, were already motivated by the dictates of practicality not to exceed the boundaries of propriety. Archer Polson, writing in 1840, noted, "Counsel . . . have sometimes pushed their privilege of treating every hostile witness as a rogue rather too far, and have received some severe rebukes from those they had hoped to make the objects either of scorn or ridicule."[50]

Another common response was to laugh the problem off with a humorous invocation of witnesses who turned the tables on their examiners. Marc Galanter, in his study of lawyer jokes, identifies the persistence of certain types of jokes as evidence of deep-seated ambivalence that the joker is unable or unwilling to confront. One of the oldest themes in the annals of lawyer humor is the badgering lawyer defeated by the lower-class witness.[51] Lawyers in the mid-Victorian period both joked about the clever witness and quite possibly believed in his or her existence. Stories of the clever witness are legion and often involve an aspersion either on the bar in general or on the individual barrister's sexual conduct.[52] For example: "Dr. Brodum, a notorious quack, was once under examination by Mr. Abraham Moore. 'Your name is Brodum, I believe,' inquired the counsel. The doctor nodded assent. 'Pray how do you spell it—Bro-dum or Broad-hum?' On this there was a loud laugh in court, which was not diminished when the quack replied with admirable self-possession, 'Why, sare, as I be but a doctor, I spell my name Bro-dum; but if I were a *barrister* I should spell it Broad-hum!'"[53] Polson also relates the classic anecdote of notorious eighteenth-century hanging Judge Jeffreys's comeuppance as a barrister. Jeffreys's wife had given birth a very short time after their marriage. "Her husband was shortly after this unfortunate occurrence examining a fair witness, who gave her evidence with tolerable sharpness. He said, 'Madam, you are quick in your answers.' 'Quick as I am, Sir George, I am not so quick as your lady.'"[54] The joke may have been on the barrister, but the underlying message served the legal profession's interests: why formalize controls on counsel when even the humblest witnesses could turn the tables on their legal adversaries?

Distinguishing the Barrister

Despite the criticisms, cross-examination came to occupy an important position in the early nineteenth-century trial, helping to distinguish barristers at a moment when solicitors were engaged in sweeping professional reform. In arguing for the centrality of cross-examination, barristers benefited from changes in the conceptualization of evidence law. By the mid-nineteenth century, jurists had come to accept that cross-examination was essential to establishing the truth of matters before the court. Evidence treatises of the time increasingly settled on the absence of cross-examination as the rationale for the hearsay rule.[55] Thomas Starkie, in a construction that would later be amplified by John Henry Wigmore, called cross-examination "one of the principal tests the law has devised for the ascertainment of truth."[56] Rather than relying on the *in terrorem* power of the oath, jurists argued that cross-examination should be the main safeguard of veracity. But the shifting rationales of the rules of evidence alone do not explain the enthusiasm with which the bar embraced cross-examination over the course of the nineteenth century.

Early attempts to reform cross-examination need to be viewed against a backdrop of widespread anxieties about the future of the legal profession. The first third of the nineteenth century was widely seen as a time of overcrowding at the bar. Barristers faced heightened competition among themselves, economic competition from solicitors, and controversies about the traditional education of barristers. Although it is difficult to isolate the number of individuals who relied on legal practice for the majority of their income, Daniel Duman estimates that the practicing bar in England and Wales grew two and half times from 1785 to 1835, far outstripping the rate of population growth.[57] This period of growth was followed by economic depression from 1837 into the 1850s. As a result, fewer barristers were able to earn a respectable living from their practices. Moreover, straitened financial circumstances threatened a particularly cherished part of the bar's self-image: the barrister as a financially disinterested gentleman, as opposed to the solicitor, who was seen as a mere tradesman.[58] James Fitzjames Stephen identified the "general theory of the distinction between the two branches of the legal profession" as the difference between superior and inferior: "the one requires the manners, the accomplishments, and the education of a gentleman, and . . . these things are not to be expected of the other."[59]

The effect of competition within the bar was compounded by the expansion of opportunities for solicitors during the nineteenth century. In the new County Courts, established in 1846, attorneys could appear for clients without engaging a barrister. This innovation proved particularly difficult for junior barristers, who suffered most from the loss of smaller cases that could now be handled by solicitors on their own in County Courts. Some barristers fought for the right to appear in the County Courts without instruction by a solicitor, but few took advantage of the opportunity.[60] As the County Courts' jurisdiction was expanded repeatedly during the nineteenth century, barristers' protests against their shrinking professional monopoly were fruitless. By the 1860s, aside from divorce cases, "the county courts were now practically courts of complete jurisdiction in civil matters."[61]

Not only did solicitors make significant inroads into courtroom practice, they also challenged the barristers' leadership of the legal profession through pioneering reforms in legal education. Under the auspices of the Law Society, solicitors introduced a lecture program in 1833, followed in 1836 by a unified admission process with formal written examinations.[62] It would take decades, however, for similar changes to be accepted by the "higher" branch of the legal profession. From the 1830s on, there was widespread interest in (as well as opposition to) reforms in legal education for barristers, as highlighted by the House of Commons Select Committee and Royal Commission reports on legal education in 1846 and 1854–55. In 1852 the Inns established a collective body, the Council on Legal Education, and agreed to make admission to the bar contingent on either attending lectures or taking a voluntary examination. This first wave of reform, however, had little in the way of practical consequences. Unsurprisingly, few would-be barristers took the voluntary examination. Moreover, attendance at the lectures declined during the 1860s, when serving a year's pupilage was accepted in lieu of the lecture requirement.[63] Mandatory examinations were not instituted until 1872.

Viewing the history of legal education simply as an inevitable—if perhaps delayed—natural course of reform misses much of the complexity of the bar's self-identification during this period. Following in the footsteps of the "lower" branch caused much anxiety among members of the bar. Barristers sought to base their claims for professional legitimacy on gentlemanly status, classical learning, and economic disinterestedness, even if competition in the legal market during the nineteenth century made their grasp on the first and the third more tenuous. In the instances where practical knowledge might be valued, many barristers still maintained that it was best acquired through the ad hoc learning experience of apprenticeship, rather than as a systematic course of study.[64] For those who wanted to maintain the traditional education of barristers, cross-examination was a convenient example of an "art" best learned at the elbow of a practicing

barrister rather than in the sterile confines of a lecture hall. John George
Witt, for example, a barrister with an extensive academic record before
turning to the law, condemned examinations because of the threat they
posed to the "principle of apprenticeship," where real preparation for a
legal career took place.[65]

From Confrontation to Mastery of Circumstance: Cleaning Up Cross-examination's Act

All of these factors combine to explain why reforming cross-
examination became so important in the mid-nineteenth century. Edward
Cox was one of the first to take up the challenge in a comprehensive way.
Writing just before the passage of the Evidence Amendment Act of 1851,
which, as we have seen, allowed parties in civil cases to testify in court,
Cox formulated new rules to guide cross-examination.[66] Cox was a barrister and a professional journalist who actively supported numerous — albeit
moderate — reform proposals through his journal the *Law Times*.[67] In particular, he lamented the lax enforcement of professional standards. In order
to describe these standards comprehensively, Cox produced a long work
titled *The Advocate*, which was published as a book in 1851 after having
been serialized over the previous four years.[68] In *The Advocate*, Cox rendered explicit the practices and techniques of the bar for aspiring students:
one modern historian calls it the "most extraordinary legal textbook of the
nineteenth century."[69] In his work, Cox drew upon two important strands
of Victorian thought in elaborating his new ideals for cross-examination:
norms of gentility and associationist psychological theories. Cox's attitude
throughout *The Advocate* might be characterized as optimistic — he praised
the first shoots of change effusively in the hope that they would take root
and spread. One reviewer described *The Advocate*'s advice as "a high les-
son and . . . a spirit of nice honour and kindly conduct, of which there are
but few living examples."[70]

In his discussion of cross-examination, Cox hopefully noted that
"advocacy has, in this respect, vastly improved of late years, and is still
improving." Yet, his tone throughout was more embattled than this

assessment would suggest. Cox began by emphasizing the difficulty of cross-examination, which he described as "the severest test of an Advocate's skills." He then laid out its goals: "there can be but *three* objects in cross-examination. It is designed either to destroy or weaken the force of the evidence the witness has already given *against* you, or to elicit something in *your favour,* which he has not stated, or to discredit him, by showing to the Jury, from his past history or present demeanour that he is unworthy of belief." Even as Cox endorsed its utility as an adversarial technique, however, he stressed the value of a more civil approach to cross-examination: "It is marvelous how much may be accomplished with the most difficult witnesses simply by good humour and a smile; a *tone* of friendliness will often succeed in obtaining a reply which has been obstinately denied to a surly aspect and a threatening or reproachful voice."[71]

Cox strongly discouraged the common Old Bailey practice of accusing witnesses of perjury. Addressing a hypothetical aspiring barrister, he wrote: "you have *no right* to charge [a witness] with falsehood unless you are in your own mind entirely convinced that [the witness] is *lying,* and not that he is merely *mistaken.*"[72] Cox urged that barristers carefully assess a witness's credibility, noting demeanor, tone of voice, level of engagement in his or her narrative, and any uncharacteristic turns of phrase, which could be signs of coaching. Only if the barrister judged the witness a deliberate liar could he confront him or her with an accusation; and even then, Cox cautioned, an imputation of perjury was likely to backfire, because juries were apt to turn the trial into a referendum on the witness's honor and punish the barrister for his suggestion. Cox's proposal that barristers assume a responsibility for prejudging witness credibility, meanwhile, ran precisely counter to the justification for knowing defense of the guilty developed at the same time. In that situation, barristers defended their conduct by claiming it was impossible to assess a client's innocence or guilt before a complete trial—the truth of the situation would be revealed by the contest between adversaries.[73]

Rather than confronting a witness with a contradiction, Cox urged an unthreatening, patient accumulation of circumstantial evidence that could later be used to destroy fabricated testimony: "The safer and surer course is to bring out the discrepancy by inference, that is, instead of seeking to make the witness *unsay* what he has said, it should be your aim to elicit a statement which may be shown by argument to be inconsistent with the former statement." In order to garner the circumstantial facts necessary to prove inconsistency, the advocate needed to appear devoid of suspicion: "there is nothing upon which witnesses of every grade of rank and intellect are so sensitive as *self-contradiction.* They suspect your purpose instantly, and the dread of being made to appear as lying, while often producing contradictions and evasions, more often arms the resolution of the witness to adhere to his original statement without qualification or explanation."[74] Rather than the intemperate confrontation of the Old Bailey, the art of cross-examination now lay in the stealthy accumulation of circumstantial evidence. Cox suggested that barristers would find much less resistance— both from the jury and from the adverse witnesses—if they argued that the witness had been mistaken. Demonstrating the possibility of mistake through a skilled cross-examination became, in Cox's view, the "triumph of [the barrister's] art," particularly when bolstered by the skilled reading of countenances and narrative sensitivity necessary to determine whether a witness was consciously lying.[75] The idea of mistake was to become a touchstone for the "new" cross-examination. The *Law Times,* for example, would explain that "what an honourable cross-examining counsel does is to use such means as will detect and expose any conscious or unconscious inaccuracy into which the witness may have fallen."[76]

Morality, Cox argued, should be the advocate's baseline: "Your duty as an Advocate is strictly limited by the rules of morality. It is no more permissible for you to tamper with the truth in others, or tempt them to confound or conceal it, than to be false yourself." Cox disagreed with any version of the duty of an advocate that was "opposed to the plainest dictates of morality, which forbid us to do an injury to our neighbours, or to lie for any purpose whatever."[77] He saw the barrister as a gentleman "subject to the curb of education and station."[78] Cross-examination, in particular, should be guided by moral principles: Cox exhorted students that their conduct should be that of a "Christian gentleman . . . which may be summed up in three words—JUSTICE, TRUTH, CHARITY."[79] This moral vision led Cox to dismiss the idea that the bench should police cross-examination. Instead, he assumed that proper (and sufficient) control could be exercised by an individual barrister's conscience.

Cox's vision of the new cross-examination as mastery of circumstantial evidence informed by a keen insight into human nature drew much of its strength from contemporary ideas about the nature of memory and the utility of circumstantial evidence. Mid-Victorian psychology was dominated by the associationist school, and many of its assumptions guided Cox's arguments, as well as giving a seemingly scientific foundation to a style of cross-examination that better fit with notions of genteel conduct. Associationist psychology originated with John Locke, who countered the earlier doctrine of innate ideas with a conception of the mind as a tabula rasa, shaped entirely by sensation and reflection. Association was the process by which these sensations were linked with concepts. For associationists, therefore, the primary question became the ways in which sensations and ideas were linked.[80] In the eighteenth century David Hartley suggested that memories consisted of the "perpetual Recurrency of the same Impressions and Clusters of Impressions."[81] Psychologists in the mid-Victorian period identified a variety of ways that memories could be contiguous, including "order in time, order in place, . . . cause and effect," and contrast or similarity.[82] Moreover, the psychologists argued, the circumstances of a memory's creation determined its longevity: memories created in a moment of strong feeling, either pleasure or pain, were likely to last longer. Associationists argued that humans were innately inclined to be truthful—indeed, that telling a falsehood led to an instinctive feeling of pain.[83] As the psychologist Alexander Bain wrote, "Contrary statements, opinions, or appearances, operate on the mind as a painful jar, and stimulate a corresponding desire for reconciliation."[84] This conception of mendacity resurfaced in Cox's advice that advocates should assume a mistaken memory before concluding that a witness had committed willful perjury.

The intersection of associationist ideas and legal practice was also reflected in James Ram's 1861 *A Treatise on Facts*. Ram quoted Locke to explain the way in which events left an impression on the mind. Memories, he argued, consisted of those impressions that persist in the mind for an extended period of time; their duration was generally proportionate to the depth of the original impression. Once triggered, memories "give up the persons or things which made the impressions; these persons or things then come before the mind's eye, and become the subject of thought." The trigger could be a question, a passing thought, or a sensory impression: the song of a field cricket could evoke "a train of summer ideas of every thing that is rural, verdurous, and joyous," for example. Even a deeply buried memory, Ram asserted, could be refreshed by external evidence, such as a diary. Such triggers could be employed by a skillful cross-examiner. Ram noted that cross-examination "is often of the utmost importance and service toward discovering the truth, and the extent to which the witnesses are to be believed." It was particularly useful when testimony was a mixture of truth and falsehood, or truth and omissions: "the witness may have spoken truth, but not the whole truth; or he may have spoken the truth, and something besides the truth; or some of the truth may not have been brought out."[85]

Both Ram and William Wills, author of a noted treatise on circumstantial evidence, questioned the assumption that any variation in testimony indicated falsity. Wills, for example, observed that inconsistencies in the accounts of the same event by different witnesses "are not necessarily to be regarded as indicative of fraud or falsehood, provided there be substantial agreement in other respects."[86] Not all sensations lodged in memory with the same force. Ram approvingly quotes the late eighteenth-century natural theologian William Paley's statement that "I know not a more rash or unphilosophical conduct of the understanding, than to reject the substance of a story, by reason of some diversity." In particular, Ram argued, variations between a witness's statement to a magistrate and his or her in-court testimony was "natural, and almost unavoidable."[87] When two witnesses differed in their accounts of a conversation, Ram found many possible explanations for a contradiction short of conscious deception. Circumstantial corroboration, in such a case, was a better tool for the identification of falsehood than simple variation.

Willful perjury, Ram argued, required a compelling motive that could mark it as something more than an accident of memory. Ram listed revelations that could damage witnesses' credit: previous involvement in court cases, having been discharged from the army or from service, financial or penal motives for their testimony, a history of enmity against the opposing party. A guilty individual was likely to tell a lie in order to parry suspicion. One needed to look for motive for perjury, because "perjury is seldom committed in mere wantonness." Typical motives, he wrote, included an interest in the outcome of a suit, envy, spite, revenge, inculpation of another, and having been bribed. Many forms of falsity existed, then, short of perjury: "To doubt of truth is not to convict of falsehood. . . . [W]here the doubt exists, it need not arise from a suspicion that the witness has willfully spoken an untruth." Like Cox, Ram urged a distinction between treatment of truthful and untruthful witnesses based not simply on the accuracy of their testimony but also on the intentions with which they delivered it: "Except in the case of a dishonest witness, one prepared to trifle with his oath, a witness may justly receive courteous or at least inoffensive, treatment at the hands of his examiner."[88]

As Ram's reliance on circumstantial evidence as a backstop for lapses in witness memory indicates, Cox's enthusiasm for it was widely shared. Paley's famous statement that "circumstances cannot lie," and his use of such evidence to prove the presence of God in the world, is testament to the prestige it enjoyed.[89] Legal scholars, for their part, made circumstantial evidence into a crucial tool for exposing perjury even before Cox. Thomas Starkie, for example, wrote in 1833:

> It is not for a witness . . . to impose upon the Court; for however artful the fabrication of the falsehood may be, it cannot embrace all the circumstances to which the cross-examination may be extended; the fraud is therefore open to detection for want of consistency between that which has been invented, and that which the witness must either represent according to the truth, for want of previous preparation, or misrepresent according to his own immediate invention.[90]

James Fitzjames Stephen also relied on circumstantial evidence as a test of veracity: "consideration of the degree to which circumstances corroborate each other, and of the intrinsic probability of the matter sworn to, is a far better test of truth than any oath can possibly be."[91] In exposing a liar, "the utmost that can be done is to tie him down to so many details and collateral circumstances that if he is lying he can be contradicted by other testimony."[92]

Lawyers, however, defined circumstantial evidence in narrower terms than Paley had. Wills, for example, defined it as lawyers do today, distinguishing it from direct evidence of the *factum probandum,* or subject of the inquiry: "circumstantial evidence is equally direct in its nature, but, as its name imports it is direct evidence of a minor fact or facts, incidental to or usually connected with some other fact," usually, the *factum proban-dum.*[93] Circumstantial evidence, as legal scholars saw it, usually involved an inference from the circumstantial fact to the fact in issue. That inference, in turn, did not have to be as firm as a presumption. Cross-examination, meanwhile, became the art of manipulating circumstantial evidence. As Richard Harris described it in his late-Victorian how-to manuals on advocacy:

> An isolated event is impossible. . . . The multitude of surround-ing circumstances will *all* fit in with a true story, because that is part and parcel of those circumstances carved out from them no matter how extraordinary it may seem: just as the oddest shaped stone you could cut from the quarry would fit in again to the place whence it was taken. It is therefore, to the rock, of which it once formed a part, that you must go to see if the block presented be genuine or false. You must, in other words, go to the surrounding circumstances.[94]

For the barrister to trap the lying witness, however, his accumulation of circumstances had to be stealthy, in order to avoid giving the opposing side the opportunity to repair the damage by corroboration from another witness.

The End of the Perjured Wretch:
Disciplining Accusatory Cross-examinations

During the 1860s and 1870s, uncertainty about the status and professional identity of the bar persisted. In addition to the preexisting competition with solicitors and controversies about legal education, common-law
barristers now also confronted the problems of competition with the equity
bar and controversies regarding the adequacy of their disciplinary systems.
From March 1869, it became apparent that the long-anticipated fusion of
law and equity would take the form of a single unified court, rather than
conferring equitable powers on common-law courts and vice versa. The
prospect of imminent institutional unification provoked professional jealousy between the common-law and equity bars. Because it was feared that
common and equity lawyers would be partial to members of their own bar,
as well as more comfortable with their own court's practices, lawyers in
each bar lobbied for the appointment of their fellows as judges in the new
courts. Lawyers from the two bars also had a sharpened sense of their own
separate professional cultures: into the twentieth century, members of the
Chancery bar maintained a deep-seated sense of a professional identity
apart from and above the common-law bar.[95] Equity barristers believed
that they were both more ethical advocates and more sophisticated legal
scholars, while common-law barristers felt that their equitable counterparts
remained deficient in courtroom representation, particularly in the fine art
of cross-examination.[96]

The 1860s also witnessed a handful of very prominent cases of barristers being subjected to professional discipline. Although there were not
many cases in absolute terms, as Wesley Pue points out, "a small number of
documented discipline cases does not necessarily mean that the Bar's powers are inconsequential." A few highly publicized disciplinary cases could
and did serve as "cultural showpieces" that allowed the bar to delimit the
outer boundaries of permissible advocacy.[97] Without such cases, as Stephen dolefully opined, the "great objection" to professional rules was that
if they were "professed without being acted on, [they] become the source of
hypocrisy and falsehood."[98] These "showpiece" disciplinary proceedings

tended to target barristers with liberal or radical political sympathies—
particularly those who had histories of challenging the professional ideologies of the bar—but their widely reported consequences discredited the
bar as a whole and built public interest in the arcane procedures of bar discipline. At the time, both a barrister's Inn and his circuit mess could claim
disciplinary authority over him, but intervention by the Inns was rare, and
a barrister could evade the largely social penalties wielded by the circuit
mess through the simple measure of leaving it.[99] Two cases brought the
problem of professional discipline to the attention of the public with particular force, introducing several concerns that would prove central to later
cross-examination controversies. The first case resembles the Tichborne
disciplinary proceedings (discussed below) in that, very unusually, it arose
in part out of in-court conduct by a barrister. The second case prefigures
issues of barristers' autonomy vis-à-vis clients that would reemerge in the
debates of the 1890s.

In 1861, the newly appointed Attorney General—a radical member
of Parliament and a Queen's Counsel named Edwin James—engendered
controversy for, among other violations of the bar's gentlemanly code, supposedly throwing his own cross-examination. James had appeared for the
plaintiff in a fraud case in 1859 and had so severely cross-examined the
defendant, Herbert Ingram, that Ingram had left court deep in a suicidal
depression. Ingram later obtained a retrial, which was settled in his favor
when James failed to pursue the case with his prior vigor. Gossip attributed James's leniency to a much-needed £1,250 loan he had received from
Ingram. In 1861, the benchers of Inner Temple held an inquiry into James's
conduct in response to the Ingram case and his rumored credit problems.[100]
While the charge in the Ingram case could not be proved, the inquiry revealed the full extent of James's debts. He had already fled England, leaving
creditors unpaid and resigning from all his public offices, but his Inn proceeded with his disbarment, a penalty James was the first Queen's Counsel
ever to suffer.[101]

James's flight took place in the midst of nineteenth-century Britain's
longest-running legal scandal, which also called the disciplinary capacities
of the bar into question. Patience Swinfen had been a servant maid when

she met and married the younger son of a landed estate owner. Her husband was promptly disinherited, but, after several years, his father, Samuel Swinfen, relented and allowed the two to return to Swinfen Hall. Samuel became fond of Patience and promised her that he would look after her; Samuel then left the Swinfen estate to Patience, enraging his older son, Frederick. Frederick sued Patience in 1856; she was represented by Sir Frederick Thesiger, but her case was short-lived because Thesiger—acting on the advice of the judge hearing the case, Sir Cresswell Cresswell—agreed to a settlement on her behalf without her consent. Patience refused to accept the settlement and eventually won back the estate, with the help of a controversial barrister named Charles Rann Kennedy.

Patience and Kennedy then took the completely unprecedented step of suing Cresswell and Thesiger, now Baron Chelmsford, Lord Chancellor. They lost the case—badly—because the legal profession acted to protect two of its most eminent members. Kennedy and Patience, meanwhile, had embarked on an adulterous affair (Kennedy was married), and in lieu of payment for his legal services, Patience conveyed to him a deed valued at £20,000. Unfortunately, their romantic association was as tumultuous as their legal partnership, and Patience fell in love with and married another man. She demanded the deed to the estates be returned; Kennedy retaliated by suing her for his legal fees in the amount of £20,000. Kennedy won the initial trial, but the Court of Common Pleas subsequently established the principle that a barrister could not sue a client for fees. Kennedy also lost his claim to the Swinfen estate—the deed was set aside on the grounds that he had exercised undue influence over Patience. While disbarment proceedings against Kennedy were never concluded, his controversial relationship with Patience highlighted the inadequacy of discipline by either the circuit mess or the Inns.[102]

The influence of the early 1860s cases persisted in an ongoing debate about the adequacy of the bar's disciplinary structure. Prompted by the question "Is the Bar a Trades Union?," the *Pall Mall Gazette* ran a series of letters in 1867 debating the role of the bar. The bar's power to enforce its rules occupied a prominent place in the debate. "A Barrister" stated that "it would be a very difficult matter to say what the rules of the bar are, or what is their sanction, and probably no two members of the profession would give the same account of them."[103] The *Law Journal* agreed that the rules were "of a very fluctuating and uncertain character" and contended that the Inns of Court "never act except where a course of conduct has been pursued at variance with the honour of a gentleman."[104] Such complaints prompted proposals to unify the Inns for the purpose of discipline and to codify disciplinary regulations and procedures. Establishment of a joint body had to wait until the mid-1880s, when the Bar Council was founded, but before then the Tichborne trials would plunge the bar into public scandal once again.[105]

These controversial trials focused public concern with the ethics of the bar on the question of cross-examination. While critics of cross-examination had decried abuses, no disciplinary proceeding had focused upon the question. Writing in 1865 Francis Parker called for making an example of a bullying, browbeating cross-examiner who had "act[ed] towards an ordinary adverse witness on the assumption that he is perjured": "It is most desirable that fit instances of this should be selected for earnest, vigorous protest."[106] Parker would get his wish. Polemics about the Tichborne trials identified in them variously the failure of cross-examination, the triumph of cross-examination, and the bounds beyond which cross-examination could not be permitted.[107] Much of the cross-examination during the course of the trials was criticized, but only one barrister was disbarred—Edward Kenealy. Kenealy, noted for his mercurial temperament, succeeded Kennedy as the bar's "professional demon" in the 1870s, and his disciplinary proceeding served to give Cox's strictures on advocacy some bite.

The lengthy litigation surrounding the Tichborne Claimant, as chronicled by Rohan McWilliams, was set into motion when the Dowager Lady Tichborne began circulating plaintive advertisements in Australia and elsewhere calling for information about her eldest son, Roger Tichborne, who had been missing for twelve years and was presumed dead at sea.[108] Since Roger's disappearance, both his father and his younger brother had died, leaving the substantial Tichborne estates and the baronetcy in the youthful hands of his brother's posthumous son. Lady Tichborne's solicitations received a response in 1866. Thomas Castro, a butcher in the outback town of

Wagga Wagga, wrote to his "Mamma" regretting his lengthy silence and requesting financial assistance. Castro quickly garnered the trust of two Tichborne family employees living in Australia. One of them, Andrew Bogle,
accompanied Castro when he went to Europe with his illiterate wife, her
illegitimate daughter, and a newborn infant in tow. Upon arrival, the Claimant, as he became known, gained the support of the Dowager Lady Tichborne, fellow countrymen from the vicinity of the Tichborne estate, and
sundry fellow officers from Roger Tichborne's time in military service—
all of whom claimed to recognize the slight form of Francophone Roger
in the much larger and defiantly non-French-speaking Castro. Almost all
of the rest of the Tichborne family refused to recognize the Claimant and
maintained instead that he was in fact Arthur Orton, the son of a butcher in
Wapping who had gone abroad at an early age. The Claimant brought suit
to regain the estate, thereby initiating what was to become first the lengthiest civil trial in English history and then the lengthiest criminal trial.

The first cross-examination took place in Chancery in 1864, based
on an affidavit the Claimant had made in Australia. It was conducted by
Mr. Charles Chapman Barber, a Chancery silk, despite the presence of
Henry Hawkins, a renowned cross-examiner also retained by the Tichborne family. Chapman Barber's restrained cross-examination, which
was limited to a recitation of facts, was much criticized after the trials as a
missed opportunity; a more aggressive set of questions could have revealed
one or more flaws in the Claimant's story, discrediting his case before trial.
Chapman Barber's supposed inadequacy in cross-examination became evidence in a larger dispute about the role of the Chancery and common-law
bars in the forthcoming fusion of the high courts of law and equity. In a
typical display of professional jealousy, common-law barristers commenting on the case held that Chapman Barber's failure revealed the inadequacy
of Chancery barristers when they attempted to assume roles traditionally
held by their common-law colleagues.[109]

At the civil trial, the Claimant retained William Ballantine, renowned
Old Bailey barrister and model for Trollope's abrasive Chaffanbrass;
the family retained Hawkins and John Duke Coleridge, the Solicitor General.[110] Thorough cross-examination ought to have been able to demolish

what was likely a fabricated story related by Arthur Orton in his impersonation of Roger Tichborne. In practice, the cross-examination provided
no real moments of drama. Because of his position, Coleridge rather than
Hawkins cross-examined the Claimant. Again, the cross-examination was
a leisurely affair, justified in retrospect by the rationale that its aim was
to get as many misstatements as possible by the Claimant on the record.
In this, the defendant's attorneys closely followed the strategy of cross-
examination by stealth, based on circumstantial evidence, advocated by
such commentators as Cox and Ram. However, this very leisureliness later
became the basis of the popular contention that the Claimant was in fact
who he claimed to be. Supporters of the Claimant frequently cited the lack
of a dramatic breakdown during the course of his cross-examination as
"proof" of his honesty.

Rather than cross-examination, therefore, the jury turned to apparently incontrovertible proofs of physical identity. Months of testimony in
the civil trial were finally brought to a conclusion by the jury's willingness
to seize upon evidence offered by the family that Roger Tichborne had
been tattooed on one arm. Many observers found both the evidence and
the jury's sudden unwillingness to proceed with the case questionable. A
sudden congeries of defense witnesses testifying to multiple tattoos was
considered suspicious, particularly given the unlikelihood of a young man
of Tichborne's status having such tattoos from an early age. The exhausted
jury, meanwhile, was thought to be reacting to the prospect (or perhaps
more accurately, the threat) of hearing another hundred witnesses. Among
the Claimant's supporters, therefore, many believed that the family's witnesses, particularly Lord Bellew, a schoolmate of Roger's, had committed
perjury.

At the Claimant's subsequent criminal trial for perjury, however, the
criticisms of cross-examination were not directed at its ineffectiveness, but
rather at the ethics of a highly accusatory style of conducting it. The Claimant's new counsel, Edward Kenealy, made a supposed Jesuit conspiracy a
centerpiece of his defense. He suggested frequently and with great vigor
that the witnesses against the Claimant, including Arthur Orton's child-
hood sweetheart, Mary Ann Loder, had been paid off.[111] He also attacked

Lord Bellew at length for seducing a friend's wife. While Kenealy admitted
that the alleged seduction had happened well before the events at issue in
the case, he professed to feeling obliged to raise the issue out of "an overwhelming sense of duty." Hawkins, now serving as prosecuting counsel,
protested strongly, calling the line of questioning a "waste of time" and noting that "there are many things of a disagreeable nature which a man does
not like to talk about," but Bellew was forced to answer nevertheless.[112]
Kenealy further alleged that the manager of the Tichborne estates, who had
appeared as a witness for the family, was guilty of criminal misconduct that
he sought to conceal by preventing the Claimant's return.

The presiding judge and Lord Chief Justice of England, Alexander
Cockburn, began his summation with a condemnation of Kenealy's conduct, criticizing his liberality in blackening the reputations of Tichborne
family members and all those associated with the family, ranging from witnesses from Chile and Australia who had testified to Arthur Orton's travels
there to the Jesuits who had educated Tichborne at Stonyhurst. He called
for censure from the bar, and the public joined in.[113] The *Guardian* declared that "in Dr Kenealy's method of conducting his case, these devices
for wasting time and insinuating the vilest charges against both Judge and
witnesses, have been more flagrant than we can remember to have heard in
any court of justice."[114] The *Pall Mall Gazette* agreed: "If there ever was a
case in which the particular Inn of Court of which Dr. Kenealy is a member
ought to feel itself bound to act, it is the present case."[115]

But what rule of professional etiquette had Kenealy violated? Edito-
rialists agreed that he had transgressed the norms of courtroom behavior,
particularly in his use of cross-examination as an occasion for accusation.
The *Pall Mall Gazette* thought that disrespect for the court was "not the
real charge" against Kenealy: "The real charge is that he attacked private
character recklessly, falsely, without proper grounds, in a great number
of cases, and in intemperate language."[116] The *Law Times* concurred:
"Dr. Kenealy . . . is charged with the most reckless violation of all the rules
which should govern the conduct of counsel in cross-examination of witnesses and in making comments upon their evidence, whilst it is said that
the Government of the country, the impartiality of the Judges, the living

and the dead who were connected with the case for the prosecution, were reviled in bitterest and coarsest terms."[117]

The legal profession united in condemning Kenealy's conduct as a threat to its reputation. In the *Law Times*'s summation, "These are not only offences against the Profession—that they do bring dishonour and discredit upon the Bar is admitted on all hands—but they are offences against public morality, and calculated to impede the course of justice."[118] What might have been acceptable during the heyday of the Old Bailey bar was no longer permissible. The *Law Journal* echoed Trollope:

> It does not follow that what was done in the time of Brougham or Denman, or at times anterior to them, can properly be done now. Morality has advanced very rapidly in the last forty years; and we do not see why the morality of the bar should stand still, as an action of doubtful propriety is not helped at all by a citation of similar actions by persons of repute in former times. Half the evils which have afflicted society have had their existence prolonged for immense periods of time, because those who were conservative of the evils could quote the opinion or conduct of some lofty personages in favour of them. Slavery, bull-baiting, condemnation for witchcraft, boiling women, hanging for theft, burning for heresy, and many other enormities which shock our age, were highly approved and stoutly defended by men whose memories are even revered.[119]

Keeping up with the march of civilization was not as easy as all that. Even committed critics of Kenealy's conduct wondered whether the Inns were being asked to intrude into the judge's sphere of authority: "it is absurd to claim for the benchers the right to do what the judges can do for themselves, and can do so much more effectually, because the judges see the offence committed, they can estimate its impropriety, and can punish it adequately."[120] The *Solicitors' Journal* protested what it saw as the assumption that the opinion of three judges and a jury censuring an advocate made it the duty of his Inn to inquire into his conduct. Such a principle would "convert the Benchers into mere henchmen of the judges, and to place into the hands of the latter a most crushing weapon against an obnoxious advocate."[121] The *Law Journal* doubted that the benchers had jurisdiction over matters: "[The benchers] ought not to attempt to exercise jurisdiction over mere conduct in Court. They are not to set themselves up as judges of manners, taste, demeanour, and the like."[122]

Another practical difficulty troubled the commentators: the evidentiary dilemma of assessing whether the context justified Kenealy's actions. "In order to [do so] it would be necessary first to measure the merits and demerits of the persons attacked by him; in other words, to try the Tichborne case over again in Gray's Inn parlor after dinner."[123] Moreover, in venturing into this new territory, the benchers were proceeding without the benefit of guideposts: a bencher would be "called to sit in judgment on Dr. Kenealy, not upon some accusation of an overt act of dishonour or wrong—not upon crimen aliquod probosum—but upon a question of discretion, of fairness, of good taste, of gentlemanly feeling, of forensic license—a question concerning which there are no laws, no rules, not even precedents worthy of a moment's consideration."[124]

Kenealy's supporters argued, with some justification, that his conduct was not unique. One wrote to the treasurer of Gray's Inn informing him of his intention to prefer a charge against Hawkins to the benchers of the Middle Temple for imputing a conspiracy to support the Claimant. The *Law Journal* rejected the comparison, commenting that "Mr. Hawkins undoubtedly used strong language in the course of the case. His diction was more choice, his manner more refined, and his bearing in all respects preferable to that of Mr. Kenealy."[125] But the charge of hypocrisy did carry some weight; later, the same periodical argued that "no worse tribunal to adjudicate upon [Kenealy's conduct] could be found than a body of men, many of whom daily and hourly hover on the very border-line between proper and improper treatment of a witness."[126]

Kenealy's defenders were swimming against the tide. On 2 April 1874, the Oxford Circuit voted to evict Kenealy from their mess, rejecting even a modest counterproposal that he be given an opportunity to respond. The mess's condemnation included Kenealy's imputations against numerous prosecution witnesses, appeals to the "Mob outside," misrepresentation of the evidence, calling of a perjured witness, mistreatment of the bench, and publication of a libel on the court.[127] The actions of the circuit were criticized by some as premature, but the *Law Times* found nothing to complain about, seeing the question in its most basic terms: "What the members of the circuit under such circumstances have to decide is, whether they wish to continue to dine and to associate in all the familiarity of social intercourse with a particular individual?"[128]

In May 1874, a designated committee at Gray's Inn charged with investigating Kenealy issued a list of alleged acts of professional misconduct, including:

1. By unjustifiably accusing members of the Tichborne family of a conspiracy to ruin the defendant in order to prevent him from recovering the Tichborne Estates, and with that view of exercising undue influence and committing bribery to induce witnesses to give false testimony on the part of the prosecution.

2. By unjustifiably accusing several of the witnesses for the prosecution [list omitted] of perjury induced and brought about in some cases by bribery, and in one case (namely that of Mr. Gosford) also by the compounding of a felony.

3. By unjustifiably accusing Mr. Bowker, Mr. Seymour, and Lord Bellew, of inventing the idea that Sir Roger Tichborne was tattooed, and of conspiring together to procure the destruction of the defendant by false evidence.

4. By unjustifiably accusing the authorities in the College of Stonyhurst of abominable and immoral conduct.

5. By unjustifiably attacking the character of several other persons [list omitted].

6. By unjustifiably accusing persons who had the conduct of the prosecution of knowingly putting forward false evidence

against the defendant, and advisedly withholding true evidence which they knew, or believed, to be favourable to the defendant.[129]

Circumstances, however, suggested an easier way out for benchers who remained uneasy. In April, Kenealy established a two-pence newspaper, the *Englishman,* which advocated the preservation of the rights of Englishmen, the establishment of female suffrage, and the thwarting of "the further march of Romanism and Jesuitry."[130] On 1 August 1874, the benchers of Gray's Inn resolved by a vote of ten to one that Kenealy's editorship of the radical *Englishman,* a "newspaper replete with libels of the grossest character," dictated the vacation of his call to the Inn's bench.[131] The benchers had also forwarded copies of the *Englishman* to the Lord Chancellor, who found them "libelous attacks on her Majesty's Judges and private individuals, and also a succession of systematic charges of bias, venality, and corruption," and informed Kenealy that he would be removed from the list of Queen's Counsel.[132] In December 1874, the Lord Chancellor proceeded, removing Kenealy.[133]

Thus, while Cockburn had called for the bar's action, control of Kenealy remained very much within the hands of the profession, not the bench. Yet, as Kenealy himself pointed out, abuses of cross-examination had occurred on both sides during the Tichborne trials. Both had raised arguably irrelevant past sexual misconduct against witnesses; both had resorted to ridicule at the expense of witnesses. And it remained an open question whether Kenealy was not performing just the function of detecting perjury that Cox and others had envisioned. Norms, however, had shifted, and Kenealy had made the error of pursuing his goals with eighteenth-century techniques. Members of the bar agreed that this type of license of counsel should be sanctioned, even if indirectly.

By the 1870s, therefore, the practice of direct and often baseless accusations of perjury during cross-examination was, if not expressly prohibited, at least widely condemned. Some of Cox's aspirations had at last been embraced by many of the leaders of the bar. Writing in 1879, Richard Harris referred to the practice of implying that a witness's previous answer was perjured as "an almost exploded style of cross-examination."[134] Instead, he reiterated the advice of earlier critics such as Edwin Chadwick that the only suitable course for a barrister to take when confronting a perjured witness was "to forbear to express the impression [the witness] has inspired."[135] In 1888, a magistrate for Great Grimsby commented during a parliamentary debate that "no Chairman of Quarter Sessions who was worth anything at all, and certainly no Judge in the land, would allow counsel to brow-beat a witness by reminding him of his oath."[136] Mr. Addison had heard counsel "remind witnesses that they were upon their oath; but he never knew, or rarely knew a counsel of experience to do anything of the kind. Such a thing was generally done by very young and inexperienced coun-sel at Sessions."[137] Baron Herschell called bullying cross-examination "the sure mark of a bumbling workman."[138] By 1897, Cox's journal informed its readers that "browbeating and annoying a witness is totally different from discrediting him."[139]

Cross-examination to Credit

For critics of abusive cross-examination, however, the Tichborne case represented one small step forward at the cost of a running leap back-wards. While the disciplining of Kenealy may have represented a grudging demarcation of the outer boundaries of accusatory behavior during cross-examination, Justice Cockburn's ruling from the bench that Kenealy could inquire into Lord Bellew's adulterous past was subsequently cited in sup-port of the proposition that *any* question tending to "shake" a witness's credit "by injuring his character" could be asked, even if it was irrelevant to the facts at issue.[140] In the 1879 edition of his *Digest of the Law of Evidence* James Stephen included the illustration of a witness testifying to a tattoo be-ing compelled to answer the question of whether he had committed adultery with the wife of one of his friends. Stephen called this "the well-established practice of the Courts," which was never "more strikingly illustrated than in the case referred to in the illustration"—which was, of course, Kenealy's notorious cross-examination.[141] Thus, while ungentlemanly accusations of perjury were now condemned, barristers still contended with the tension between their own sense of honor and their role as character assassins, not unlike their Old Bailey predecessors.

Everyone agreed that cross-examination as to character was necessary on some level; in the opinion of George Bramwell, First Baron Bramwell, "the grossest injustice is done when a man of undoubted good character is opposed to one of undoubted bad character, and yet they are treated as on an equality."[142] But Victorian lawyers were also keenly sensitive to the importance of reputation and the dangers posed by revelations of old misconduct in an age that treasured character above all else. As Ram described the problem:

> The temper of a witness is often tried, and his feelings hurt, by his cross-examination on his past conduct. He may have been charged with this or that offense; he may have been in prison. Questions on these matters are often properly put, with a view to see how far the witness is now entitled to credit; yet if the conduct inquired into is that of some years ago . . . it may be great and needless cruelty to bring again to light such bygone stains on his character.[143]

The plight of the otherwise virtuous witness forced to confess to long-ago misdeeds seems to have preoccupied Victorian jurists. Baron Herschell, in his lecture on legal advocacy, criticized even arguably relevant evidence of past dishonesty: "To require a witness who has long lived a respectable life to avow that very many years ago, he was convicted of dishonesty, is in general as cruel as it is unjustifiable."[144]

Anxieties regarding cross-examination to character were heightened by an 1883 decision that exempted counsel from defamation charges for words uttered in the course of a judicial proceeding.[145] While it had long been recognized that such actions could not be brought against judges, witnesses, and counsel in the ordinary course of judicial proceedings, *Munster v. Lamb* established that this protection extended even when counsel's statements were both malicious and completely irrelevant to the issue at hand. The counsel whose in-court statements were at issue in this case was

Charles Lamb, who was actually a solicitor. Henry Munster, the plaintiff and himself a barrister, had previously prosecuted William and Ellen Hill for a theft that had taken place in his lodging house in Brighton. William was convicted and Ellen was acquitted. Subsequently, Lamb defended Ellen against a charge that she had unlawfully administered soporific drugs to Munster's servants in order to prevent them from raising an alarm. According to Munster, during the course of the defense Lamb implied that Munster was in fact keeping a bawdy house and that the drugs were present there for some illegal purpose, such as facilitating rape or procuring abortions. In response, Munster sued Lamb for defamation. Reasoning that counsel had a need for protection at least equivalent to that already extended to judges and witnesses, the court took the opportunity to decide this case on the broadest possible basis—assuming both malice and irrelevance. Two members of the court commented that the absolute privilege of counsel was counterbalanced by the judge's power to check inappropriate conduct.[146]

Perhaps not coincidentally, 1883 also saw the first official formulation of the judge's power to curtail cross-examination. The Judicature Act of 1875 establishing the unified court system also set up a rule-making committee charged with codifying existing practice. In 1883 the committee issued the consolidated Rules of the Supreme Court. Order 36, Rule 38 provided that "the Judge may in all cases disallow any questions put in cross-examination of any party or other witness which may appear to him to be vexatious, and not relevant to any matter proper to be inquired into in the cause or matter."[147] Despite some initial misgivings as to whether the committee had exceeded its powers by including, for the first time, a measure explicitly giving judges the right to curtail cross-examination, the rule was generally praised.[148] It was also generally ignored in practice. More than three years later the *Solicitors' Journal* noted what it believed was the first instance the rule was invoked. Significantly, it was a case in which a party was conducting a pro se cross-examination.[149]

Although judges may have been given the power to curtail cross-examination, they remained chary of exercising it, particularly when the questions were posed by leaders of the bar. In December 1891, the weakness of the judicial reed was made abundantly clear in two cases: the

Russell divorce case and the so-called Pearl case. In these two cases, cross-examinations to character were conducted in a fashion that generated outbursts of public indignation. In 1891, the young wife of John Francis Stanley, the Second Earl Russell, petitioned for judicial separation from him on the grounds of cruelty. This was the second earl's first wife; he would subsequently acquire (and lose) two others, becoming along the way a fervent activist in the campaign for reform of England's divorce law.[150] The first Lady Russell was Mabel Edith Scott, whom Lord Russell wed after becoming infatuated with her mother, a beautiful widow. Mabel and John Francis, commonly known as Frank, were married on 6 February 1890 and separated a short five months later, in June 1890. Mabel's case came to trial in December 1891.[151]

Lady Russell alleged numerous acts of cruelty. She said that the earl had forced her to stay up until two or three o'clock in the morning doing accounts, that he had insisted she see after a restroom used by both male and female servants, and that he had demanded she dress him before he went out to a formal event. In order to prove that his cruelty had damaged her health, Lady Russell enumerated a series of disputes during which her husband had grabbed her by her wrists, thrown her onto the carpet, and, once, caused her to bleed at the wrists where her bracelets had torn into her skin. After one incident, she came to consciousness naked and in pain on the floor. They fought about money and about whether she could meet with individuals who the earl felt were not suitable company. She said that he kept a pistol in their house, and threatened to use it. Nor was his cruelty limited to the human species: he had also behaved badly toward her cat by tossing it repeatedly toward the ceiling. As a result of these disputes, she feared by the summer of 1890 that her health would be permanently impaired if she remained with the earl.

Most sensationally, Lady Russell accused her husband of going upstairs on consecutive evenings, undressed, to spend several hours in a bedroom with a male guest from Oxford. Lady Russell's accusation was incendiary because it resonated with Lord Russell's mysterious expulsion from Oxford as an undergraduate, which involved allegations of an inappropriate friendship with the poet Lionel Johnson. During the trial, Lady

Russell testified that it was only after she discussed the incident with several of Russell's relatives that she realized it was something "very grave."[152] There was, however, a great deal of ambiguity about the status of her accusation. Her own barrister pointedly remarked that the charge had been drawn from her only on cross-examination and had not been included in the petition. The judge hearing the case commented that her barrister, Solicitor General Sir Edward Clarke, argued as if "he would rather have had nothing to do with this part of the case."[153] During the presentation of Lady Russell's case, Clarke remarked that he was not going to make the serious accusation implied in her story.

Russell's defense painted his wife as a fiscally irresponsible woman who came into the marriage burdened with debt and who suffered from nervous complaints. The only motive for the suit was, they argued, a bid for an allowance. Lord Russell testified that Lady Russell was, according to him, a young woman who was used to having her own way and that he had to "exercise some restraint very early in the married life."[154] He was fond of cats and had never been cruel to any of them. He may have asked Lady Russell to look into bathroom supplies, but they were for a different bathroom that the servants did not enter. As for the incident in which she awoke naked on the floor, it was because she had fainted and he had attempted to revive her, removed her wet nightdress, and wrapped her in a comforter.

Clarke cross-examined Lord Russell. In the course of discussing a letter from Lady Russell requesting that the earl not rehire a servant, Clarke managed to plunge the case still deeper into controversy. Russell was forced to explain that he had previously engaged as servants a family called Williams. He had seduced the eldest daughter, Kate, about four years ago and remained intimate with her until just before his engagement to Lady Russell. Russell had arranged to pay one pound a week to Kate's mother, but she nonetheless brought a breach of promise suit that had been settled for five hundred pounds. In his reexamination, Russell testified that he had told both Lady Russell and her mother of this affair before the marriage. The following day, Russell commented that the story of his affair with Kate Williams had not been known publicly until this trial, a theme that Charles Russell, the earl's counsel, returned to with great zeal during his closing argument. Kate Williams, he said, had been earning her own livelihood and "had been able to hold up her head in the eyes of the world; but for the base purpose of endeavouring to still further prejudice Lord Russell in the eyes of the [jury, Lady Russell] had not hesitated to sacrifice ruthlessly the happiness of one of her own sex."[155]

Lord Russell's plight seemed to touch a popular chord. When he was cross-examined about his history at Oxford, "there was applause in the Court, notwithstanding the protests of the learned Judge."[156] The President, in a summing-up that tended to stress the tenuousness of Lady Russell's case, condemned the questions regarding Kate Williams in a thinly veiled criticism of Lady Russell: "he could not help thinking that whoever had instructed the Solicitor-General to put these circumstances before the jury was actuated by nothing but malice." Similarly, the incident at Oxford seemed to have no purpose except "making the jury believe that he was a young man addicted to such practices as were suggested." Yet he called Clarke "far too honourable" to make such a charge and praised Charles Russell for zealous service on his client's behalf in cross-examining Lady Russell.[157] The jury retired for little more than half an hour and quickly returned to announce that they agreed Lord Russell had not been guilty of cruelty toward his wife. As a result, the unhappy couple remained married to one another.

Less than a fortnight after the conclusion of the Russell divorce case, many of the same legal luminaries returned to court in a slander case, *Osborne v. Hargreave & Wife*. Charles Russell appeared for the plaintiff, Mrs. Osborne, a recently married young woman who had been known under her maiden name, Ethel Elliot, at the time of the events in question; Edward Clarke appeared for the defendants, Major George Hargreave and his wife Georgiana, who was a distant relation of Mrs. Osborne's.[158] The Osborne case was commonly known as the "Pearl case" after the missing pearl and diamond earrings—with pearls as "large as filberts"—whose secret travels lay at the heart of the dispute.[159] Russell deemed it a case "fraught with mystery," but its widespread public appeal may have had more to do with the unusual spectacle of a slander action between two respectable society ladies regarding an accusation that one had stolen the other's jewels while visiting her house.[160]

Miss Elliot had visited Mrs. Hargreave in Torquay in February 1891. The two women were second cousins but had only recently resumed contact after an estrangement of some years (the reason for the estrangement was never fully explained in the course of the trial). Major Hargreave, meanwhile, had recently left for an extended trip to Aix-en-Provence for health reasons. The two women enjoyed a visit of more than a week; Mrs. Hargreave expressed admiration for Miss Elliot's hat, which Miss Elliot promptly gave to her, and the two had photographs taken. Miss Elliot returned to her London home on February 18 to make arrangements for her April wedding. On February 19 a young woman claiming to be Alice Price sold Mrs. Hargreave's diamond and pearl earrings to a London jeweler for £550. Miss Price first gave a Hyde Park address, but when the jeweler noticed that no one named Price lived at that address, she said she was visiting from Yorkshire. On February 23, the same young woman returned to the jeweler to change the check she had received on the 19th to one payable to cash.

Back in Torquay, Mrs. Hargreave noticed that her earrings were missing from their secret cabinet after Miss Elliot's departure. The earrings, which Mrs. Hargreave had inherited from her grandmother, had been kept in a specially designed escritoire with a secret compartment that Mrs. Hargreave had demonstrated to Miss Elliot during her visit. Police in Torquay were notified, and the Hargreave's house was searched several times, with the assistance of a friend of the family, Mr. Engelhart. Major Hargreave returned briefly from Aix on March 1 but went back there on March 4. As the search progressed, suspicion fell on Miss Elliot. On March 9, Mr. Engelhart took the photos of Miss Elliot to London where the jeweler and several of his assistants identified her as the young woman who had sold them the jewels. Mr. Engelhart went to Miss Elliot's brother with his suspicions, and the two of them, together with Miss Elliot and her elder sister, returned to the jewelers. There, Miss Elliot was once again identified as the young woman in question, both by the jewelers and by the bank clerk who had cased the check on February 23. The witnesses, however, differed significantly in their recollections of the young woman's attire. Subsequently, the Hargreaves successfully sued the jewelers for return of their earrings, but rather than prosecuting the recently married Mrs. Osborne, they demanded a written confession from her.[161] She refused, and sued them for slander instead.

Mrs. Osborne's slander suit provided a full measure of drama. In her testimony, she claimed that Mrs. Hargreave had complained about Major Hargreave and that the Hargreaves and their friend Engelhart were hard up. Mrs. Osborne's sister recounted an incident in which Major Hargreave said that he would commit any crime for money, and her brother insinuated that the major had probably taken the jewels himself. When Major Hargreave took the stand, Charles Russell questioned him repeatedly about his trips to Aix: what illness, precisely, was he receiving treatment for? The major responded that it was a combination of general poor health, a recent bad fall, and the recurrence of an illness he had contracted in India. Russell pressed for a more specific description of the nature of this recurring illness; the major said it was blood-poisoning, and Russell skeptically commented that he had not known blood poisoning could recur over a period of twenty-one years. The exotic origin of the illness, its persistence, and the major's decision to seek treatment in France allowed Russell to imply that the major suffered from venereal disease.

Before the defense testimony was complete, however, the trial came to a sudden and curious halt. It was adjourned after Justice Denman received a letter from a firm of tailors informing him that they had been visited by a woman matching Mrs. Osborne's description who had asked them to change a large quantity of gold into notes. Subsequent investigation revealed that one of those notes had been signed by Mrs. Osborne. When the trial reconvened, Charles Russell and the rest of Mrs. Osborne's legal team informed the court that they could no longer appear as her counsel. Moreover, Russell expressed their regret "that we have in any sense been the medium of conveying" imputations against Major Hargreave and Mr. Engelhart. Edward Clarke, for his part, said that Russell "only did his duty in acting upon instructions he had no reason to doubt." Finally,

Justice Denman—in a fit of ill-judged enthusiasm—announced that the case had been "nobly conducted throughout": "I do not think that any human being can impute the slightest blame to any one engaged in it. On the contrary, everybody who is acquainted with the working of our law must feel the highest honour and respect for the counsel who have conducted the case."[162]

The conclusion of the Pearl case was met with widespread consternation. The *Times* greeted the news by lamenting that young ladies moving in good society might not be what they seemed: "we are confronted with possibilities of evil under the most plausible exterior which are at least as appalling as any rapidity of descent from integrity."[163] But Mrs. Osborne's legal travails were not over by any means. Within a week an arrest warrant was issued for her, describing her appearance as "rather Jewish," but she had already fled to the Continent.[164] In February 1892, Mrs. Osborne surrendered to the public prosecutor to stand trial for theft and perjury.[165] After she pleaded guilty in March 1892, the Hargreaves; her husband, Captain Osborne; and her reconstituted legal team, headed again by Charles Russell, argued for leniency, contending that her behavior had been caused by "hysteria" and that she had undoubtedly brought the slander case without understanding its consequences. He played on a Victorian tendency to explain "bad" behavior by "good" women by assuming that such conduct must be indicative of madness, particularly madness caused by physical instability, such as pregnancy or childbirth.[166] Despite a recent pregnancy, Mrs. Osborne was sentenced to nine months' hard labor, much to the shock of her friends and relations. Meanwhile, the Hargreaves benefited from the notoriety of the trial by selling their jewels at auction for more than a thousand pounds.

The Hargreaves, Elliots, and Osbornes mounted a campaign for clemency, citing Mrs. Osborne's history of hysteria and her recent pregnancy. The idea of a "respectable" young woman—even one who had admitted to theft, perjury, and slander—facing such a sentence struck an empathetic chord among the reading public. *Woman* magazine called for the "strong arm of the law" to be relaxed in her case, arguing that her public humiliation amounted to punishment "quite as much as that of a woman in a humble position of life sentenced to a term of imprisonment." Mrs. Osborne's criminal acts were reframed as gestures of marital love: "for the sake of [her husband's love] she had faced judge, jury, and counsel in the forlorn hope of winning her action, and convincing her husband of her innocence."[167] A public appeal for mercy on her behalf was signed by leaders of the British medical profession. In the end, Mrs. Osborne served less than two months of her sentence: she was released in April 1892.

Public attention remained focused, however, on the conduct of the trial, and in particular the role cross-examination had played in it. The *Times*'s editorial question as to how this trial could be deemed to have been "conducted 'nobly'" struck a nerve.[168] It immediately provoked an outpouring of correspondence on the license of counsel with regard to cross-examination. Dozens of correspondents wrote to the *Times*, while the legal professional press carried on its own debate. Even humorists entered the fray. Edward Manson published a satirical piece titled "Cross-Examination: A Socratic Fragment" in which Socrates and his interlocutor progress from an initial assertion that "the object of cross-examining witnesses is to elicit the truth" to a conclusion that "the special excellence of the advocate is to advertise himself and make himself popular with solicitors" because "law is in the nature of a cock-fight, and that the litigant who wishes to succeed must try and get an advocate who is a game bird with the best pluck and the sharpest spurs."[169]

Trollope's rhetoric of cruelty dominated the discussion. One writer called the courts "the torture chambers of the end of the 19th century."[170] Another compared cross-examination to blood sports, perhaps alluding to barrister Henry Hawkins's notorious fondness for Sunday dog and badger fights:[171] "We have put down prize-fighting, bull-baiting, and badger-drawing. It is high time we should put down Chaffinbrass [*sic*], and with him witness browbeating, the last surviving of these 'noble' sports."[172] The *Times* used the language of torture in an editorial exploring the statement, "The discretion of counsel is practically the only security against the transformation of a Court of law into a torture chamber, and this security is rapidly disappearing."[173]

Why did nineteenth-century critics turn so readily to the language of torture and cruelty? One answer may lie in the fear of status degradation. James Whitman's account of heightened revulsion concerning degradation in the nineteenth century is echoed in English concerns about the conduct of late Victorian trials.[174] Punishment involved status degradation, particularly in Europe, where there was a recent history of differentiation between high- and low-status forms of punishment. In England, the demarcation between high and low punishment was not as clear, but cross-examination to character and prior history threatened high-status witnesses with severe reputational costs. Degrading cross-examination transferred the norms of the Old Bailey, where most defendants and many witnesses were lower class, to the higher-status realm of civil litigation. In the witness box, a lord, a lady, or even the Prince of Wales could be reduced to the same ignominy as the rude criminal defendant.[175]

Other critics focused on the practical consequences of unrestricted cross-examination: anxiety that a zealous barrister's questions might lead witnesses to refuse to testify and make justly wronged plaintiffs reluctant to bring cases for fear that unrelated past embarrassments might be "raked up." One firm of solicitors reported that a preeminent engineer who frequently testified as an expert witness raised his fees to a "prohibitive" level upon discovering that Charles Russell would be representing the other side.[176] One "J.H.P." wrote to say that, although he had been defrauded by his broker, he would not prosecute because he feared that the broker would employ "forensic bullies" and "his defense would, no doubt, be 'nobly' conducted."[177] Several correspondents noted that "commercial men" no longer brought their disputes into court for fear of degrading treatment.[178] An "Equity QC" took the occasion to tout the superiority of the equity bar: "I do not remember to have ever heard a question asked by any member of the Equity Bar which could be considered even by the most morbid sensitiveness as unfairly put for the purpose merely of terrifying or inflicting pain."[179]

Many correspondents wondered why judges did not intervene. They speculated that judges had often been "smart cross-examiners themselves"[180] or that they were "too habituated to the present mode of cross-examination to perceive its abuses and protect witnesses from them."[181] "Counsel" argued that judges failed to check the abuse of cross-examination "through timidity, and the natural desire to shun a passage of arms with the big bullies of the Courts."[182] The *Law Times* criticized Isaac Butt and Denman for commending "where everyone condemned" and opined that "none of our judges appear to be strong enough to stop in mid career the leading advocates at Nisi Prius."[183] The *Solicitors' Journal* concurred, noting that the checking of abusive cross-examination "ought not to be left solely in the hands of the judges."[184]

A number of correspondents suggested vigorous application of the rule of court against vexatious cross-examinations. The *Law Journal* believed that the rule had never been invoked since its adoption in 1883.[185] The *Solicitors' Journal* called for a formal definition of "vexatious" that would give force to the rule, which was otherwise a dead letter, but it also cautioned that stopping cross-examination is a "matter of extreme difficulty" and that longstanding practice permitted "the greatest latitude."[186] The *Law Journal* suggested that a similar provision against vexatious questioning be incorporated in the Divorce Court rules.[187] Other correspondents urged, as Stephen had before, turning to India or to the armed forces for a new model. W. T. Dooner of the Royal Inniskilling Fusiliers wrote to suggest that civil courts "might do worse than follow the procedure which is adopted . . . in courts-martial" whereby judges are required to determine that questions would "seriously affect their opinion as to the credibility of the witness" before requiring a witness to answer.[188]

Baron Bramwell, writing from the standpoint of forty-seven years of practice, served as the voice of the legal profession at its most unrepentant. He declared that he believed Charles Russell's improbable posttrial assertion that "he did not know that Aix was resorted to for such affections [*sic*] as suggested." Bramwell dismissed the accusations against the bar, stating that he did not know of any counsel notorious for bullying. Instead, he argued that the barrister stood in the client's shoes and was obligated to exercise all the rights that belonged to the client; therefore, he had the right to conduct any cross-examination that bore upon a witness's intelligence or honesty. Any roughness that might result was justified by the outcome: "Let us judge by the result. By our system is not truth got at, is not justice done? I say yes confidently."[189]

Others agreed that cross-examination was necessary and placed the blame on recalcitrant witnesses and unscrupulous solicitors. "R.A.M." found it necessary not only against the perjurer and the fraudulent criminal, but also against a far larger class of "conceited and self-satisfied witnesses, whose inaccuracy of observation, weakness of memory, bias, and prejudice can be exposed by cross-examination and cross-examination alone."[190] Bruised witnesses, another writer suggested, should look to their own consciences:

> No doubt some witnesses have a rough time of it, but they generally have only themselves to blame. If they are truthful, frank, and intelligent, the most powerful cross-examiner is powerless. [But many witnesses are] willful liars; more are gross exaggerators and prevaricators, and others are over-zealous partisans. It is the task of the cross-examiner not merely to get evidence out of the witness, but to show what manner of man he is. And frequently the sole method of doing this is by means of questions on apparently immaterial points.[191]

"A Good Witness" agreed: "Thirty years' experience in courts of law has convinced me . . . that men and women are so prone to espouse the cause of the side upon which they are 'called' that they require, as a rule, to be well 'shaken up' in order to bring their minds back to the proper balance."[192]

The defenders of cross-examination would concede to only limited prophylactic measures. Barristers needed to be more careful in their evaluation of their clients' accusations: "to examine upon a speculative hypothesis, upon the chance that the witness may admit something to his prejudice, is, we think, a most reprehensible practice."[193] At the same time, however, Baron Bramwell criticized the suggestion that a barrister should second-guess his client: "Counsel . . . I do not say is blindly to think his client is right, but I do say he is to think he may be right till it is shown he is not."[194]

Little changed as a result of the controversy caused by the Russell and Pearl cases, but the heightened emotions revealed the intimate link between cross-examination and the barrister's identity as a gentleman. "A Barrister of Twelve Years' Standing" touched off an outcry by challenging the gentility of the bar. He asserted sardonically that "barristers are, of course, all gentlemen before they become barristers. They change rapidly afterwards."[195] In a subsequent letter, he deplored the way "conduct which, if in man who was a gentleman and not a barrister would be considered disgraceful, in a barrister is not only passed over but is called 'noble' by a kindly Judge, and excused by the whole profession."[196] More readers responded to this letter than any other. A barrister of "nearly 24 years' standing" proclaimed, "The truth is that if a man is a gentleman he cannot cease to be one, and such a man is as incapable of a 'brutal' cross-examination as he is of any other ungentlemanly conduct."[197] The *Law Journal* brought the topic of abusive cross-examination back to the playing fields, declaring that it "savours rather of terrorism than fairplay."[198] Moreover, professional identity both conferred and ensured gentility: "To charge Sir Charles Russell or Sir Edward Clarke with such a wicked misuse of their power is about as ludicrous as it would be to charge Sir James Paget with using a surgical instrument merely to inflict pain."[199]

The question of the barrister's role as a gentleman brings us back to the cases that ignited the correspondence in the *Times*. Both trials featured young female litigants using barristers to advance accusations of serious sexual misconduct against respectable men. In Lord Russell's case, it was homosexuality, and in the Pearl case, it was the coded accusation that Major Hargreave suffered from a venereal disease, indicating that he had had contact with prostitutes. In both cases barristers took refuge behind their instructions, even though the plaintiffs' cases were tenuous at best. The outrage, therefore, also conveys a criticism that the barristers had departed from their specifically masculine role as gentlemen. The *Law Journal* called on barristers to fulfill their role as the "sterner sex," employing a "chivalrous sense of duty."[200] Lord Russell saw his case as a battle of the sexes for control of the forensic arena. After the divorce case, Russell wrote his friend George Santayana, proclaiming that the verdict showed "men in general that women should not have all their own way in law courts."[201]

Many participants in these controversies took pains to emphasize the broader principle that the barristers should have at least enough autonomy from their clients and instructing solicitors to reject potentially degrading lines of inquiry. Baron Herschell declared that "this conception of independence of the advocate . . . is of vital importance. If it were lost sight of, and counsel were to become the mere creature of the party who had engaged his service, the profession of advocacy would be a source of public danger."[202] It required the advocate "never to yield to the solicitations of a client, however pressing, to blacken the character of an adverse witness by a line of questioning which his own judgment condemns."[203] Richard Harris agreed, opining that in cross-examination to credit "the greatest mistake an advocate can make is to let his client dictate to him the mode in which his case is to be conducted."[204] Nor should counsel succumb to the equally dangerous desire to please instructing solicitors by following their suggested lines of inquiry. Such admonitions were more than a little self-serving in their suggestion that abusive cross-examination had its origins in either the client or the solicitor's flawed judgment. But they did serve to couple zealous advocacy with a duty of restraint. Barristers justified the latitude they claimed for themselves in cross-examination by taking on a new responsibility for policing the boundaries of reasonable inquiry.

The New Rules of Embarrassment

Barristers' conduct in cases like the Russell divorce or the Pearl suit was made possible by a shift in the rules of evidence relating to cross-examination. Increasingly, barristers were allowed more latitude when cross-examining on subjects that tended to degrade witnesses without subjecting them to criminal liability. Where previously the law had entertained some ambiguity as to either whether such questions could be put or whether a witness could be compelled to answer them, the last quarter of the nineteenth century saw the emergence of a consensus that such questions were permissible, although most commentators were unwilling to go so far as to say that witnesses could be compelled to answer them.[205] At one level, this absence of solicitude for a witness's public character is puzzling. Reputation, as many cultural historians have noted, was crucially important in late nineteenth-century Britain. Chief Baron Frederick Pollock, for example, was reported to have burst into tears when an apparently respectable witness was forced to admit to "a conviction years gone by."[206] The resolution to this apparent paradox lies in the redefinition of cross-examination as a gentlemanly art—one governed and limited by the barrister's own honor and moral sense.

During the early decades of the nineteenth century, legal authorities debated the existence of a privilege protecting witnesses from questions that tended to damage their reputations. Thomas Starkie, for example, wrote that "it has been held that a witness is not bound to answer any question which tends to render him infamous, or even to disgrace him," but he questioned the extent of the privilege.[207] Samuel Phillipps commented that opinion was divided on the question. Although at least two cases held that "a question, the object of which is to degrade the witness's character, cannot properly be asked," Phillipps noted that one of the authors of these opinions countenanced similar questions in his courtroom in other cases.[208] Other treatise writers found the privilege uncertain. Andrew Amos, in his 1838 edition of Phillipps's *A Treatise on the Law of Evidence,* doubted the continuing validity of some earlier precedent suggesting that even putting such questions would be illegal, but thought it more likely that a witness could refuse to answer such a question: "there seems to be no reported case, in which this point has been solemnly determined; and in the absence of all express authority, opinions have been much divided."[209] By the 1850s, the window of uncertainty had narrowed. While debating the Common Law Procedure Act in 1853, Lord Brougham commented that judicial opinion was divided as to whether a witness was protected from answering questions "which did not tend to implicate him in the confession of any offence, which did not expose him to the risk of any indictment, but which only went to disgrace and degrade him." In Brougham's opinion, the privilege did not extend that far.[210] John Pitt Taylor questioned the weight of "older dicta" indicating that a witness was not bound to answer an immaterial and degrading question: "the privilege, if it still exists, is certainly much discountenanced in the practice of modern times."[211]

This era of ambiguity drew to a close with the Tichborne trials. After the ruling on the Bellew testimony in the first Tichborne trial, Stephen, writing semianonymously in the *Pall Mall Gazette*, declared, "It appeared to be the law of England that if a witness is called to testify in any court of justice upon any subject whatever his opponent has a legal right to ask him any question whatever as to any incident in his past life, the existence of which would in any degree affect [his credit]."[212] The 1877 edition of William Russell's *A Treatise on Crimes and Misdemeanors* doubted whether a witness could refuse to answer a question tending "merely to disgrace and degrade him."[213] The legal periodical press, meanwhile, took the question as definitively settled by the Tichborne case: counsel could ask any question of a witness, no matter how embarrassing, if it had the potential to degrade the witness's credibility.[214]

What had previously been seen as a form of abuse increasingly came to seem like acceptable practice if the case at hand justified it in the barrister's estimation. Once this change occurred, commentators suggested that abuses of cross-examination could be stemmed by greater attention to distinctions between "character" and "reputation" and between relevant and irrelevant inquiries. Ernest Bowen-Rowlands, for example, carefully delineated the difference between character as general reputation and character as disposition in an 1895 article on character evidence.[215] Other writers called for more stringent restrictions on impeaching a witness's credibility on matters irrelevant to the issue at hand.[216] Still other legal commentators sought to distinguish between previous noncriminal misconduct that actually bore on credibility from that which was peripheral or solely intended for embarrassment's sake. The *Law Journal* complained that "when an attempt is made to forge a link between what is called character and veracity, the main difficulty lies in deciding what are and what are not proper materials for the purpose. Into the inquiry a whole host of moral, social, even of religious problems are apt to thrust themselves—problems upon which the greatest masters of casuistry might agree to differ."[217] Sexual misconduct in particular, it was argued, should not be taken as indicative of lack of credibility. The *Law Journal* thought that "because a man has for some cause or other separated from his wife and has committed adultery, it does not follow that he will be guilty of the crime of perjury."[218] Similarly, adulterous immigration to the United States, leaving behind a family, had no bearing on the credibility of witnesses testifying to the quality of wool yarn.[219] In a later article, the *Law Journal* advised its readers that "it is much safer to proceed upon the principle that sexual immorality has no bearing at all on the credibility of the witness."[220] Despite the clarity of the principle, the trials of the 1890s provided ample demonstration that the temptations of sexual innuendo still proved irresistible for some counsel. Adultery proved fertile ground for cross-examination as to credit both inside and outside the Divorce Court, as will be discussed in chapters 4 and 5.

The problem was that "the line is hard for any one but the cross-examining counsel himself to draw; and that the matter must chiefly be left to his honour and discretion."[221] The *Solicitors' Journal* thought the "practice of the English bench is, with few exceptions, *not* to check any question, however painful to the witness, but to leave the matter to the honour and discretion of the Bar." The bar's honor and discretion were, in turn, insulated from scrutiny because "the advocate knows what is in his brief; the judge and public do not."[222] Moreover, the barrister was also protected by his lack of knowledge of the other side's case: "The most scrupulously honourable and fair practitioner cannot know with certainty that allegations of which prima facie evidence appears are unfounded when the rebutting evidence is in the possession of the other side."[223]

Instead of rules and precedent, then, control of cross-examination was largely reliant on the artistic instincts of the barrister, as tempered by his sense of honor as a professional man. The *Law Journal* waxed lyrical on this subject, presenting cross-examination as both aesthetic and moral: "Cross-examination constitutes the fine art department of the profession of counsel. . . . Like painting, sculpture, poetry and music, it commands a multitude of critics, but boasts a limited number of experts." Given the intuitive nature of the activity, cross-examination was best governed by the individual counsel's conscience. While the extent of cross-examination permitted at law inevitably encompassed the potential for abuse, "there are many extreme rights which no sane man enforces." Instead, the *Law Journal* placed its reliance on the lawyer's self-restraint: "counsel is bound in honour and out of respect to himself and his profession to consider whether the question ought to be put, not whether his client would like it to be put."[224] As the *Law Journal* saw it, then, barristers were to be trusted with the reputations and honor of others, because their own honor as gentlemen was unquestioned. The construction of this notion of gentlemanly restraint, and its paradoxical-seeming reconciliation with the sometimes decidedly aggressive exigencies of cross-examination, complicates the usual assumption that the triumph of the adversarial model was an unqualified one.

By the end of the nineteenth century, cross-examination had emerged as the main engine of truth in traditional common-law trial contexts. There were, however, situations in which cross-examination was still thought to be inadequate to the challenge of ascertaining truth. In both the colonial courts in India and the new Divorce Court in London, the impetus toward mendacity was thought to be too strong for even cross-examination to counter it. We now turn to the Victorian experimentation with innovative sanctions against deceit in these two novel circumstances.

PART TWO

Experimentation Abroad and at Home

CHAPTER THREE

Perjury and Prevarication in British India

IN 1858, THE GOVERNOR GENERAL OF INDIA, Charles Canning, passed on a remarkable petition to the Court of Directors of the East India Company in London. The petition was from Ishri Pershad, described by Canning as a "native of respectability" in the city of Allahabad.[1] Writing in the aftermath of the Indian Rebellion of 1857–58 that had sorely challenged British rule, Pershad had a simple message for the British government of the North Western Provinces in India: I told you so. Pershad reminded the government that in 1856, before the outbreak of the rebellion, he had proposed a scheme of governance. If only they had listened to him, Pershad wrote, "the mutinies of some 40 or 50 regiments would never have occurred."[2] Pershad's scheme was a curious one: he advised that sweepers, the so-called untouchables who could pollute higher-caste Hindus through even slight contact, be specially attached to each criminal court. These sweepers would be employed to spit into the mouths of natives convicted of perjury, thereby defiling them. Those convicted of perjury and defiled could then be converted to Christianity and employed as a regiment to defend Allahabad.

The British never seriously considered Pershad's suggestions; Canning forwarded his petition to London merely as evidence of popular belief among inhabitants of the North Western Provinces that the British sought widespread conversions. The Court of Directors, for their part, noted that Pershad "wish[ed] to recommend himself to the authorities and to obtain preferment for himself and his brother" and urged the government in India to "strictly abstain from all measures" that might support the belief that the British wished to force Indians to become Christians.[3] But Pershad's letter is evocative nonetheless. His linkage of effective control of perjury to colonial governance uncovers the complicated consequences of an ideology of colonialism based on the rule of law.

Pershad did not hit on perjury by accident. Perjury loomed large in the colonial imagination because of the British conviction of its prevalence. British administrators in India tended to see most, if not all, witnesses as likely perjurers. Pershad appears to have known this; certainly, he seems to have thought that the British would accept his assumption that the ranks of perjurers were numerous enough to provide a credible defense for a large city like Allahabad. In part because of their unshakeable belief that perjury was rampant in India, British administrators returned repeatedly to the question of identifying, regulating, and punishing lies and liars. Pershad might be forgiven for thinking that his suggestion would simply have been the latest in a long series of related legal innovations.

Nor, for that matter, was Pershad's solution as far out of line as it initially seems. In proposing a quasi-religious sanction—defiling contact with a sweeper—the proposal combined two other themes that characterized British attempts to combat perjury under the East India Company's rule. First, Pershad's suggestion employed shame as a crucial tool of governance. During the period when the Company formally controlled the Indian legal system, which lasted until the Indian Rebellion, the British sought a sanction or form of oath that would mobilize community sentiment against perjury. They identified lack of ignominy as a key reason why their efforts against perjury appeared to fail and tried to develop ways of cultivating the revulsion they felt was missing. Pershad would have been familiar with other British attempts to inculcate shame, such as tattooing offenders' foreheads or forcing them to blacken their face and ride backwards on an ass; in this context, his suggestion looks rather less bizarre. Second, Pershad's framing of his punishment within a religious context—in this case Hinduism—is consonant with the British history of placing their criminal law in India within indigenous religious traditions. The British radically transformed the Islamic law of perjury, ostensibly the law that they administered, while maintaining at least the façade of continuity with Islamic tradition. Finally, Pershad's linkage of a criminal offense with military defense suggests that forensic deceit was a question of order as much as it was of law.

This chapter explores the process by which the British redefined perjury in response to the perceived exigencies of colonial rule. British legislative efforts in India stand in stark contrast to the history of law reform in England, where little redefinition of the substantive law occurred during the same period. British legislative creativity in the subcontinent was driven by anxiety about the ability of British administrators to uncover the truth in disputes before them. Perjury justified colonial rule by separating rulers from ruled—with the British convinced that they were honest and Indians were inherently mendacious—but it also complicated it by suggesting that colonial administrators were constantly at risk of being duped. Perjury's contradictions crossed the boundaries between substantive and procedural law, challenging both the definition of the crime and the legitimacy of the judicial system in British India. The tension between these contradictory aspects of the ideology of the rule of law forced administrators to revisit the question of perjury constantly, searching for a solution to a dilemma created, in large part, by the very nature of colonialism. British interest in redefining perjury took multiple forms. The British were not only concerned with the evidentiary requirements of the crime and its punishment; they also sought to develop an analogous offense—prevarication—that would strengthen their control over the colonial legal process without extensive investigation into underlying facts or the intent of the accused. We trace this process through two broad phases: first, a period of innovation that lasted until the early 1830s, and second, a period of retrenchment and Anglicization between the Charter Act of 1833 and the Indian Evidence Act of 1872. These efforts to develop novel strategies for the production of truth in the courtroom generated unexpected problems and contradictions that cast the development of common-law trial practice in a new light.

Perjury and the Colonial Project

Perjury had a special role to play in maintaining the legitimacy of the legal system in India. Belief in widespread perjury challenged administrators' and spectators' confidence in the validity of judicial decisions; combatting perjury, therefore, was crucial to maintaining colonial rule. Many imperialists have advanced the rule of law as one of the central rationales for colonial rule.[4] As Peter Fitzpatrick writes, "law was a prime justification and instrument of imperialism."[5] With specific reference to India, Thomas Metcalf similarly argues that "in place of a religious faith shared with its subject, the British colonial state . . . found its legitimacy in a moralization of 'law.'"[6] Examining the struggle over perjury in the British administration of India highlights profound anxieties and contradictions in the use of the rule of law as a sustaining ideology of colonial rule. It can therefore contribute to the growing interest in looking at contradictions and conflicts within the colonial project. Scholars such as Martin Chanock have pointed to the tensions caused by embedding the universality promised in the rhetoric of the rule of law within a framework of colonial difference.[7] But these tensions should not be seen as limited to the colonial setting: the rhetoric of legal equality in the metropole was both undergirded and in some ways contradicted by a notion of police power that drew upon profound distinctions between the ruler and the ruled, between the head of the family writ large and the subordinate members of his household.[8]

British notions of the prevalence of perjury in India paradoxically served both to destabilize and to sustain faith in the rule of law as colonial justification. For those closest to the administration of law in India—the magistrates and judges working for the East India Company—belief in the ubiquity of perjury caused them to doubt the practical benefits of the vaunted rule of law. Unsure of the veracity of much of the evidence that they relied on in their decisions, magistrates and judges questioned the justice of their judgments. A. Tufton, magistrate in Bahar, complained along these lines in 1801: "In short, to speak my mind without reserve, this crime is so common and audacious, that it has excited in me the most complete scepticism with respect to all evidence which is offered, and I seldom pass a judgment, without having cause to doubt if I have not been imposed upon."[9] For the lawgivers, the rule of law was a hopeful pretense, covering up the awkward reality of justice based on guesswork. In John Comaroff's apt description, the search for truth in British Indian courtrooms was one of the "disarticulated, semicoherent, inefficient strivings for modes of rule that might work in unfamiliar, intermittently hostile places a long way from home."[10]

Yet, at the same time, British ideas about perjury helped deflect criticism of the practical workings of the colonial state. Native perjury could explain why the rule of law seemed to bring little in the way of actual progress in its wake. In Metcalf's summary, "if Indians were people without moral principles, then inevitably they lied in court, pocketed bribes, and wilfully rejected the benefits of British justice."[11] As James Mill argued, Indian vices tended to "enfeeble the arm of justice" in British India.[12] The British, as they saw it, brought the horse to water, but the Indians, habituated to perjury by centuries of despotic government, refused to drink. Perjury and prevarication, in the form of prosecutions and discourse regarding their prevalence, also sustained colonial ideology by providing a concrete location for and confirmation of beliefs about native mendacity.[13] Metcalf has pointed out that British ideology depended on the construction of polarities, among them "honesty" and "deceit," with the British as paragons of the former and Indians as embodiments of the latter.[14] As the previous chapters have shown, nineteenth-century jurists were hardly sanguine about witness veracity in the metropolitan courts. In India, however, this inconvenient fact disappeared: perjury prosecutions and discussion of the prevalence of perjury and prevarication ceaselessly created and re-created the imagined polarity between honest Britons and deceitful Indians, giving it the imprimatur of juridical truth. This differentiation echoed the treatment of slaves in the United States: there, testimony by enslaved people was strictly limited, and degrading punishments for perjury, such as public whipping or pillorying, were adopted to combat what was seen as an inherent mendacity and irreligiosity.[15] In both cases, the distinction between ruler and ruled justified methods of control within the procedural structure of the courts that were directed at entire populations.

Perjury, moreover, speaks to the recent interest in understanding colonialism as a system of production and control of knowledge. As Nicholas Dirks writes, "colonialism was made possible, and then sustained and strengthened, as much by cultural technologies of rule as it was by the more obvious and brutal modes of conquest that first established power on foreign shores."[16] Bernard Cohn has identified one of the most important of these "cultural technologies": British colonialism's assumption that society could be represented as a series of facts and that administrative power stemmed from efficient use of those facts. The British therefore needed to collect the facts, through what Cohn calls "investigative modalities." These modalities took a variety of forms, from historiography and museology, surveys and the census, to sciences such as economics and ethnology.[17] Subsequent historians have pointed out that British production of knowledge occurred on different levels of generality, from the broad-ranging ideological constructions of James Mill or William Jones to what C. A. Bayly calls "the level of practical, *ad hoc,* 'satisficing' administration."[18]

Perjury was a problem at the level of "satisficing" administration, and like other problems on this level, it has received little scholarly attention. When the British administration depended on native informants, there was almost inevitably fear of deceit.[19] Anxiety about perjury and prevarication in courtroom testimony was yet another "knowledge panic" of the sort that periodically occurred in the British attempt to develop systematic knowledge despite their dependence on the opaque "native" informant. Approaches to perjury and other types of deceit took a variety of forms during the period before the Indian Rebellion. Until the 1830s, British administrators in India exhibited great inventiveness in defining and policing the twin offenses of perjury and prevarication. Between Thomas Macaulay's arrival in 1833 and the passage of the Indian Penal Code in 1860, administrators continued to be concerned by the dangers posed by deceit, but the rate of innovation slowed. Finally, as we will see below, the question of Indian perjury reappeared in 1872 with James Fitzjames Stephen's influential new Indian Evidence Act, which codified practices in India and was subsequently proposed as a model for changes in Britain itself.

"A Liar You Are"

The British not only saw perjury everywhere, they also had an unprecedented level of agreement among themselves as to its ubiquity. Britons of all political orientations and statuses in India saw perjury as a significant threat to colonial administration. Joachim Hayward Stocqueler, author of popular guidebooks on India, warned newcomers that the "prevalence of perjury among all classes of native witnesses" constituted one of the greatest obstacles to the administration of justice.[20] Phrasebooks also inculcated the expectation that Indians would lie. George Hadley's *A Compendious Grammar of the Current Corrupt Dialect of the Jargon of Hindostan* taught its readers to declaim "a liar you are!" and "false news do not bring!" for the edification of servants and sepoys.[21]

The idea that perjury was common because there was no community sanction against it had its roots in missionary attempts to discredit Hinduism. Although missionaries were not allowed to proselytize in British India until 1813, evangelical critiques of Indian religions dated back to the late eighteenth century, with Charles Grant's condemnation of Hinduism. Missionaries were eager to dispute the Conservatives' support for native beliefs by demonstrating that lying was a vice encouraged among Indians by religious ideas and community sentiment. As the missionary J. Statham wrote in 1832, "Lying is not considered a vice with them; but on the contrary, the man who can dissimulate most successfully is most applauded; and the greatest lies, so far from being considered as worthy of censure, are extolled."[22] Another missionary tied this affection for rule-breakers to the example set by Hindu gods, noting that "as most of these gods are thieves or liars, the practice of theft and falsehood among men, cannot be looked on, in a very serious light."[23] But the idea spread beyond missionary circles to become one of the most common British analyses of perjury: legislators, as we explore below, sought repeatedly to create community revulsion against perjury through manipulation of either the religious oath guaranteeing testimony or the punishment awarded to perjurers.

Those Britons who sought to maintain local traditions in India, meanwhile, turned the missionary analysis on its head. In their view, British education and institutions did not bring progress but instead had a demoralizing effect. The longer the British controlled Indian territory, they argued, the more prevalent perjury became. In 1844 William Sleeman, Commissioner for Thuggee and Dacoity, devoted an entire chapter of his memoirs to the question of Indian mendacity. He argued that honesty was universal in India among the wildest hill tribes, because members of small communities depend on the veracity of others, but that experience with British rule quickly convinced Indians that the British judges and magistrates were incapable of detecting falsehood.[24]

These dissenters, however, were a small minority. As Metcalf notes, "the British saw deception and deceit everywhere in India." He links this fear to colonial anxiety, a British sense of their own "inability to know and control their colonial subjects."[25] Because the anxiety stemmed from an inescapable condition of colonial rule, no amount of legislative reform or vigorous enforcement of the law could quiet it. Nonetheless, the British sought to do precisely that—to invent new laws and ways of enforcing them that would finally put to rest their own anxieties about perjury. As we will see, they pursued this largely futile quest with remarkable creativity.

Finding the Law

The British decided early on that they would govern India through local law. As a result, they had to discover that law, or be entirely dependent on their native law officers, the Hindu pandits and Islamic *maulavi, kazis,* and *muftis.* Bernard Cohn and J. D. M. Derrett record how the British attempted to cement their power by imposing a rigid structure, particularly on Hindu law. This endeavor stemmed from their belief that the law could be made stable by locating and identifying the oldest exposition as the most authoritative. In short, the British sought to locate India's "ancient constitution."[26]

As the British assumed control of the criminal justice system in Bengal in 1790, they confronted a law in which even the categories were alien to them. Crimes, they discovered, were divided in Islamic law by type of punishment: *qisas* (retaliation), *diyut* (blood money), *hadd* (fixed punishment), and *tazir* or *siyasa* (discretionary or exemplary punishment). In some cases, moreover, control of prosecution remained in the hands of a victim's family members. The crimes for which the punishment was fixed—such as illicit intercourse, wine drinking, and robbery—were limited in number.[27] Perjury was not among them. It was considered punishable by *tazir,* a category of discretionary punishments that could include imprisonment, exile, corporal punishment, reprimand, or humiliating treatment. The British saw Mughal administration of Islamic law, however, as at once too harsh and too lenient. Corporal punishments such as mutilation seemed too severe; by contrast, the actual punishments normally inflicted in cases of perjury struck British observers as too lenient. In the last years of Mughal criminal administration, British commentators observed, prisoners convicted of perjury had received "inadequate" sentences: they were released without any punishment at all.[28] The British, therefore, sought to work within the flexibility provided by the amorphous category of *tazir* to ensure that perjury received consistent and stringent punishment. Among the possible forms of *tazir* applicable to perjury was *tashhir,* or exemplary punishment. The history of *tashhir* in Mughal India combined both Islamic and Hindu precedents.[29] It was to become, as we see below, one of the favored British responses to the never-ending problem of perjury.

The first English treatise on Islamic law, Charles Hamilton's *The Hedaya,* published in 1791, provided the basic outlines of perjury's position in Islamic law. *The Hedaya* declared that "a false witness must be stigmatized."[30] According to the Hanifite authorities relied upon in *The Hedaya,* perjury should be punished with shaming, or *tashhir.* What exactly constituted shaming, however, was a matter of dispute. Public shaming, scourging, and imprisonment all had some form of precedential authority according to *The Hedaya.* The authorities cited in *The Hedaya* were silent on a number of other questions, including the definition of perjury and the standard of proof to be applied.

Hindu law proved even more elusive for British officials. In part because the Mughal government had enforced Islamic criminal law, the British found it difficult to determine the parameters of Hindu law on perjury. The earliest attempt to translate Hindu law was Nathaniel Halhed's *A Code of Gentoo Laws* published in 1776. Halhed's work was an English translation of a Persian translation of the work of a committee of eleven pandits assembled by the first Governor General of Bengal, Warren Hastings, to compile a digest of Hindu law on various topics.[31] In the words of one modern commentator, "The Hindu criminal law as presented in the 'Gentoo

Code' is full of impracticable and absurd direction which cannot represent any systematic practice."[32] Halhed's section on the punishments for false evidence must have deeply puzzled English lawyers. "The crime of false witness," he translated, "is the same as if a man had murdered a Brahmin, or had deprived a woman of life, or had assassinated his friend; or of one, who, in return for good, gives evil; or who, having learned a science or profession, gives his tutor no reward; or of a woman, who, having neither son, nor grandson, nor grandson's son, after her husband's death, celebrates not the seradeh [feast in honor of the dead] to his memory."[33] But from there, Halhed's translation went on to detail the ways in which moral culpability changed in relation to the nature of the dispute. For example, false witnessing in a matter concerning a horse resulted in guilt "as great as the guilt of murdering one hundred persons" while that in a matter concerning gold resulted in guilt equivalent to that "incurred in murdering all the men who have been born, who shall be born in the world."[34] Despite these extravagant declarations of culpability, Halhed's text was strangely silent (to legal ears) about what, if any, punishment might be imposed in these cases.

These scholarly pursuits were, however, a matter of pressing concern to British administrators as they sought to establish control over their new subjects. It seems likely that perjury under the Raj was an "everyday" form of resistance, defined by scholars as a "form . . . of struggle present in the behaviours and cultural practices of subordinated people at times other than overt revolt."[35] It would be surprising if there were not some elements of everyday resistance in the perjury cases that plagued British officials in India. Similar anticolonial resistance has been described by John Rogers in colonial Sri Lanka, where popular support for the illegal activity of gambling led to what he calls "resistance within the law" marked by false accusations and misleading testimony. "Faced with the necessity of dealing with an alien but effective form of power," Rogers observes, "Sri Lankans treated the colonial courts as morally neutral, and manipulated them to their own advantage. They regarded testimony not as true or false, but as effective or ineffective."[36]

Anecdotal evidence from perjury cases appealed to the Sadar (literally high) Courts in India suggests that, at the very least, Indian witnesses were likely to put loyalty to family members, friends, or perhaps employers above legality. There are a surprising number of impersonation cases, in which relatives pretended to be unrelated witnesses.[37] The Bengal Sadar Court opted for mercy in the case of an ailing seventy-year-old man who had pretended to be unrelated to his son, citing his age.[38] Nor were the impersonators just relatives. Mahommed Alee, for example, impersonated the son of a local official.[39] Unrelated impersonators or friends also figure in the cases.[40] Still other cases present circumstances suggesting that British fears of paid, professional witnesses were not unfounded. One convicted perjurer, for example, gave evidence twice in the space of a month, each time under a different name.[41] While it is difficult to discern precise motives from the terse accounts of reported cases, the number of impersonation cases suggests that giving false testimony on something as basic as one's own identity was fairly common.

Colonial Courts

During the period of the East India Company's control of India, there were two court systems in Company-ruled territory. The first, the Supreme Courts within the Presidency towns themselves, operated as English courts, staffed by common-law judges and possessing jurisdiction over suits involving British citizens and Company employees. The second, the *adalat* or *mofussil* system, administered justice in the *mofussil*, or countryside outside the Presidency towns. It was staffed by a combination of Company civil servants and native officials and applied local law. Although the East India Company had initially been content to assume a merely supervisory role, leaving the previous Mughal system of government largely unchanged, successive administrations toward the end of the eighteenth century dramatically expanded the Company's control. This process culminated during the governor generalship of Lord Charles Cornwallis, from 1786 to 1793.[42]

Under the criminal justice system Cornwallis instituted in 1790, the Indian official previously in charge of the criminal side of the judiciary was divested of that power, and the Governor General and Council of the Bengal

Presidency served as the Sadar Court.[43] At the apex of the *mofussil* system were the Sadar Courts: the Sadar Nizamat Adalat on the criminal side and the Sadar Diwani Adalat on the civil side.[44] The 1790 system also reorganized the lower criminal courts. Bengal was divided into four divisions, or circuits, which were in turn composed of several districts. All criminal cases were to be heard by the Court of Circuit, which consisted of two East India Company civil servants assisted by native law officers. The role of these native officers, or *kazis* and *muftis,* was to decide the law applicable to the case and issue a fatwa, or statement of that law. When the judges disagreed with their law officers, the dispute was referred to the Nizamat Adalat. The magistrate, also a Company civil servant, was the principal officer in each district and was responsible for the investigation of cases. This magistrate, however, had authority only to try offenders and inflict punishment in petty cases; all serious cases had to be committed for trial before the Circuit Court. After 1790, therefore, the Company had assumed direct control over the administration of criminal justice, ousting Indians, with the exception of the native law officers.[45]

The process of law-making in India under the East India Company proceeded through a variety of means. Islamic law formed the basis of the criminal law in Bengal and Madras, and for many of the residents of Bombay, but it could be and was modified through legislation. Before the Charter Act of 1833, legislation was passed separately in each Presidency, and new laws were referred to as "regulations"; after 1833, law-making was consolidated for all of British India, and new laws were referred to as "acts." Below the level of legislative enactment, however, the picture of law-making becomes rather more murky. The principle of stare decisis was not adopted by the Sadar Courts of Bengal, so although selected case decisions were published, they provided an erratic guide to the nature of the law. In addition to case law, the Sadar Courts of each Presidency issued two types of general letters distributed to all inferior judges, known as "circular orders" and "constructions." These letters reflected the Sadar Court's bureaucratic role in supervising the lower courts and responding to queries and problems raised in monthly reports from the judges. Constructions, in theory, provided just that: the authoritative construction placed by the Sadar Court on regulations.[46]

In this hybrid legal system, perjury presented an immediate problem. While the British sought to retain Islamic criminal law in Bengal, they found it impossible to maintain Islamic law regarding perjury. After 1790, when the British first fully assumed direct control over the administration of criminal justice in Bengal, selected aspects of Islamic law were changed because the British found them unworkable—most notably, the law of evidence, certain punishments such as mutilation, and the law of murder, which had left prosecution largely within the discretion of a victim's relations.[47] These changes have been ably studied by Jörg Fisch;[48] what is less well-known is that the British quickly discovered that redefinition of the substantive law of perjury and its punishments was also crucial to their assumption of judicial control. In this context, the demands of colonial governance drove change in both the procedural and substantive laws.

Bengal: Inscribing the Sentence

In 1797 the government of Bengal moved to amend the law of perjury, one of the first changes made to the substantive criminal law outside of the law of murder. As already mentioned, British judges feared that the discretionary punishment administered to perjurers was too mild. While the British were, in theory, administering Islamic law, the impetus for this change clearly came from the British judges themselves, not from their Islamic law officers. In October 1797, the Third Judge of the Circuit Court, Dacca Division, reported to the Register of the Nizamat Adalat on the state of affairs he had observed while on circuit in Chittagong. He complained that "[perjury] is prevalent to a most gross and notorious degree in this district. Hardly a trial occurred before me, in which I did not find reason to impeach the veracity of the witnesses on one side or the other."[49] The Third Judge had a solution that he believed other British judges would concur with: imposing harsher penalties than those possible under Islamic law. Specifically, the Third Judge recommended that a convicted perjurer be tattooed, both to create the stigma of infamy and to alert subsequent judges to the unreliability of his or her testimony.

The Nizamat Adalat was inclined to agree with the Third Judge but felt that his suggestion should first be circulated to and approved by its Islamic law officers.[50] They suggested use of a form of permanent tattooing, called *godna,* which women commonly used for decoration.[51] A month later, the judges of the Nizamat Adalat obtained a representation from the law officers that the proposed punishment was not forbidden under Islamic law. The law officers pointed out that discretionary punishments for perjury already included blackening an offender's face and public exposure upon an ass. New discretionary punishments, such as the tattooing proposed by the Third Judge, were permissible by analogy. Moreover, they interpreted the Qur'an's prohibition on *wusheer* (tattooing) as designed to stop women from ornamenting themselves. As to the question of what text to tattoo on the face of the unfortunate perjurer, the law officers recommended *der gowahe duroogh go asteen* ("this person is a perjured witness"), which they assured the Nizamat Adalat could be read in both verse and prose.[52]

Satisfied by this, the Nizamat Adalat submitted a draft regulation allowing a judge to impose a "mark of ignominy" in addition to the usual punishment of exposure.[53] Adopted as Regulation XVII of 1797, it noted "the prevalence of perjury" in the courts. Under it, judges who determined that the prisoner would not be sufficiently punished by the "usual mode of public exposure" could direct "the words 'derogh go,' or such other words as, in the most current local language, may concisely express the nature of the crime, to be marked on the forehead of the prisoner, by the process commonly denominated 'godena.'"[54] The regulation warned judges that it should be used with "utmost deliberation and caution" to ensure that only offenders truly deserving of the lifelong stigma of tattooing be thus punished.[55] Finally, in passing, it defined the crime of perjury, declaring it to be "the wilful delivery of false evidence on oath, or under solemn obligation esteemed equivalent to an oath, in some judicial proceeding; and in a matter material to the issue thereof."[56]

The use of *godna* as punishment was innovative on a number of levels. As Radhika Singha points out, it "was probably the Company's pecu-

liar contribution to punishments of infamy."[57] British authorities had previously used *godna* to reduce the danger of escapes by convicts sentenced
to life terms. By extending it to perjury, the Company administrators responded to specifically colonial anxieties by attempting to make the lie visible. They attempted a (literally) Kafkaesque unification of the criminal and
the identity of the crime, immediately and indelibly comprehensible to all
who might encounter the convicted offender. This emphasis on visibility
was both an attempt to create public infamy and a practical tool for colonial
magistrates who could prohibit convicted perjurers from any subsequent
testimony in court.[58]

Ironically, despite the role of the judges in suggesting the new punishment, they proved extremely hesitant to use it. In 1801, magistrates responded
to a survey from Governor General Richard Colley, Lord Wellesley. They
were asked about the frequency of perjury in their districts and what measures they had taken. Eight magistrates, one-quarter of the respondents, said
that they had not used the punishment of *godna* even once over the previous
four years.[59] Another five respondents said they had seldom used *godna*.[60]
Nor were these respondents from quiet districts in which perjury cases were
unheard of: in Patna, a district in which few usages of *godna* were reported,
there had been thirty-two convictions for perjury over the same four years.[61]
Similarly, Nuddea, where *godna* had never been used, saw twenty-nine trials of forty-five individuals, yielding twenty-six convictions.[62] The judges,
it would seem, were squeamish about their new powers. Curiously, this did
not stop some of them from suggesting that still stronger sanctions were
needed. The magistrates of Chittagong, Jelalpore, Shahabad, and Juanpore,
for example, recommended extending the punishment for perjury to include
transportation as well, while the magistrate at Dinagepore wanted to add the
pillory to the repertoire of discretionary punishments.[63] The magistrate at
Bahar wanted to go still further and called for the power to impose confisca-
tion of all property, permanent disqualification from testifying, prohibition
on inheriting property in the future, and transportation in cases where the
perjury could have led to the imposition of the death penalty.[64]

At almost the same time as Wellesley's survey, the Nizamat Adalat received another suggestion from a local judge that resulted in a new

amendment in the law of perjury. The report of the Third Judge of the Moorshedabad Court of Circuit prompted the Nizamat Adalat to propose another
regulation altering the law of perjury.[65] The Third Judge complained, and
the Nizamat Adalat agreed, that "a practice has become very prevalent in
different parts of the Company's provinces, for parties in civil suits to prefer
unfounded charges of perjury against the witnesses of their opponents, and
against their own witnesses, where their evidence does not establish every
point which they may have been brought to prove, and similar charges of
subornation of perjury against the adverse parties in such suits."[66] Not only
did perjury tend to multiply exponentially under these circumstances, with
perjured evidence brought in to support charges of perjury, but this practice also compounded the difficulties of getting witnesses to testify in the
Company courts, as any potential witness feared prosecution, either from
his or her own side or from the opposing party.[67] Accordingly, the Nizamat
Adalat proposed a regulation that, as adopted, prohibited magistrates from
receiving charges of perjury proffered by parties in civil suits against their
own witnesses or those of the other party, and held all witnesses, plaintiffs,
and defendants in civil suits not liable to be prosecuted for perjury unless
they were committed by the *zillah* (local) judge.[68]

The new regulation diminished the power of the Indian legal profession, which was then in its infancy, having begun to be regulated by law
only in 1793.[69] This innovation also placed the problem of perjury in India
on substantially different footing than in England. In England, as we saw
in chapter 2, the absence of a system of public prosecution until late in the
nineteenth century meant that the responsibility for detecting and prosecuting perjury fell almost entirely on the opposing party's counsel. Detection of perjury in England relied on cross-examination by the opposing
party's barrister. In India, by contrast, the judge was expected both to detect perjury and to initiate prosecutions. The regulation prohibiting party-
initiated perjury prosecutions explicitly countenanced cross-examination
by the judge: "leave it in the discretion of the Judge to determine when any
witnesses brought before him are guilty of perjury, which he may always
be able to do by cross-examining them minutely, and by confronting them,
when necessary, with the witnesses of the adverse party."[70] By severely re-

stricting the power of citizens to initiate perjury cases, the colonial government confirmed its primary responsibility for policing the populace.

Administrators remained uncomfortable about leaving so much
power—both in evidentiary determination and in sentencing—in the
hands of the native law officers who sat alongside British judges. The Bengal government went so far as to propose vesting the circuit judges with the
power to determine guilt or innocence, but the suggestion was rejected by
the Nizamat Adalat.[71] Instead, the court proposed a regulation specifically
tailored to meet complaints about the administration of Islamic law, giving
judges the power to overrule native law officers' fatwas.[72] Regulation II of
1807 had already provided for submission to the Nizamat Adalat when the
law officers and the Company judges disagreed about the punishment;[73]
the new Regulation XVII of 1817 went further, authorizing the judge, on his
own initiative, to alter sentences. At the same time, the limitation banning
party-initiated perjury prosecutions in civil cases was extended to criminal
cases.[74]

The changes of 1817 demonstrate just how far the British had strayed
from Islamic law. The convoluted treatment of perjury in Regulation XVII
of 1817 bears out Fisch's thesis that, by this time, the British version of Islamic law was largely, but not entirely, superficial. In Fisch's description,
"with Regulation 17, 1817 the foundation of the British system of criminal
justice was laid. It was the last regulation concentrating on basic issues between the European and the Islamic conception of justice."[75] Overall, the
Sadar Court opted not to abolish the structure of Islamic law but instead
assumed complete control over the decisions of the officers interpreting
that law. Similarly, the Bengal Sadar Court subsequently continued to refer
to Islamic legal authorities in determining perjury cases, while enforcing a
law of perjury almost entirely derived from statutory enactments.

At the same time that British authorities were restricting the ability of
Indians to initiate perjury suits, they also legislated to expand the domains
of potential perjury. In Bengal, this process began almost as soon as the British took control of the criminal justice system. In 1793, *putwarries,* or local
revenue-collecting officials, were made liable to the penalties of perjury for
any falsification in their accounts.[76] Statements before land assessors were

also made subject to the penalties of perjury, as were statements before col-
lectors regarding land assessments.[77] Other Presidencies followed Bengal's
lead.[78] The result of this expansion was to bring much of Indian interaction
with the colonial government under possible perjury penalties. Not only
did British administrators see perjury everywhere, they also gave themselves the power to prosecute for perjury in almost any interaction.

Given the attention paid to making prosecution for perjury easier,
what were the consequences of these reforms? In the late 1820s, Henry
Strachey, a retired judge who was a member of a prominent family of Indian
civil servants, and whose work was praised by James Mill in the *History of
British India,* compiled figures on perjury in Bengal.[79] Strachey was no
advocate of ideas of character; he took violent exception to Mill's assertion
of a distinctive Indian national character, for example, noting the difficulty
of forming "a correct judgment on such a subject."[80] Nevertheless, his figures reveal frequent prosecutions for perjury among Bengalis: according
to his numbers, convictions for perjury in Bengal alone outstripped those
for all of England and Wales. For 1826 and 1827, for example, there were
219 convictions in both the Lower and Western Provinces of Bengal. In England, meanwhile, there were approximately twenty perjury cases yearly,
resulting in around ten convictions.[81] While direct comparisons are difficult to make, not only because of differences in population, but also because of access to the judicial system, Strachey's figures suggest that despite
the complaints of colonial magistrates about the difficulty of prosecuting
perjury cases, many more cases were being brought in India, and many led
to convictions.

Overall, however, while the British in Bengal had ensured that they
remained in control of judicial decisions, redefined the law of perjury to
correspond with the common law, specified the standard of proof, and
searched for shame sanctions meaningful to Bengalis, they nonetheless remained attached to the idea that they were administering Islamic law. Their
native law officers were frequently called upon to render opinions. In other
Presidencies, however, this level of solicitude for at least the façade of Islamic law was noticeably lacking.

Madras: The Invention of Prevarication

After 1817, innovation in the law of perjury came from the south, in the Presidency of Madras. Under the governorship of Edward Clive in 1802, a judiciary was established in Madras largely in imitation of that in Bengal.[82] The Company's highest criminal court, however, was called the Foujdari (as opposed to Nizamat) Adalat in Madras. The law of perjury there was initially borrowed from Bengal, albeit in piecemeal fashion. One of the first regulations establishing the criminal justice system in 1802 provided for punishment by *godna* in cases of perjury and echoed the definition of perjury adopted in Bengal.[83] Prosecution of cases by parties in civil suits was prohibited in 1810; this was reenacted in 1816 after the reorganization of the lower courts, extended to criminal cases in 1822, and extended to all tribunals in 1829.[84] Meanwhile, concern that sentencing discretion was allowing the law to be applied too leniently led to a tightening of the law of perjury in 1811. Under Regulation VI of that year, imprisonment was to be between four and seven years only, banishment was provided for, a reward was offered, and the offense was made nonbailable except under special circumstances.[85]

The Foujdari Adalat offered its own contributions to the law of perjury during this period, through circular orders. In 1814, the court instructed lower tribunals on procedure in perjury cases. It noted that prosecutions for perjury against Indians were frequent but "generally unsuccessful." Warning that "it is scarcely to be expected that an uneducated native should, of himself, state facts and circumstances with the precision here required," the court placed the responsibility for developing a complete record on the criminal judge. A proper charge should contain the words spoken by the accused, the place and time, the judicial proceeding in which they were relevant, and the falsehood of the accused's statement. In particular, the court reminded judges that "no person should be made the object of a prosecution for perjury, who has not been cautioned against committing himself on his oath, and has, subsequently, persisted in maintaining falsehood for truth."[86] Seven years later, the court intervened again to clear up confusion as to the standard of proof required for conviction in perjury cases.[87]

In 1822, the law of perjury in Madras began to depart significantly from that of Bengal. Prodded by the discontent of local judges, Madras innovated first through the invention of a crime of prevarication, and second through legislation against false accusations. As in Bengal, local judges took the lead, but in Madras their suggestions met resistance from the Sadar Court. The Foujdari Adalat was at best a reluctant partner in legislation. Thomas Warden, the Second Judge on Circuit, Western Division, wrote the court angrily in 1822, annoyed that it had focused on the question of materiality in responding to his complaints about perjury. Instead, Warden wrote, "it is where contradictory evidence by the same witness is given on points material to the issue that I wish to engage the consideration of the Court."[88] Warden protested that the requirement of some evidence demonstrating the falsehood of the alleged perjury prevented the prosecution of cases of contradiction apparent on the face of the depositions. He suggested instead the creation of an intermediate crime, between perjury and contempt of court, if the law of perjury itself could not be altered.

The Foujdari Adalat, however, was not immediately swayed by Warden's plea. It responded by dismissing the two scenarios Warden had posed: first, a witness testifying successively to a murder happening by "torchlight" and by "daylight"; and second, an actual case where witnesses had testified that death resulted from different causes, despite the fact that the alleged deceased's relatives seemed unconvinced that he was, in fact, deceased.[89] The first, the court argued, was merely speculative, while the second called for more diligent investigation by the police and magistrates, not a change in the law. Nonetheless, it was willing to consider penalties for prevarication that would be less severe than those for perjury, but more severe than those for contempt of court.[90] Accordingly, a draft regulation was prepared to create a new crime of prevarication that would respond to administrative concerns about the limited investigative abilities of colonial officials. R. Clarke, secretary to the Regulation Board, explained: "The difference between [perjury and prevarication] consists in this, that perjury is a distinct assertion of that which can be proved not to be, or a denial of that which can be proved to be; whereas prevarication is the giving of contradictory or inconsistent evidence, which affects the credibility of the evidence, though neither the extent of the witness's falsehood, nor the precise points in which he has departed from the truth be capable of ascertainment."[91] Under the proposed regulation, prevarication would be punishable by a fine of one hundred rupees, six months' imprisonment, or up to a year's imprisonment if a convict could not pay the fine.[92] Despite approval from the Foujdari Adalat, the regulation was not enacted.

Insight into why the question of conflicting depositions appeared so critical to Madras judges can be found in George Campbell's description of criminal procedure in British India.[93] Campbell described a process that repeatedly created depositions. Beginning with the original complaint, each police station was required to keep a diary of daily events, including statements from witnesses, which was forwarded to the local magistrate for his review each morning. The magistrate would then take depositions in the course of investigating the cases forwarded to him. If a case was committed for trial, all the witnesses would appear for a third time before the judge, generating a second set of depositions.[94] All of this happened before the trial itself, generating a dossier of statements and depositions for review by the trial judge. As Archibald Galloway, a military officer and chairman of the Court of Directors of the East India Company, observed, because of what he saw as the overall tendency for Indian witnesses to lie, "the necessity of written documents is therefore greater in India than in our own country; and any expedient suggested with the view of multiplying them ought of all things to be encouraged."[95] Making lying discoverable merely through contradictory depositions, therefore, responded to the largely written nature of judicial proceedings under the Company. While the use of *godna* united convicted perjurers with their sentences, the invented offense of prevarication reduced the complexity of testimony and credibility assessment to a simple dossier. Both made the crime legible to officials who feared its obscurity.

The following year, the process of criminalizing prevarication began anew. This time C. M. Lushington, Second Judge on Circuit, Western Division, initiated the process with a report claiming that "the most common case of perjury as it appears in our Courts, is totally unprovided for," namely, swearing to opposite facts before the magistrate and circuit judge respectively.[96] Unlike three years previously, the Foujdari Adalat was extremely resistant to the suggestion of change, declaring peevishly, "It seems extraordinary to the Court that explanation to the extent to which it has already been required and seems still called for, should be necessary to the understanding of so clear a point as that the wilful falsehood of a witness's false assertion must mainly be established by proving the fact he has denied." The Foujdari Adalat then concluded that it "will here dismiss the subject."[97]

Despite this attempt to close the door on the topic of prevarication, the matter was soon forced back into the court's purview. The Presidency government took the unusual step of referring the question to the Advocate General, a solicitor employed by the East India Company to manage the Company's legal affairs with respect to English law, asking him whether an individual swearing to two contradictory depositions in England would be liable for the punishment for perjury.[98] The Advocate General responded that there was some precedent for taking two contradictory depositions as evidence of perjury.[99] The government forwarded his letter to the Foujdari Adalat, along with a pointed hint that "Governor in Council is satisfied of the expediency and propriety of admitting the same kind of proof to establish perjury in the Company's Courts" and suggested that the Foujdari should effect this object, either by issuing a circular order or by drafting a new regulation.[100] The Foujdari Adalat balked, respectfully taking issue with the Advocate General's interpretation of English case law.[101] The court also noticed the problem of possible reprosecution for perjury, with the accused tried twice, first on the basis of a contradiction and subsequently on the falsity of one or another of his or her statements. After further prodding from the government, the court agreed that the law could be changed but insisted on a new regulation, rather than making the change through a circular order.[102]

At the suggestion of the Foujdari Adalat, the law as eventually enacted contained a number of protections for potential defendants.[103] First, the court urged that prosecution be used "exclusively for cases where the contradiction is direct and positive" and where a distinct corrupt motive could be discerned.[104] Second, the regulation expressly prohibited subsequent trial for perjury by the usual way of proving the falsehood of one of the two statements.[105] Finally, the regulation required evidence that the defendant was duly sworn and that before affixing his or her signature to the contradictory depositions, their contents were distinctly read over to him or her.[106] Shortly after passage of this regulation, the Foujdari Adalat issued a circular order clarifying the new requirements for composing indictments.[107] Contradiction had been made a crime, albeit one amalgamated into the definition of perjury. This, however, did not appear to be enough for the judges of Madras. Six years later, they supported another bill to create a separate offense of prevarication, this time punishable by one month's imprisonment or a fine of fifty rupees.[108] While the court had stressed determination of a corrupt motive in the earlier regulation, later commentators concluded that motive could be inferred from the depositions themselves, relieving the courts of any additional factual inquiry into intent.[109]

Perhaps chastened by this unusually contentious process, the Foujdari Adalat actively consulted the local judges before embarking on its next initiative. In February 1827, the court sent out a request for input from the judges on a new regulation that would make preferring false accusations a crime.[110] As with the earlier prohibition against accusations of perjury by opposing parties, the effect would be to further concentrate the power of policing in colonial hands. The response to the suggestion was overwhelming. Judges from throughout the Presidency wrote to complain of the problem in their districts. W. Lavie, the assistant criminal judge at Combaconum, saw the practice as spanning social classes: "the better class of native are for the most part rich, and are in consequence enabled to purchase evidence, and . . . the lower orders are so very depraved that a person possessing the means may at any time procure as many witnesses as he pleases."[111] J. Monro of Tinnevelly attached a multiple-page accounting of some of the false accusations brought over the previous four years.[112] A. Sinclair estimated that the average number of false complaints seen yearly was "around 76."[113] S. Nicholls, a criminal judge at Madura, attributed most false accusations to a desire for revenge.[114]

The judges differed among themselves as to the best means of de-
terring false accusations: fines, degrading punishment, imprisonment and
fines, or lashings.[115] Magistrate E. Smalley of Nellore wanted to discriminate among classes in punishment: men of property, he wrote, should be
fined up to three hundred rupees; "persons without property but above the
lower orders" should be confined for two months with hard labor; members of the lower orders should be flogged.[116] Still others thought that the
best way to prevent false accusations was to create a more stringent form
of oath, such as requiring an accuser to swear "in the village Pagoda."[117]
After reviewing all of these suggestions, the Foujdari Adalat recommended
a graded approach based on the severity of the accused offense. The police
were authorized to administer a solemn declaration to the complainant in
all nonbailable offense cases, along with a warning about the penalties for
perjury. For bailable offenses, a Criminal Court could punish the complainant by a fine of up to two hundred rupees, or imprisonment with or without hard labor for up to one year. For nonbailable offenses, the offender
would be committed for trial before the Court of Circuit and liable to punishment of up to seven years' imprisonment with hard labor and lashing
with the cat-o'-nine-tails.[118] This structure was subsequently modified, and
the distinction between bailable and nonbailable offenses was abandoned.
Instead, all false charges could be punished by imprisonment of up to six
months, although the regulation noted that judges could consider "the apparent motives and tendency" of the charge in sentencing.[119]

Taken together, the two innovations in Madras worked to extend the
purview of perjury and to greatly ease detection of the offense. They responded to fears about the duplicitous native informant, as either witness
or accuser, with new penalties and new technologies for detection.

Bengal Sequel: Making Innovations Islamic

While the original outlines of the law of perjury had been settled in
Bengal, the innovations in Madras left judges in Bengal with a dilemma:
should they join their southern colleagues in expanding the definition of
perjury? In an early decision, the Nizamat Adalat had rejected the argu-

ment that perjury could be proved simply through contradictory depositions; instead, it demanded that, in conformity with English practice, one
of the depositions be proved false.[120] The Madras law, however, revived
the question. In 1841, the Nizamat Adalat changed course and adopted the
Madras rule. Henceforth, "the mere fact of a witness having wilfully given
two statements directly at variance with each other, on a point material
to the issue of the case in which he gives the testimony, must be held to
be perjury."[121] This decision was prompted by evidence that prisoners in
Bengal were already being convicted of perjury on the basis of contradictory depositions. In the monthly report of H. Nisbet, a session judge of
Sarum, five individuals were listed as convicted for perjury on the basis of
contradictory depositions, including one in which two years had elapsed
between the original statement before a magistrate and the testimony given
at trial.[122]

But the judges of the Nizamat did not justify their volte face by reference to the Madras law; instead, they argued that it was merely a recognition of Islamic law. In their circular order, they referred to a ten-year-
old construction that contained an extended opinion by the Islamic law
officers of the Calcutta Sadar Court. The opinion responded to a query
asking what evidence was sufficient to convict in cases of perjury. Among
the circumstances the law officers considered was the delivery of contradictory evidence by the same witness before different courts. According
to the law officers, if a witness claimed to have witnessed a crime and then
dropped the accusation, it became the responsibility of the judge to assess
the witness's motives. If "the retraction be made under a proper sense of re-
pentance and contrition," the witness was not liable to *tazir* (discretionary
punishment); but if it was made "with contempt and boldness," then the
witness was liable.[123] If a witness subsequently remembered details initially
forgotten, he or she was not liable to *tazir*. The law officers went further
than the Madras law by declaring that witnesses who made statements that
were "highly improbable, and bordering close upon impossibility" were
also punishable by *tazir*.[124]

At the same time, however, Bengal judges sought to soften the impact
of the innovation. In a circular order of 1850 they cautioned session judges

against indiscriminately using their power to commit parties for perjury on the basis of contradictory depositions. The court warned:

> By an indiscriminate or injudicious use of the power vested in the sessions judge, witnesses would be forced to adhere to any perjury, which they may have committed before the magistrate, whereas by abstaining from punishment of those witnesses who may appear to correct at the sessions the falsehood of their first evidence, and limiting the order of committal to those who manifestly make a false deposition before the sessions judge, the ends of justice would be more satisfactorily attained.[125]

Like the earlier opinion by the Sadar Court law officers, and unlike their counterparts in Madras, the Bengal judges sought to discriminate between motives for inconsistency and thereby temper the new law. Interestingly, however, they did not once again invoke Islamic or Hindu precedent to justify this qualification, although both types of precedent could be found. While consistency with Islamic law seems to have been a powerful trope in Bengal jurisprudence, it was not always employed by the Sadar Court in grounding its opinions.

Macaulay and the Indian Penal Code

After passage of the Charter Act in 1833, law-making in India was centralized in a single legislature. At the same time, an Indian Law Commission was appointed to create a shared law for all residents of British India. Back in England, Thomas Macaulay had lobbied actively for appointment as Law Member of the Legislative Council. Among his duties in this post was service on the Law Commission, which, aside from Macaulay, consisted of Charles Cameron, an English barrister; John McLeod, a civil servant from Madras; and George Anderson, a civil servant from Bombay who had taken part in the drafting of the Elphinstone Code.[126] Much of the work of the commission was, however, the result of Macaulay's nearly solo effort, as his fellow commissioners either fell ill or proved themselves of little use.[127] Remarkably, over the course of three years in India, from 1834 through 1837, Macaulay was able to complete a draft of a comprehensive system of criminal law, the Indian Penal Code.

En route to his employment, Macaulay had an encounter with Indian justice that may have proved crucial in shaping his views on the problem of false evidence.[128] As he prepared to leave Ootacamund for Madras, his manservant was arrested on a charge of seduction and adultery. Macaulay offered to settle the suit by paying the aggrieved husband, but, as he wrote, "the prosecutors of my servant interfered, and insisted that he should be brought to trial in order that they might have the pleasure of smearing him with filth, giving him a flogging, beating kettles before him, and carrying him around on an ass with his face to the tail." Macaulay commented, "I have a very poor opinion of my man's morals, and a very poor opinion also of the veracity of his accusers."[129] Macaulay was irritated because his servant's detention prevented his travel; when his first request for an immediate trial was denied, he wrote an irritated letter to the station commandant asking him to intervene. The servant was tried that evening and acquitted. As Macaulay prepared to leave at last, there was a riot during which his servant was dragged out of a palanquin and stripped naked. Macaulay returned to the commandant and had the rioters arrested, remarking with satisfaction, "Nothing can be well imagined more expeditious than the administration of justice in this country when the judge is a Colonel, and the plaintiff a Councillor."[130] While Macaulay nowhere mentioned the influence of this episode in his subsequent work as Law Member, the fear of false accusations for profit and a revulsion toward the shame sanction of *tashhir* are apparent in the Indian Penal Code.

Publicly, however, perjury figured in the project of codification as an example of the problem of disparity in punishment among the three Presidencies, one of the primary reasons for the establishment of the commission. Macaulay seized upon uniformity as the guiding principle of his efforts. His much-quoted baseline was, "the principle is simply this; uniformity when you can have it; diversity when you must have it; but, in all cases certainty."[131] Perjury served Macaulay as a convenient example of existing inconsistency. In Bengal, he noted, forgery was punished with a term of imprisonment double that inflicted for perjury, while in Bombay, the situation was reversed, with perjury punished with imprisonment double that for forgery; in Madras, the two crimes were punished equally.[132]

Though Macaulay's debt to Bentham and also the English common law is apparent, his sympathy for existing laws under the East India Company is less clear. The Elphinstone Code had little specific influence on him; he even dismissed it outright, asserting that "the penal law of the Bombay Presidency has, over the penal law of the other Presidencies, no superiority, except that of being digested."[133] Elsewhere, Macaulay wrote contemptuously, "the Bombay Criminal Code is the description of Code which I should expect from a laborious and experienced zillah judge."[134] (Unfortunately, the response to this comment is unrecorded.) By contrast, Macaulay's code was written in a clear and concise style, with reference to illustrations to clarify potential ambiguities.[135]

In the draft Indian Penal Code submitted to the Governor General in October 1837, perjury was renamed "false evidence" and included in the section of "offences against public justice."[136] Giving false evidence was defined as when "in any stage of any judicial proceeding, being bound by oath, or by a sanction tantamount to an oath, to state the truth, [a man] states that to be true which he knows to be false touching any point material to the result of such proceeding."[137] The offense of "fabricating false evidence" was defined as "caus[ing] any circumstance to exist, intending that such circumstance may appear in evidence in some stage of a judicial proceeding" in order to mislead the decision maker.[138] Both giving false evidence and fabricating false evidence were to be punished with imprisonment for a term between one and seven years, with the possibility of an additional fine. Macaulay, however, excepted fabrication of false evidence by the accused from his definition. His greatest departure from the common law came in his linking the punishment for false evidence to the severity of the accusation. Giving or fabricating false evidence in a capital case was treated more severely: transportation for life or imprisonment for a term between seven years and life. Doing the same in noncapital cases that were punishable by more than seven years' imprisonment, the falsifier was to be punished just as a person convicted of the offense would have been.[139]

While Macaulay could have argued that discriminating among lies according to their consequences and motives had Indian antecedents—as we have seen, both Hindu and Islamic law made similar distinctions—he did not. Unfortunately, none of his writings on the Indian Penal Code identifies the source of his ideas on this topic, so whether they arose from Macaulay's own inclinations or local inspiration remains unclear.

Macaulay's use of imprisonment, fines, and transportation represented a decision to reject the punishment of *tashhir,* or public exposure. In his "Notes on the Penal Code" on the draft Indian Penal Code, Macaulay explained that the commission had considered this punishment carefully before deciding to abandon it. A primary reason for their rejection was the inherent inequality of the punishment, which weighed heavily on those with refined sensibilities while having little effect on "hardened and impudent delinquents." Prisoners who preserved a sense of shame were, for Macaulay, prime candidates for rehabilitation, a goal that the stigma of public shaming would make more difficult to achieve. As he wrote, "If it were possible to devise a punishment which should give pain proportioned to the degree in which the offender was shameless, hard-hearted, and abandoned to vice, such a punishment would be the most effectual means of protecting society. On the other hand of all punishments the most absurd is that which produces pain proportioned to the degree in which the offender retains the sentiments of an honest man." Underlying Macaulay's objection to the disproportionate, and therefore un-Benthamite nature of shame sanctions, was a fear of the vagaries of the Indian mob: "That the amount of punishment should be determined, not by the law or by the tribunals, but by a throng of people accidentally congregated, among whom the most ignorant and brutal would always on such occasion be the most forward, should be a disgrace to an age and country pretending to civilization."[140] Thus, bringing forty years of experimentation to a close, Macaulay set the stage for an end to the long search for an appropriate shame sanction in British India.

With regard to the question of perjury specifically, Macaulay acknowledged that it was one of the instances in which his proposed penal code had been modified for local, Indian conditions.[141] The offense of perjury, he commented, was "not one of very frequent occurrence in western countries. It is notorious, however, that in this country the practice is exceedingly common." Macaulay described judges in India as doubting the veracity of all testimony and therefore being prone to seize on circumstantial evidence in preference to witness testimony. The consequence, according to Macaulay, was that wily litigants turned to fabricating evidence: "in India, where a judge is generally on his guard against direct false evidence, a more artful mode of imposition is frequently employed. A lie is often conveyed to a court not by means of witnesses, but by means of circumstances."[142] Macaulay therefore advocated punishing the fabrication of evidence with the same severity as the giving of false evidence. He concluded a note on "Offences Relating to Public Justice" with a plea for punishing falsity in pleading as perjury, but, despite his passionate Benthamism, such a measure was not incorporated into the draft.[143]

After the publication of Macaulay's "Notes" and his return to England in 1838, debate on the code continued in India. It was during this phase of the debate that a number of policies developed by the three Presidencies were incorporated into the penal code. In 1847, the law commissioners published a *Second Report,* detailing responses to the code and suggesting changes. The inquiries answered by the commissioners covered a wide range of issues. Mr. Hudleston wondered "why the word 'perjury' which is perfectly intelligible to the people of India, and has been so long in use, is discarded." A. D. Campbell, one of Macaulay's successors on the Law Commission, responded that the commissioners decided to abandon the "technical terms" of English law where they did not adopt its definitions. Henry Seton, meanwhile, questioned the exception made for those who fabricated evidence designed to exculpate themselves. The commissioners wrote, "we answer, that . . . the temptation to escape from death or infamy though deserved, by means of fraud which injures no individual, is greater than the weakness of human nature can in general resist."[144]

Some suggestions were received more favorably than others. John Fryer Thomas, a judge on the Madras Sadar Court, wrote to urge "lowering the penalty of the offence, and enjoining frequent prosecutions." The commissioners found Thomas's argument "valid" and advocated omitting the minimum one-year sentence in a revised code. Thomas also suggested incorporating the Madras innovations that made contradictory depositions punishable as perjury and prevarication a separate crime. The commissioners doubted whether an individual could be convicted of "false evidence" merely on the basis of contradictory depositions. They wanted to differentiate the forgetful witness who later recalled the truth from the witness who sought all along to mislead the court. The latter witness, they suggested, could be apprehended through two successive prosecutions, because a successful defense on the first charge would entail failure on the second. They also thought that "if necessary, a special rule might be enacted to sanction this mode of procedure." As for the crime of prevarication, the commissioners wrote that they were "disposed to think a Clause for the punishment of persons who being on oath, &c., in any judicial proceeding, shall prevaricate or make contradictory or inconsistent averments in a manner indicating a deliberate intention to conceal the truth, would have a very salutary effect."[145] They recommended punishment of up to six months' imprisonment or a fine.

After the Indian Rebellion, the Indian Penal Code finally became law in 1860.[146] In its final form, it incorporated many of the suggestions mooted in the *Second Report*. While preserving most of the original Macaulay-authored sections, it also added substantial new material. In keeping with one of the suggestions made by Thomas, the minimum of one year for imprisonment was dropped. In another response to Indian circumstances, impersonation of another person was specified as an enumerated offense, to be punished by up to three years' imprisonment, or fine, or both.[147] But the suggestions derived from the Madras innovations—either a separate crime of prevarication or special rules for serial prosecutions for false evidence in contradictory depositions—were not included. As the law became more centrally controlled, the innovations of the Presidency legislatures fell by the wayside.

In the years between Macaulay's draft penal code and its eventual passage in 1860, several reforms relating to the law of perjury were passed: first, the abolition of religious oaths, and second, the end of *tashhir*. Both had originally been part of the attempt to spur community sentiment against perjury, and their abolition marked a movement away from the strategy of working within what the British thought were local religious beliefs.

Abolition of the Religious Oath

Macaulay's desire to end religious distinctions in the law eventually bore fruit, although in a more attenuated form than he might have desired and for motives other than his own preference for uniformity. Two years after his draft penal code, the government of India considered replacing oaths tailored to the deponent's religious belief with a single affirmation referring only to "Almighty God" that could be used by all native witnesses.[148] The change, however, appears to have been motivated by fear that Indian upper classes were avoiding testifying in the Company's courts out of repugnance to the previous form of oath.

This proposal met with decidedly mixed reactions. The judges of the Bombay Sadar Foujdari Adalat agreed without reservations.[149] The judges of the Madras Sadar Adalat, meanwhile, disagreed violently among themselves. The majority of the court felt that abolition of oaths was ill-conceived and "would be attended with pernicious effect."[150] They forwarded to the government of India a letter they had previously written to Macaulay's law commissioners arguing against the abolition of the oath. In it, they noted that "a general impression prevails among the native community in the territories subject to this Presidency . . . that evil will be visited through supernatural agency upon the perjurer." Not only that, "we learn from history, that by the common consent of all mankind, in all ages, reverence has been attached to these 'appeals of a religious nature.'"[151]

One member of the Madras court, however, disagreed. Acting Puisne Judge A. D. Campbell submitted an extensive minute surveying his reasons for supporting the abolition of all oaths. He rejected the appeal to conventional wisdom, tartly noting that the majority of mankind in earlier times was as liable to have been on the side of error as that of truth. Instead, Campbell argued that truth was most likely to be found in communities in which the use of oaths was unknown. If attention had been given to crafting a form of oath that was truly binding on the conscience of natives, Campbell allowed, some good might have resulted, but as it was, the oath as administered was "mere mummery and an empty form binding on the conscience of few or none." European affection for empty oaths had "driven from our courts all the more reputable classes of the community."[152] Campbell found in the Indian experience confirmation of Bentham's prediction that increased reliance on the oath would only drive truth out of the courtroom. Instead of modifying the oath to meet the religious scruples of Hindus and Muslims, Campbell concluded that it should be abolished.

Despite Campbell's enthusiasm for more dramatic measures, the act as proposed was limited to the substitution of a solemn affirmation for the previous ceremony of swearing on the Qur'an or water from the Ganges. The Sadar Court of Bengal suggested extending the act to all native witnesses and taking great care in translating "Almighty God" into vernacular languages.[153] The judges of the Sadar Court of the North Western Provinces at Allahabad, meanwhile, requested that the use of the new oath be declared imperative. They cited a recent case in which a Muslim witness was able to escape conviction for perjury by pretending to be Hindu, swearing upon Ganges water, and then, in his criminal trial for perjury, claiming that the oath he had taken did not bind his conscience. Mysteriously, he was acquitted on this basis.[154]

The Indian law commissioners then commented on the debate. They called for an even broader application of the new affirmation: not just to witnesses, but to all judicial testimony; not just to Hindus and Muslims, but to all who came before the courts.[155] Andrew Amos, Macaulay's successor as Law Member, took a narrower view. He opposed his fellow commissioners' proposed expansions.[156] The act as eventually passed followed Amos's suggestions closely. Its scope was limited to Hindus and Muslims and replaced the previous oaths with an affirmation: "I solemnly affirm, in the presence of Almighty God, that what I shall state shall be the whole truth, and nothing but the truth."[157] False statements made following such an affirmation were to be subject to the same penalties as perjury. Nonetheless, even this somewhat limited expansion of the right to affirmation caused great interest and consternation among those in London considering the question of the oath.

The judges, however, were never entirely reconciled to the abolition of the oath. In 1847, the government of India collected statistics to show that perjury had increased since its abolition. In Bengal, the number of cases doubled: from 289 in 1834–39 to 605 in 1840–44. In Bombay, meanwhile, the number of convictions increased from 325 in 1834–39 to 609 in 1840–45. Madras alone reported a fall in the number of cases, from 428 to 331 for the same two periods as Bombay.[158] The authorities in London, however, responded without excitement, blandly noting that the reader's "attention may be directed to this subject."[159] The register of the Sadar Foujdari Adalat in the North Western Provinces reported that the judges of the Sadar Court, as well as all but one of the *zillah* judges, attributed the increase in perjury in the North Western Provinces to the consequences of the 1840 act. They rejected an alternative explanation that the increase resulted from the more expansive definition of perjury embraced by the Bengal and North Western Provinces in 1841, according to which evidence of contradiction alone was sufficient to prove perjury.[160] Given that Madras was the one place to report a decline, and that the broader definition of perjury had previously existed only there, the alternative explanation was stronger than the Sadar Court acknowledged.

Ten years after the act's passage, the government of Bombay returned to the same question.[161] Compilation of crime figures from the previous decade revealed that not only had the overall number of commitments for perjury risen dramatically, but also the percentage of convictions had increased.[162] Judges consulted tended to blame the increase in perjury on the abolition of the oath; as summarized by the register of the Foujdari Adalat: "the general impression appears to be that the increase noticed by the Honorable Court is chiefly attributable to the substitution of the declaration now in use for the oath formerly administered to Hindoos and Mahomedans."[163] A. Elphinston, magistrate at Khandesh, ascribed the increase in the rate of convictions to an even greater increase in the number of cases from which magistrates could select the most "glaring cases of perjury, more susceptible of clear proof."[164] Some judges advocated a return to pre-1840 forms of oath used in Bombay: "to command truth by the placing of the hand on the Geeta, the cow, the child or the grain must be reverted to."[165] But, as happened four years earlier, no changes followed on the judges' recommendations.

The abolition of the oath remained a bone of contention for the judges. As J. F. Thomas of the Madras Sadar Court wrote, in commenting on the Indian Penal Code: "It is not apparently sufficiently borne in mind, that we have no oath by which we can bind the conscience of the Hindoo. He does no violation therefore to his conscience, in forswearing himself; and he neither does nor can he perceive, and feel with us the enormity of perjury."[166] In their dogged affection for the religious oath, the judges maintained the conviction, identified by Lata Mani in her work on *sati*, that India was best governed through the idiom of religion.[167] They did so out of a belief that religious ritual could affect community sentiment, which they thought crucial to preventing crime. But, after the centralization of law-making with the 1833 Charter Act and the creation of the Indian Law Commission, the initiative in law-making had passed out of their hands. Moreover, the Indian Law Commission was more likely to be dominated by individuals like Amos—English-trained lawyers who steered Indian law closer to the English common law and away from the precedents of the East India Company. A similar progression can be seen in the abolition of *tashhir*.

The End of *Tashhir*

Macaulay's arguments against the punishment of public exposure, or *tashhir*, had a striking effect in India, even while passage of his Indian Penal Code was delayed for more than twenty years. In 1848, Charles Baynes, in his treatise on the criminal law of Madras, saw fit to quote Macaulay's condemnation of *tashhir* almost in its entirety.[168] In Bengal the reaction was even more rapid. The Sadar Court at Calcutta issued a circular order addressed to the Courts of Circuit and session judges requiring them to suspend execution of sentences of *tashhir* for three months.[169] The immediate objective of the circular order was to allow for appeals to the Nizamat Adalat, but it seems to have been a preliminary step toward the abolition of tattooing.[170] The President in Council for the government of India responded to this, conveying his support for an even broader abolition of all forms of *tashhir.*[171] Macaulay's argument against shame punishments seems to have been widely adopted among legislators in India, bolstered by the abolition of pillory in England.[172] Judges, meanwhile, pointed out that *tashhir* was rarely inflicted in their jurisdictions.[173]

Despite this apparent consensus, however, no general abolition of the punishment of *tashhir* was enacted in 1838. The reason for this appears to have been the separation of the issue into two questions: first, expanding the power of the judges to order transportation in perjury cases, and second, ending *tashhir.*[174] The first was passed, while the second was allowed to languish for another decade.[175] It reemerged in 1848 as an amendment to legislation specifically aimed at abolishing the remaining use of *godna,* which had been limited to cases of imprisonment for life. Governor General James Dalhousie offered his support for the broader abolition of all forms of *tashhir,* citing the reasoning of the law commissioners and the abolition of similar punishments in Europe and wondering about "the causes which have led to its being dropped out of sight" since its discussion ten years previously.[176] Dalhousie's proposal was met with widespread support from officials in Bengal, with the judges of the Foujdari Adalat in Madras dissenting ineffectually on the basis that Indians in the south wear such "very scanty clothing" that inmates could not reliably be identified by distinctive prison wear alone.[177] Unswayed by this argument, the government proceeded to abolish *tashhir* throughout India.[178]

As with the abolition of the religious oath, judges remained skeptical of this innovation long after the act's passage. Less than a week before the act was sent to the Governor General for his formal assent, the judges of the Bombay Foujdari Adalat belatedly voiced misgivings. They argued that imprisonment had little apparent effect on Indians and that public disgrace was necessary to "stigmatize" certain selected crimes, including perjury and forgery.[179] The government was unmoved, noting only that "the reasons urged by the authorities at Bombay have not in any degree altered the opinion of the President in Council."[180] Dissent persisted nonetheless. Chief Justice of Bombay Matthew Sausse minuted authorities in London in 1859 requesting a return to shame punishments.[181]

Though Sausse was described as having a "frigid, morose, and taciturn temperament," and was known by contemporaries as "Sausse the Silent," his minute was voluble on the problem of perjury, albeit in a strikingly unsympathetic fashion.[182] He called the 1849 act a "very grave error," attributing it to a misguided impulse to treat Indians and Europeans alike. This overlooked, in Sausse's view, the distinctive nature of India, where "falsehood is the rule, truth the exception." Sausse thought that the change had been motivated by "two or three instances" of suicide among perjurers who had been publicly exhibited riding an ass backwards. He took this as an indication of the success of the punishment, arguing that "I should have thought it a great point to be gained to have discovered a punishment so intrinsically harmless that could produce so deep a sense of humiliation" and concluding that the repression of perjury was "of infinitely greater moment to the community at large, than the contingent suicide of a few convicted perjurers."[183] Sausse the Silent appears to have spoken in vain; no change in the law of perjury or its punishment was proposed as a result of his minute, and the Indian Penal Code, passed shortly thereafter, was not altered to incorporate punishments other than imprisonment, fines, and transportation.

This period of innovation in the law of perjury and prevarication in India was brought to a close by the eventual adoption of the Indian Penal Code in 1860, followed by the Indian Evidence Act in 1872. By the time Ishri Pershad wrote the curious letter that began this chapter, British administrators' attempts to confront what they saw as widespread mendacity in India, and what Indians may well have seen as justifiable resistance to an imposed judicial system, amounted to little more than an enduring obsession. Justice in many cases had become a quixotic attempt to discern which of the parties was honest, not who had the better case. Disturbingly, judges confronted with the same case could come to radically different assessments of the credibility of witnesses. More than half a century of attempts to control perjury through legal innovations had led not to more efficient application of the law, but to the creation of a cadre of judges ruling on the basis of the perceived mendacity of witnesses. The imperatives of policing the courtroom had come to overshadow the touted gift of impartial justice according to law.

Coda: James Stephen and a Law of Evidence for India and England

Further Anglicization and codification followed on the heels of the Indian Penal Code. James Fitzjames Stephen, already a prominent scholar of evidence law in Britain, arrived in India in 1869 to take up the position of Legal Member of Council. Over the next three years, Stephen wrote much of the 1872 Indian Evidence Act as well as revising the Indian Criminal Procedure Code.[184] Although Stephen arrived in India with pronounced views on the underlying logic of the evidence law, he also adapted to what he saw as the situation on the ground, in particular, the dilemma of governing cross-examination. In Stephen's description, it was "little more than an attempt to reduce the English law of evidence to the form of express propositions arranged in their natural order, with some modifications rendered necessary for the particular circumstances of India."[185] As it happened, one of the modifications deemed necessary for the "particular circumstances of India" related to cross-examination.

Stephen's first version of the Indian Evidence Act contained unusually rigorous restrictions on cross-examination. It exempted witnesses from answering any question injurious to their credit when the matter inquired into was unrelated to current proceedings. Moreover, it required a barrister to obtain "express written instructions" from his client regarding any questions as to credit.[186] The motivation for these restrictions appears to have been the continued employment of judges in the Indian countryside who were not legally trained and therefore thought to be at risk of being bullied by counsel. Suspicion of Indian advocates who had been appearing in courts both as *vakils* (pleaders) and as barristers also probably played a role.[187]

Stephen's proposal raised howls of protest from the bars of Bombay, Calcutta, and Madras. The Calcutta bar declared that "the combined effect of these sections seems to be an almost absolute prohibition of any question affecting the character of witnesses."[188] The Bombay bar suggested that if the bill were to pass, "it would be better to abolish private cross-examination altogether, and entrust it solely to judges."[189] In the final form of the Indian Evidence Act the express instruction provision was eliminated, and the court was instructed to exercise its discretion on questions as to credit only after deciding that "the truth of the imputation would seriously affect the opinion of the Court as to the credibility of the witness."[190] The judge was also instructed to consider the remoteness in time of the alleged imputation and any disproportion between the importance of the imputation against the witness's character and the importance of his or her evidence.[191] Even with the revision, the judge was granted significantly more power in India to determine the boundaries of cross-examination.

Although the Evidence Act had been written in part in response to lo-cal circumstances, such as the prevalence of legally unsophisticated judges, Stephen soon decided that what was good for the colony would also be good for the metropole. Shortly after his return to England in 1872, he was invited by Attorney General Sir John Coleridge to propose a codified law of evidence for England based on the Indian Evidence Act.[192] The bill failed, but Stephen tried again in 1877 with a criminal code bill that contained provisions for testimony by criminal defendants.[193] Again, his attempt at codification failed, wrecked by Irish opposition and the intransigence of the Lord Chief Justice.[194]

Undeterred by his earlier failure, in 1886 Stephen again advised the Lord Chancellor that he favored redefining perjury along the lines of his Indian codes. Punishment for perjury would be determined by what was at stake in the underlying case: perjury in capital cases or cases that could result in imprisonment would result in a more severe sentence.[195] As in India, Stephen recommended limitations on the examination of prison-ers. Prisoners would not be examined on oath, and the judge would be responsible for questioning, not the prosecution. Notably, however, by the 1880s there was less support among reformers in the legal community for limits on cross-examination. Sir Harry Poland wrote the Lord Chancellor and opposed this aspect of Stephen's reform. "I have changed my opinion on the subject & now think that there should be no limit," he confessed. "The accused, if called, must be treated as an ordinary witness, leaving the cross-examination as at present to the good taste, judgment and discretion of the [prosecuting counsel]."[196] Like Stephen's earlier attempt, this proposal also failed.

Despite this failure, Stephen's codification efforts represented a new era, one in which solutions pioneered in the colonial context were reintroduced in England in an attempt to resolve the enduring issue of counsel's discretion versus the judge's authority in cross-examination. In fact, even after his attempts at parliamentary codification failed, Stephen remained convinced that his Indian Evidence Act had important lessons for English evidence law. During the Tichborne controversy, he insisted that a solution to this dilemma might be located in the Indian Evidence Act of 1872.[197] Enthusiasm for Stephen's work continued to play a role in debates on the law of evidence in England. In the flurry of letters regarding cross-examination, the Indian experience again came up as a model. One writer proposed giving the judge the power to ask prisoners about disputed points in testimony and also to invite prisoners to respond to the evidence against them, as in the Indian Criminal Code.[198] As late as 1898, "B.C.S." wrote to the *Times* to suggest that the model for English reform could be located in India: "So far as a single observer can judge from his own limited experience, and from conversation with others, the Indian system is completely successful."[199]

India was not the only venue for experimentation with novel approaches to the legal production of truth during this period, however. The Divorce and Matrimonial Causes Act of 1857 created a situation in the metropole that had revealing similarities to the colonial one: in the eyes of jurists, parties to divorce cases, like "natives" in India, were assumed to be liars. If mendacity was a given, and the normal sanctions of gentlemanly honor and the oath were assumed to have no weight even among respectable parties, how could the truthfulness of witnesses be guaranteed? Working within the traditional system of common-law crimes seemed, as in India, not to be an option. Dramatically new circumstances appeared to call for innovations that went beyond conventional rules. In divorce proceedings, rather than looking to invented Hindu or Muslim traditions, British jurists opted to turn to a source less exotic but also novel: inquisitorial justice.

CHAPTER FOUR

The Queen's Proctor:
An Inquisitorial Experiment

IN 1878 THINGS BEGAN TO GO badly for the Castles. James Castle, a gas-fitter, and his wife, Elizabeth, had been happily married for three years, but early in 1878 Elizabeth started drinking heavily, or in the parlance of the time, she became "addicted to habits of intemperance." The following year James learned that Elizabeth had committed adultery with another gas-fitter, Walter Wombwell. James responded by throwing Elizabeth out of their house; he also filed a petition for divorce against her, naming Walter as a co-respondent. At the Divorce Court, James was represented by counsel, but Elizabeth and Walter neither appeared nor responded to the charges. The judge granted James a provisional divorce, or a decree *nisi*, subject to intervention by the Queen's Proctor.[1]

Unfortunately for James, his case attracted closer scrutiny. An initial investigation by the Queen's Proctor showed that James had entered into a bigamous marriage before filing a petition for divorce and had committed adultery himself. This discovery ended James's chances for a smooth divorce. First, at the Queen's Proctor's direction, James was prosecuted for bigamy and convicted at London's Central Criminal Court; meanwhile, hearings of the Queen's Proctor's motion to rescind James's decree *nisi* were postponed until he finished serving his three-month sentence.[2] Once released from jail, James still had to appear in the Divorce Court, where the Queen's Proctor was prepared to prove his case with the marriage certificate from James's second, bigamous union.[3] Unsurprisingly, James chose not to contest the Queen's Proctor's intervention.[4] With his divorce petition rescinded, James remained married to Elizabeth. Except for his prosecution for bigamy, James's story is a typical example of the kinds of action taken during the late Victorian era by the Queen's Proctor,

a prominent Victorian law officer responsible for uncovering deceit in divorce cases.

Though it may be tempting to dismiss the Queen's Proctor as an
anomalous institution, rooted in peculiarly Victorian moral standards and
irrelevant in an era of no-fault divorce available on the same grounds to
both husband and wife, it provides an opportunity to consider the revealing intersection of important questions in the history of adversarial trial
procedure and family law. As we will see, this anomalous institution, more
inquisitorial than adversarial, was yet another experiment in ensuring witness veracity undertaken in the environment created by nineteenth-century
legal reform—an experiment pursued and then abandoned in the face of
growing criticism. The Queen's Proctor's failure reveals much about the
nature and limits of the common-law system in practice: where cross-
examination fit comparatively smoothly into an adversarial model, the
Queen's Proctor generated a steadily tightening knot of contradictions. We
are increasingly accustomed to thinking about marriage as a contract with
three parties: husband, wife, and the state.[5] The Queen's Proctor instanti-
ated the participation of the state in an unusually direct fashion, not only
specifying the terms of the marriage contract, but actively trying to determine the true circumstances of marital disputes brought before the Divorce
Court. He represented community interests within the context of an adversarial proceeding, drawing upon community sentiment while compensating for the inadequacies of party-controlled fact-finding.

The history of the Queen's Proctor also contributes to our growing
understanding of how social norms as expressed through narratives and
legal regimes interacted in marital cases. The analysis of law's use of stories has been particularly fruitful in the study of marital disputes, in which
strong social norms structure (often conflicting) ideas of the "just" resolution of a problem. As Austin Sarat and William Felstiner have demonstrated
in their work on contemporary divorce cases, marital litigation brings a
broad range of people into contact with the law, many of whom seek vindi-
cation of their own narratives rather than having specific financial and legal
goals.[6] Scholarship on the history of marriage in the United States by Norma
Basch and Hendrik Hartog also demonstrates the influence of the narrative

approach. Basch's work uses the idea of narrative framing to structure her analysis; in her introduction she devotes particular attention to the role of narrative construction in divorce suits, where stories are shaped to meet formulaic legal requirements.[7] Hartog, meanwhile, describes the same concept as role-playing, noting that legal subjects "assume[d] identities recognizable in law" and attempted to "impose identities on their opponents." Failure to undertake this project of narrative adaptation might deprive one of legal recourse: many adulterers, for example, "lived complicated lives that might never fit into the stories that the law recognized as justifying divorce."[8]

Nineteenth-century English divorce cases introduce an additional complication to our thinking about storytelling in such cases. What happens to social expectations of stories when all the participants are expected to lie? As we have already seen in chapter 1, the nineteenth-century Divorce Court was considered a "playground of perjurors."[9] According to received wisdom, the extraordinarily harsh social penalties for such transgressions guaranteed that women would always lie when accused of adultery; although the consequences for men were less severe, their chivalrous desire to protect the reputations of their paramours made them equally unreliable. Indeed, under the circumstances, honesty from the male partner in the relationship could seem downright ungentlemanly. In the course of an 1859 parliamentary debate, for example, the Lord Chancellor noted that "his experience had shown him that it was considered a point of honour for a man to shelter the partner of his guilt" in cases of adultery.[10] Given these social norms, even the most artful cross-examination seemed powerless to bring the truth forward. As a result, England's response to the problem of mendacious divorce plaintiffs was both extreme and unique.

While suspicion of party-controlled narratives and wistful comparisons with continental criminal procedure form a significant current in U.S. legal thought, little attention has been directed to the possible results of any attempt to graft inquisitorial elements onto common-law procedure. The experience of the Queen's Proctor provides a cautionary tale for those who seek to circumvent party-controlled narratives. In nineteenth-century Britain, "facts" susceptible to proof—in particular, the act of adultery— were thought superior to the unreliable stories that parties presented. By reducing the analysis of complicated divorce cases to a simple "did he or didn't he?," the Queen's Proctor made it seem as if such cases were simple to resolve—a matter of applying a bright-line rule to relatively uncomplicated facts. This apparent simplicity, however, concealed an array of new difficulties. Most importantly, these evidentiary preferences effectively rewrote the substantive law of intervention in divorce cases, shifting the emphasis away from collusion and toward adultery, creating a harsher regime than even England's conservative lawmakers had intended.

Despite the Queen's Proctor's anomalous status in Anglo-American legal history and highly public role in regulating divorce, it has received surprisingly little scholarly attention.[11] This chapter seeks to fill this gap with a more detailed study of the first quarter century of the Queen's Proctor's activities, from 1861 to 1884. In particular, it employs archival records and newspaper accounts of unreported cases to generate a more comprehensive portrait of those activities than can be gleaned from the highly selective minority of cases that were reported at the time. During these twenty-four years, the Queen's Proctor intervened in at least 216 cases, of which only 33 were reported.[12] This chapter examines 171 cases, of which 146 provide details on the case from decree *nisi* through final disposition.

The Divorce Court

England was comparatively slow in legislating for divorce, unlike both the United States and France. The Divorce Court was established only in 1857 in London.[13] While the creation of a judicial court to hear divorce cases was path-breaking, given that divorce had previously been obtainable only through a private bill in Parliament, the new legislation was less innovative in its substantive definition of divorce.[14] Divorce was available to the husband on the basis of his wife's adultery; a wife, meanwhile, had to prove adultery combined with some other marital offense, such as cruelty, desertion, incest, bigamy, rape, or sodomy. Critics thought that this double standard prompted collusive cases, as adulterous husbands either feigned aggravating circumstances or asked their wives to pretend to commit adultery. The court was headed by one judge—known as the Judge Ordinary until 1873, after which he was known as the President—and had jurisdiction over admiralty and probate matters, as well as matrimonial causes.

Shortly after the Divorce Court's establishment, moves began to reform it. The original structure of the court was thought to be deficient on a number of grounds. First, one judge could make scant headway on the hundreds of cases that arrived yearly. Second, the publicity of divorce cases was thought to endanger public morals, particularly given the attention they received in newspapers. Third, lawmakers feared that collusion was making a mockery of the substantive law. This third concern became the justification for the Queen's Proctor's role in the Divorce Court.[15]

In 1859, the Lord Chancellor proposed that the Attorney General be notified as part of every divorce petition; the Attorney General, in turn, would be able to institute inquiries if he felt there was reason to suspect collusion. Critics maintained that this new responsibility would be an imposition on the already overworked Attorney General, so the Lord Chancellor soon modified his proposal to have the judge of the Divorce Court notify the Attorney General "whenever they thought it desirable."[16] The House of Commons, however, defeated this proposal. Members objected to the apparent duplication of proceedings and to the lack of provisions giving the Attorney General the power to conduct the investigations for which he was asked to assume responsibility. As one member concluded, "Altogether the clause was so crudely framed and seemed so insufficient for the objects desired, that, unless it could be amended, he must vote against it."[17] Nor were members of Parliament the only ones with reservations: the *Law Times* quoted the Lord Chancellor's opposition to the proposal, saying that the true question "is not whether collusion is possible in one case in five hundred, but is it right to burden the 499 honest cases with the needless cost, delay and inconvenience of an investigation."[18]

The following year, the proposal reappeared. In addition to authorizing the Queen's Proctor to appoint counsel to represent the undefended side in cases where the respondent failed to appear, a new bill gave the Queen's Proctor power to investigate suspected cases of collusion.[19] By making the Queen's Proctor the responsible official, rather than the overburdened Attorney General, the main objection to the previous year's bill was overcome. The Queen's Proctor was a part-time office held by a civilian—a lawyer trained in canon law—who was responsible for looking after the crown's interests in cases of intestacy and other causes. Intervention in divorce cases would substantially expand his responsibilities but would not swamp an already busy office. Robert Rolfe, Lord Cranworth then offered the amendment that would become the basis for the Queen's Proctor's jurisdiction: all divorce decrees were henceforth to be decrees *nisi*, subject to rescinding by the court.[20] The Queen's Proctor had three months after the decree *nisi* to file a motion to intervene on the grounds of suspected collusion or suppression of material facts. If the Queen's Proctor received the Attorney General's permission to proceed with the case, he could retain counsel and subpoena witnesses for what was effectively a second trial before the Divorce Court.[21] Despite some grumblings from the House of Commons as to the expense of the new office, the bill passed without further incident and became law in August 1860.[22]

Two areas of crucial importance for the later development of the Queen's Proctor emerge from the parliamentary debate and contemporary reactions: community participation in identifying abuses and the definition of collusion. Parliament expressed an unusual concern with encouraging community participation in the activities of the Queen's Proctor. The task of rooting out collusion, a number of lords suggested, should be partially delegated to the neighbors of the petitioners seeking a divorce. Speaking for the bill in Parliament, the Attorney General expressed skepticism of the ability of the Divorce Court judge to provide a sufficient bulwark against collusion in undefended cases, noting from his experience overseeing the court that "the Judge was unable to ascertain anything relative to the antecedents of the parties to a suit, or the position of the witnesses, beyond that which the counsel for the petitioners might think proper to furnish from his instructions."[23] To remedy this problem, Lord Cranworth proposed a system of community notification: the court would grant a provisional decree *nisi* and then "issue notices to the neighbourhood in which the parties lived, so as to afford any person who was aware of any collusion between the parties an opportunity of coming before the Court before a final decree was pronounced."[24] Advocates of the Queen's Proctor held out particular hope for friends and relatives as informants.[25]

Lord Henry Brougham's speeches and writings before the act's passage provide a clue to the origin of this somewhat unusual recourse to popular input outside the traditional channel of the jury. In a proposal submitted to the Law Amendment Society, Brougham referred to the experience of the House of Lords as a model to draw upon: "In the House of Lords," he wrote, "divorces have often been prevented in consequence of suggestions made to individual peers, which led to sifting of the case, brought forward by collusion, and as it were conspiracy, of parties—suggestions which of course cannot be made to the judges of a court."[26] By adopting the practice of the House of Lords, the Divorce Court reformers preserved an element of popular participation and laid the groundwork for presentation of the Queen's Proctor as representative of the public interest.

This element of popular participation also attracted criticism, however, albeit from an enraged minority. One contributor to *Law Magazine and Review* compared the Queen's Proctor to the Venetian stone receptacles for anonymous accusations, or *bocce del leone:*

> In Venice there existed a much-prized institution. Whoever knew too much of his fellow-man or woman disburdened himself of his plethora of knowledge by imparting it into the mouths of one of the Lions which stood on the Giant's staircase [at the Doge's palace]. This valuable institution, long since disused in the place of its birth, has . . . been transferred to a new locality, viz., London. The Attorney General and the Queen's Proctor have become the lions' mouths, and are to tell the Court all that the public in general, or spies in particular, know about any petitioner or any respondent.[27]

By invoking Venice, the contributor played on a favorite Victorian anxiety: the fear of becoming a mercantile empire fallen into tyranny and despotism with a democratic citizenry co-opted into the service of a police state.[28]

In the second topic appearing throughout the House of Lords' debate, agreement on a definition of collusion proved elusive. Shortly after the act's passage, the *Solicitors' Journal* sought to distinguish the varieties of collusion:

> we may class the cases generally as follows:—first, cases where one party commits adultery with the connivance of the other, for the purpose of qualifying the adulterer for, or of enabling the other party to procure, a divorce; secondly, where, without adultery, the parties conspire to impose upon the Court, and obtain its judgment by putting forward a false case, or keeping back the true one . . . ; and thirdly, where there has been mere passive connivance or insensibility to dishonour, and it is impossible to discover the real motives of the parties.[29]

It was only in the second case, the *Solicitors' Journal* thought, that a Queen's Proctor could conceivably protect the court from abuse. The indefatigable Lord Brougham, a law reformer for all seasons, tried to develop his own typology: "There are two types of collusion, one from the mere common purpose of the parties, who being . . . equally desirous of divorce, make almost all such cases really undefended; the other when there has been such connivance as shews that the offence was committed with the design of causing a dissolution of the marriage."[30] The dividing line between the two was action. Parties committing acts with the sole design of attaining a divorce fell into the second category. While he considered the former less culpable than the latter, Brougham argued that the court should be able to investigate both sorts of collusion.

Skeptics argued that with these new measures, Parliament had dangerously broadened the definition of collusion. Previously, in the ecclesiastical courts, collusion had been narrowly defined as the agreement for one party to commit (or appear to commit) adultery in order to obtain a divorce; under the new parliamentary definition, collusion included any agreement to present and prosecute a false petition.[31] As one essayist in the *Law Magazine and Review* observed in 1874, collusion under the Divorce

Act had come to encompass any "agreement between the parties as to the institution or conduct of the suit itself."[32] Later, the definition of collusion would become still more expansive, so that by 1880 collusion included any agreement between parties to withhold material facts that might be adduced as evidence in support of a countercharge.[33] The link between these definitions was an agreement between the parties; as we will see, however, by the end of the nineteenth century collusion would be defined by some as concealing relevant facts from the court, whether or not the other party agreed to hide them.[34]

After the establishment of the Queen's Proctor, several minor changes were made. Six years later, for example, Parliament opted to lengthen the time for intervening from three months to six months.[35] In 1873, this was followed by an extension of jurisdiction to cases involving suits for nullity of marriage.[36] Concern about the Queen's Proctor's ability to force opponents to pay his costs led to legislation in 1878 making provisions for a victorious party to charge costs to the Queen's Proctor.[37] This measure, however, seems to have been a dead letter until the early years of the twentieth century. Finally, as mentioned in chapter 1, in an abortive reform attempt in 1888, Mr. Darling, a Queen's Counsel and member of Parliament, offered a bill that would enable either the judge or the jury in Divorce Court to immediately consider whether a co-respondent had been guilty of perjury and pass sentence as if he or she had been indicted and convicted through the regular process. Darling withdrew his bill within two weeks of introducing it, but the extreme measures he proposed suggest the extent to which perjury in the Divorce Court was publicly perceived as a threat.[38]

Outside of the law regarding the Divorce Court itself, one other significant change affected divorce suits during this period. The prohibition on parties giving evidence in suits "arising from adultery" was finally abolished in 1869. As we saw in chapter 1, adultery and breach of promise had been exempted from previous legislation allowing interested parties and witnesses to testify.[39] Even Lord Denman, an otherwise stalwart proponent of admitting all possible evidence—his father wrote the first legislation to allow interested witnesses to testify—expressed his reservations about this reform by asserting that in adultery cases he "would never consent to

put a man into the position of either being obliged to commit perjury or
to betray the partner of his guilt."[40] Furthermore, other critics noted that
such perjury would be virtually immune from prosecution, because it was
seen as excusable.[41] Nonetheless, despite the strong resistance to allowing
evidence on adultery, momentum for reform came from the frustration of
Divorce Court judges, who protested that the law was irrational, given that
parties could testify to adultery in other proceedings. The judges' views
eventually carried the day, and in 1869, after several abortive attempts, the
Evidence Further Amendment Act became law, allowing parties to be competent (but not compellable) witnesses in suits arising from adultery.[42] This
change, discussed in more detail in chapter 5, meant that the Queen's Proctor had access to testimony delivered in court, by the parties, regarding
adultery from 1869 on.

The Queen's Proctor in Action

In 1909, a Royal Commission on Divorce and Matrimonial Causes
was convened to reconsider the law of divorce, particularly its accessibility
to the poor and the ongoing controversy regarding the publicity of Divorce
Court proceedings.[43] Among the witnesses were Hamilton Cuffe, the Earl
of Desart, who had just stepped down after fourteen years as the King's/
Queen's Proctor; Lord Chief Justice Richard Webster Alverstone, who, as
Attorney General, had supervised the activities of the King's Proctor; the
current President of the Divorce Court; and numerous solicitors and barristers who practiced before the court. Many of these individuals had experience with the Divorce Court dating back into the 1880s. By combining
their published testimony with the limited records of the Queen's Proctor
from the late 1870s and 1880s preserved in the Public Records Office at
Kew, and with other sources, we can piece together a general description
of the Queen's Proctor's practice, including how the Queen's Proctor obtained information about suspicious cases, investigated them, and selected
a few for intervention.[44]

The first step toward an intervention began with the Queen's Proctor's receipt of information alerting him to something suspicious in a di-

vorce case before the decree *nisi* was made absolute. Over time, the Queen's Proctor moved from largely passive reception of information to a more active role. Testimony before the Royal Commission describes the later, more active role, in which a majority of cases were identified either by the judge of the Divorce Court or by the Queen's Proctor himself. According to one solicitor testifying before the commission, the Queen's Proctor was usually "put on the scent" by aspects of divorce cases that the judge singled out as requiring further investigation.[45]

Sir John Bigham, President of the Divorce Court, described the selection of cases by judges: "It depends on the judge, who may notice during the evidence some circumstances that he thinks suspicious. He may then put questions himself to the witnesses, and if his suspicions appear to be well founded, or if he thinks they are well founded, then what he does, of course, is to send the case to the King's Proctor." The judge, in turn, relied in part on the cooperation of the bar. As Bigham pointed out in his testimony, "it is supposed to be the duty of the counsel in an undefended case to bring to the notice of the judge any circumstances of which he may be cognizant pointing to collusion, a duty which I know has been admirably performed by counsel in the court."[46]

Another way in which the Queen's Proctor was able to monitor ongoing cases without actually attending the Divorce Court was through shorthand transcripts. All cases heard in the Divorce Court were taken down in shorthand. If the judge found a case suspicious, he could order the shorthand notes transcribed and sent to the Queen's Proctor. These notes were used in another way as well. According to the Earl of Desart, all the shorthand notes of undefended cases were transcribed and sent to the Queen's Proctor for review.[47] Undefended cases were of particular interest because they were common, with some six hundred to seven hundred cases per year, and were typically heard in ten to fifteen minutes.[48] It was widely thought that collusion in undefended cases was both more common and harder to detect, because the judge had so little information to go on.[49] Hard-fought cases, meanwhile, were thought to be relatively unproblematic.[50]

Beginning around 1880, the records of the Queen's Proctor increasingly refer to the Queen's Proctor himself as the source of information.

Between 1880 and 1885, approximately two-thirds of the interventions are listed as being based on information from the Queen's Proctor.[51] This designation appears to encompass a variety of ways in which the Queen's Proctor monitored ongoing cases. In one case, the registry records that the Queen's Proctor's suspicions were triggered by a police report from the *Daily Telegraph*.[52] More frequently, however, the registry notes visits by the Queen's Proctor's assistant to the Divorce Court to peruse case registers. Given that around the same time the records cease naming the judge as a source of information, referrals from the judge must be included in this latter category.[53]

A large number of cases, however, were based on information from individuals in the community. Before the 1880s, letters provided the main source of the Queen's Proctor's information. After 1880, information provided by outsiders continued to play a role in generating cases, albeit a reduced one. Most of the letters the Queen's Proctor received were identified as coming from solicitors. Occasionally, other types of individuals appeared—including an estate agent, a plasterer, and the relieving officer of St. Pancras.[54] Some solicitors were identified as representing the parties, or their families and friends; others were similarly employed even if they were not identified as such. Still other letters were anonymous. Newspaper coverage of divorce cases made it possible for community sentiment to generate the kind of protest Brougham envisioned when he argued for the establishment of the Queen's Proctor.

In general, however, an aggrieved losing party or a close relative was the most likely source of the Queen's Proctor's information. Early on, the court established the acceptability of hearing evidence from parties or relations of parties, although it was occasionally contested by counsel.[55] A favorite story of the supporters of the Queen's Proctor related the anguish of the mother of a man involved in an adulterous relationship with a married woman. Upon seeing the news that her son's paramour had been granted a divorce, the mother sought to inform the court of her unfitness to receive a decree; but, under the previous restrictions on intervention, there was no way for the mother's testimony to be communicated to the court.[56] By contrast, by the end of the period studied here, it had almost become expected that the source of information would be a relative.

Turning to the investigation of suspicious cases, the Queen's Proctor was often in possession of a surprising amount of information from letters alone. In one case, the respondent's solicitor sent the Queen's Proctor five signed affidavits; in another, an anonymous letter writer provided photographs.[57] The Queen's Proctor's staff frequently met with letter writers and parties during the early stages of investigation. We know from the Queen's Proctor's registry that many investigations were conducted by solicitors working in the vicinity of the alleged malfeasance, and that some solicitors performed a great deal of this work. In 1884, the Queen's Proctor Augustus Stephenson described the role played by London-based investigators, saying that while he did employ local investigators, he "usually sends down persons from London to make inquiries" because "it is difficult work and local agents are often interested."[58] On at least one occasion, however, the Queen's Proctor hired the author of a letter to act as his local agent.[59] Many of the published accounts of cases mention affidavits, so it is probable that local solicitors sent affidavits to the Queen's Proctor's office in London; unless the case was contested, there was little reason to compel witnesses to travel to the capital.

The expenses for the cases give a rough indication of the amount of effort involved in their preparation. From 1861 through 1873, costs ranged from £56 to £1,522, with twenty-nine cases coming in at more than £300.[60] While the Queen's Proctor could ask the judge to award costs when he successfully proved collusion, the infrequency of such victories meant that Parliament paid for most of the Queen's Proctor's expenses until 1878, when the grounds for requiring defeated parties to reimburse the Queen's Proctor were broadened. Moreover, the Queen's Proctor did not hesitate to conduct extensive investigation of many more cases than those in which he eventually intervened. Investigations could easily go on for months, involving dozens of interviews and prepared affidavits, as well as participation by both local and London solicitors, and by hired detectives, only to have the Attorney General decide at the last minute not to request leave to intervene.[61] In his testimony before the commission, the Earl of Desart reported investigating between 306 and 631 cases per year over the previous fifteen years and intervening in only between 11 and 33 cases.[62] While it is difficult to determine how many cases were investigated in earlier periods, the relatively small number of interventions is typical. Parliamentary returns on the Queen's Proctor's activities from 1861 through 1876 show between zero and thirteen interventions yearly.[63]

Given the disparity between cases investigated and those in which the Queen's Proctor intervened, what made the difference? From 1879 through the early 1880s, we have records of the cases that were brought to the Queen's Proctor's attention. During this period at least, no type of case or source of information appeared to result in automatic intervention. The Queen's Proctor refused to intervene in cases brought forth by the Judge Ordinary, by outraged aunts alleging collusion, by other relations, by anonymous letters, and by discontented losing parties.[64] Provision of incriminating affidavits, photographs, or trial notes was also not necessarily enough to spur the Queen's Proctor to intervene.[65]

The Queen's Proctor was clearly hesitant to intervene in cases in which the respondent claimed poverty as a reason for failing to put up a defense. In one instance, however, he intervened when a respondent, James Bakey, wrote from the Mountjoy Convict Prison explaining that his incarceration had prevented him from defending his wife's petition. Bakey also disclosed details of his wife's adultery. The Queen's Proctor then investigated, leading to an intervention that resulted in Caroline Bakey's decree *nisi* being rescinded.[66]

While the witnesses before the Royal Commission in 1909 identified undefended cases as particularly interesting to the Queen's Proctor, the early registries reveal a more complicated attitude. The registry shows the Queen's Proctor's assistant searching the lists of *defended* cases.[67] Undefended cases, meanwhile, seem to have drawn more attention when they were defended at the outset. When a respondent or a co-respondent dropped a countercharge, or if there had previously been a cross-petition for divorce or a suit for judicial separation by the respondent, the Queen's Proctor was likely to notice. The Divorce Court judges, meanwhile, seem to have also responded to countercharges put forward by the respondent in selecting cases to refer to the Queen's Proctor; evidence insufficient to block a decree *nisi* could serve as the basis for an intervention.[68]

The Queen's Proctor's interest in dropped countercharges reflects a suspicion that sudden silence might indicate collusion; and it also points to what was arguably the most crucial factor in determining which cases would be selected for intervention: the probability that convincing proof would be forthcoming. Lord Alverstone, who was responsible for approving interventions as Attorney General, suggested why so few cases progressed to intervention. He insisted on a standard of full proof before proceeding to trial: "I never allowed the King's Proctor to intervene unless I thought he was certain to be successful."[69] But what constituted convincing proof? We turn now to that question.

From Suspicious Stories to Incontrovertible Facts

On a pleasant Saturday in July 1876, a horse brought to a close the first chapter in the history of the Queen's Proctor. Francis Hart Dyke, who had held the office since 1851, was thrown by his mount while riding near Windsor and subsequently died from his injuries. Dyke had a long history as a civil lawyer, beginning practice in Doctor's Commons in 1825 and serving as the Registrar of Canterbury. When he assumed the office of Queen's Proctor, his responsibilities were largely limited to obtaining letters of administration for the crown in intestacy cases.[70] The 1860 statute giving the Queen's Proctor power to intervene in divorce cases dramatically expanded his role. Dyke adapted to the change and served as Queen's Proctor for the next sixteen years. As a civilian, Dyke represented the continuity of the new Divorce Court with previous ecclesiastical law governing marriage, but his successor came from quite a different background. Augustus Keppel Stephenson, the son of the Chief Commissioner of the Inland Revenue, had been called to Lincoln's Inn in 1852 and took a position with the Treasury Solicitor's office in 1856.

One year before Dyke's untimely death, Stephenson had been appointed Treasury Solicitor. His appointment as Queen's Proctor, therefore,

marked the institutional incorporation of the Queen's Proctor within the
Treasury Solicitor's office. Subsequently, Stephenson would become the
second Director of Public Prosecutions in 1884, as the work of that office
was also incorporated into the Treasury Solicitor's office. Stephenson, a
"man of strong opinions," is credited with that "naked 'take-over'" through
his "sheer forcefulness."[71] Stephenson also accelerated changes in the selection of prosecution of divorce cases. During Stephenson's tenure, the
trend toward focusing on adultery cases solidified, largely determining the
pattern of interventions for the remainder of the century.

The Queen's Proctor's approach to intervention thus changed from
the first period, when the office was held by Francis Dyke, to the second,
when it was held by Augustus Stephenson, with adultery overshadow-
ing collusion as the dominant rationale. This shift was a consequence of
the difficulties the Queen's Proctor encountered in bringing cases based
on collusion. Under the statute establishing the Queen's Proctor's responsibilities in divorce cases, intervention was authorized in cases of collusion or where parties withheld material facts from the court; other reasons
cited for intervention echoed the grounds for preventing a divorce under
ecclesiastical law, including condonation, connivance, conduct conducing
(for example, a husband's desertion or cruelty might be taken as conduct
"conducing" his wife's adultery, even if it fell short of grounds for divorce),
and, of course, the petitioner's own adultery. Collusion was the Queen's
Proctor's clearest mandate, but straightforward cases of collusion proved
few and far between.

From the beginning, the Queen's Proctor encountered substantial
problems establishing proof of collusion, understood as an agreement between parties to mount a false case. As the counsel for the Queen's Proctor
in *Gethin v. Gethin* dolefully informed the Judge Ordinary in a case he
was about to lose, "collusion, like bribery, could never be directly proved;
it could only be established by results."[72] The *Law Journal*, meanwhile,
thought that the Queen's Proctor's lack of success was "because parties
who act in collusion manage matters very skillfully."[73] The Queen's Proctor's difficulty proving collusion may have been exacerbated, indirectly, by
a statutory provision in force until 1878 that allowed him to recover costs

from a defeated opponent only when the intervention alleged and proved collusion.[74] As a result, the Queen's Proctor may have been tempted to charge collusion in cases where he had little possibility of substantiating the allegation.

Even cases in which the circumstantial evidence of collusion seemed highly persuasive were liable to be dismissed. In *Cox v. Cox,* for example, no collusion was found even though the petitioning wife was represented in her suit by her supposedly estranged husband's solicitor.[75] In *Poore v. Poore and Lake,* the Queen's Proctor demonstrated the "attendance of the respondent, co-respondent, and co-respondent's mother at the office of the petitioner's solicitor during the preparation of the suit," which the Judge Ordinary thought "most suspicious" but nonetheless did not find to be conclusive evidence of collusion.[76] Similarly, the Solicitor General, appearing for the Queen's Proctor, confessed in another case that "he had no legal proof of collusion, although there was probably a good legal understanding between the parties, as the co-respondent, who was a wealthy man, had lived with the respondent and Mr. Gavaron [the petitioner] had for the last 10 or 11 years lived with another woman at his chambers in Clifford's-inn."[77]

One of the few cases in which the Queen's Proctor successfully established collusion, *Barnes v. Barnes and Grimwade,* is the exception that proves the rule. In *Barnes,* the petitioning husband not only granted his estranged wife an allowance, but also had several interviews with her both before and after petitioning for divorce, promising that if she did not oppose the petition he would "be a friend to her" and "would not hurt a hair of the co-respondent's head." One of these interviews apparently took place in a public house.[78] With this as the standard, it is unsurprising that the Queen's Proctor rarely succeeded in proving collusion.

The cases examined reveal that, in the early years, the Queen's Proctor often charged the petitioner with collusion and adultery but succeeded in proving only the adultery.[79] In what is probably a response to these early verdicts as well as an effort to expedite cases, Divorce Court judges often decided cases, or urged juries to decide cases, solely on the question of adultery, even when the Queen's Proctor offered other allegations.[80]

Occasionally, judges even refused to hear evidence of other charges. In *Ravenscroft v. Ravenscroft, Smith and Whitney,* the Judge Ordinary cut off testimony after the question of adultery, saying that "it was unnecessary to go into any further evidence, because the end of the intervention was attained as soon as it was proved that the petitioner had been guilty of an act of adultery, for his petition must then be dismissed."[81]

Shortly before Francis Dyke's death, the Queen's Proctor had been tarnished by several high-profile defeats, particularly in what the *Law Times* called "the two recent and notorious trials of *Van Reable* v. *Van Reable,* and *Gladstone* v. *Gladstone.*"[82] *Van Reable* involved a dispute between two foreigners working in England as language instructors. Amelie Van Reable accused her husband Alphonse of adultery and cruelty and received a decree *nisi* after he made no official answer to her charges. He did, however, submit an affidavit to the court containing countercharges. The court then passed the affidavit along to the Queen's Proctor, who decided to intervene, accusing Amelie of adultery and collusion. In an unusual example of an allegation of physical cruelty committed by a wife, the Queen's Proctor alleged that she "pulled and tore his whiskers, and scratched his neck and hands with her nails, and, on one occasion in the end of the year 1871, threw herself on the respondent and seized him by the throat nearly suffocating him, saying at the same time she wished he was dead."[83]

The trial was unusually lengthy, lasting five days, and focused on the accusation that Amelie had committed adultery with Captain Brutton, the son of a next-door neighbor. Captain Brutton had rented a room from Amelie, and the Queen's Proctor urged the jury to consider that "this intimacy was inconsistent with innocence." Amelie maintained that they were merely good friends and strongly protested their innocence in what the *Times* called "a remarkable conflict of testimony."[84] Despite a strong summation in the Queen's Proctor's favor by the judge, who deemed Amelie's friendship with Captain Brutton "calculated in the highest degree to excite suspicion," the jury was clearly unconvinced. After only ten minutes' deliberation, they rejected all the Queen's Proctor's allegations.[85]

The Gladstone's divorce case, meanwhile, was still more hotly contested than the Van Reables'. Like *Van Reable,* this was a petition for divorce

brought by the wife, and the Queen's Proctor intervened on the basis of collusion and adultery. Unlike the *Van Reable* case, however, the respondent
had vigorously defended himself. In fact, Mrs. Gladstone's counsel argued
against the charge of collusion on the basis of the "pertinacious nature" of
the divorce suit. The Queen's Proctor also revived accusations of adultery
presented by Captain Gladstone in the divorce trial, leading to an angry
rebuke by the judge, who reminded the Queen's Proctor that he could not
call for a retrial of questions already determined by a jury. After a lengthy
and contentious trial, in which the Queen's Proctor was forced to withdraw the charge of collusion at the eleventh hour, the jury found against the
Queen's Proctor on the remaining charge of adultery without even leaving
their box.[86]

These two prominent failures resulted in unprecedented public
criticism of the Queen's Proctor. The *Law Journal* called for making the
Queen's Proctor liable for costs in the cases it lost. While the Queen's Proctor could receive costs from a defeated petitioner in cases in which collusion was proved, no such provision allowed parties to recoup costs from
the Queen's Proctor, even where the interference might have been reckless or frivolous. As the *Law Journal* noted, the defense costs in both *Van
Reable* and *Gladstone* undoubtedly exceeded £1,000. The Queen's Proctor
"is fallible," the *Journal* noted, "and as his mistakes inflict grievous loss on
innocent persons, it is only just that some means should be found either of
limiting his actions or of compensating those who so suffer."[87] Both Parliament and the legal community responded to the call for reform. Parliament,
as already noted, passed a measure in 1878 enabling the judge to award
costs when the Queen's Proctor failed to prove his case. The Legal Departments Commission, apparently wanting to rebuke Dyke without removing
him from office, recommended that, upon Dyke's retirement, the business
of the Queen's Proctor be transferred to the Treasury Solicitor, rather than
remaining an independent office.[88]

Because of Dyke's fatal accident, the transfer occurred shortly after
the commissioners' recommendation. The new Queen's Proctor, Augustus Stephenson, was clearly mindful of the criticisms mounted against his
predecessor. He brought a new consciousness of costs to the selection of

cases.[89] He was also much more hesitant than his predecessor in intervening in highly contentious cases. Instead of searching for collusion in murky
and suspicious cases such as *Van Reable* and *Gladstone,* Stephenson had a
pronounced preference for the easy mark. He liked incontrovertible cases,
particularly ones in which he could obtain a reversal without proceeding
to trial. He also appears to have learned from *Gladstone* to differentiate the
Queen's Proctor's intervention from countercharges raised in the divorce
trial. Even where the divorce trial generated a detailed list of allegations of
adultery, the Queen's Proctor was certain to provide additional names.[90]
All of these changes served to accelerate the shift away from accusations of
collusion toward proof of adultery.

By the early twentieth century, this shift had become so pronounced
that the Queen's Proctor's trials were referred to as "adultery trials." In
contrast, in one early case, counsel for the petitioner questioned whether
the Queen's Proctor could intervene on the basis of alleged adultery alone,
given that the statute authorizing interventions mentioned only collusion.[91]
Once the emphasis shifted to adultery, what did the Queen's Proctor have
to show to persuade a judge or a jury that the alleged act had occurred?
Although proving adultery was easier than proving collusion, the Queen's
Proctor still needed to provide a sufficiently detailed allegation.[92]

Proving adultery in court had literary parallels in the growing genre
of novels concerned with the discovery of adultery. At the same time as the
Queen's Proctor searched for "irresistible inferences" of adultery, novels
featuring adultery and divorce grew in popularity.[93] Barbara Leckie identifies parallels between the way in which sensational novelists of the late
Victorian period conveyed the slow realization of a partner's adultery and
the practice of the Divorce Court.[94] In the typical novelistic formula, initial
suspicion of a husband's adultery is followed by an unwelcome disclosure
by a servant. The distraught wife then seeks a formal denial from her husband, but the denial's effect is soon overwhelmed by the wife's discovery
of a written record, usually notes in her husband's hand that trace the history of his infidelity. In the final phase of discovery, the wife spies on her
husband's meeting with his paramour. Forensic discovery of adultery in
the Queen's Proctor's cases both coincided with and departed from the tra-

jectory of literary discovery that Leckie describes. Testimony by servants and spies and evidence in the form of letters did feature in Queen's Proctor's cases, but they were overshadowed by the Queen's Proctor's preferred forms of evidence: legal documents and physical evidence. Where novels located the discovery of adultery in narratives—servants' stories, diaries, and letters—the Queen's Proctor shied away from stories in favor of facts less susceptible to contested interpretations.

Perhaps unsurprisingly, the Queen's Proctor favored facts with a legal imprimatur. Conclusions generated in other court cases, witnessed marriage certificates, and legal complaints signed by petitioners in other circumstances were seen as highly influential. As in the case of Elizabeth and James Castle, a marriage certificate from a bigamous second marriage was effective evidence. In a case of bad timing, one woman's petition for divorce was defeated because she was named as a co-respondent in an uncontested divorce suit before her own decree *nisi* was made absolute.[95] Similarly, a respondent's prior criminal conversation suit against the petitioner's lover was taken as convincing evidence against his claim that he did not know of his wife's adultery.[96]

When legal documents were lacking, the Queen's Proctor often turned to evidence from the body, specifically illegitimate children and venereal disease, both of which had the potential to be interpreted as conclusive evidence of adultery. The existence of an illegitimate child constituted almost insurmountable evidence against a petitioner.[97] Lavinia Sparks, for example, tried to contest evidence that she had given birth to a child while estranged from her husband, despite testimony from a nurse who identified her as the mother, though she had used the name Mrs. Fisher. Sparks's lover, Mr. Fisher, claimed that he had escorted a prostitute, not Mrs. Sparks, to the hospital and registered her under his name. The President would have none of the story, because Fisher had subsequently registered the child's mother as "Lavinia Alberts Watkins," Mrs. Sparks's maiden name. Fisher protested that he was using an old friend's name only for convenience, but the President was unsympathetic. He complained that Fisher had not only committed "a criminal act" if his story was true, "but the man who would say he had committed it was capable of any falsehood."

Mrs. Sparks lost her case, and her decree *nisi* was rescinded.[98] Another surefire way to get one's decree *nisi* rescinded was to testify while pregnant with an illegitimate child: the Divorce Court came close to deeming such behavior contempt of court.[99]

While an illegitimate child was evidence generally used against a wife, children could be proof of a husband's adultery, too. In *Bowen v. Bowen and Evans,* the petitioning husband was discovered to be living with another woman who had given birth to a child since the date of the decree *nisi;* he was presumed to be the father and the decree was rescinded.[100] In another case, the Queen's Proctor was able to present evidence of *both* bigamous remarriage and an illegitimate child, when the petitioner was found to have married a very pregnant bride, who gave birth two months later. The bigamous husband subsequently abandoned his petition for divorce.[101]

Another form of evidence from the body—the communication of venereal disease—invariably told against the husband rather than the wife. Venereal disease acquired after marriage was considered "practical proof of adultery," and communication of the disease constituted legal cruelty.[102] The Queen's Proctor periodically included venereal disease and its communication among its allegations.[103] But evidence of venereal disease was not as incontrovertible as an illegitimate child; in at least two cases the Queen's Proctor intervened in response to countercharges of venereal disease but failed to prevent the decree *nisi* being made absolute.[104]

Many cases turned on evidence of cohabitation or frequent visitations, although this was less definitive than the birth of a child or a bigamous marriage certificate. Two unmarried people living together as man and wife was considered definitive evidence of adultery.[105] Neighbors testifying to frequent visitations by unmarried acquaintances could also serve as proof of adultery.[106] In one case, Mr. Stocker, an engineer, tried to defend himself against testimony that he was often visited at his lodgings by various women. He explained that "he was engaged in inventing a washing machine, and that he required [women's] assistance in the experiments he was conducting." The women in question, he maintained, were all experienced laundresses. The Judge Ordinary was unimpressed, and Stocker's petition was dismissed.[107]

As in novels, another form of commonly used evidence included testimony from servants and hotel keepers, but this could be treacherous for the Queen's Proctor. Hotel keepers and landlords could testify to parties' simultaneous stays in shared bedrooms, but they could also be accused of misidentification, particularly in the case of hotel chambermaids, who were thought unreliable.[108] While the standard for identification was lower in Queen's Proctor's interventions than in divorce cases, errors could still count against the Queen's Proctor.[109] One of the most dramatic defeats of the Queen's Proctor came at the hands of an actress, Mrs. Wilson, who decisively refuted the testimony of hotel staff. Mrs. Wilson, who worked at the Birmingham Theatre under the name of Lillie Lonsdale, had received a decree *nisi* after complaining of her husband's adultery and cruelty. The Queen's Proctor intervened, accusing Mrs. Wilson of committing adultery with John Smith, a family friend and Birmingham solicitor, at the Eagle Hotel in Stafford. A chambermaid identified Mrs. Wilson as the veiled lady she saw with Mr. Smith. Mrs. Wilson, however, was able to establish an alibi by showing that she had been at Llanbrynmair, in North Wales, and had gone to the train station there both the day of the alleged adultery and the following day to inquire whether a hamper had arrived for her. The stationmaster, a local shopkeeper, and the hotel landlady in Llanbrynmair were all able to testify to Mrs. Wilson's presence there on the two days in question, making travel to Stafford a practical impossibility. The Judge Ordinary in the case did not even call on petitioner's counsel to make a closing statement, but instead found for Mrs. Wilson immediately.[110]

In contrast to their dispositive role in adultery novels, letters could be ambiguous evidence in court, as the Queen's Proctor found when he attempted to prove collusion in *Marris v. Marris and Burke* on the basis of a letter from the petitioner's wife to her lover, which read as follows: "I went to Warser-gate yesterday, felt disappointed there was no note or message for me. Just had your whereabouts. The important question is finally settled, and the *article* is waiting your claim. I have not felt so happy for years as now. Come or write me what you wish me to do; better telegraph."[111] The Queen's Proctor argued that this letter, because it came with the apparent endorsement of the petitioner (he had written the address on the outside), proved collusion or connivance. The petitioner, however, argued that the "article" in question was not a reward or payment for the co-respondent, but rather was his wife herself, whom he was evicting from his house. The Judge Ordinary agreed, granting the petitioner his decree. The Queen's Proctor had better luck in *Mayes v. Mayes*, where the petitioner admitted in letters to being the father of his estranged wife's child. He denied they were in his handwriting, but a special jury did not believe him.[112]

Like the unconvincing denial by husbands in novels, parties' testimony was rarely credited by the judge. In *Boardman v. Boardman*, the Judge Ordinary celebrated the fact that the parties could testify but cautioned the jury that their testimony was not to be believed:

> Whatever may be the result of the case, we must all rejoice that we have had the husband and the wife and the person alleged to have committed adultery with the wife in the witness box. Do not suppose that I mean to suggest that the assertion of those witnesses, that they did not commit adultery, is a very serviceable fact in the case, for we all know what human nature is, and the interest they have in denying the truth of such a charge; but the value of their testimony is that it has enabled them to answer or explain all the little things which have been suggested about them.[113]

Similarly, in the divorce case of *Ricketts v. Ricketts*, the President dismissed the testimony of the respondent, saying that "he did not think the respondent was a person worthy of credit."[114] But when the case came before Justice Butt, sitting in the Divorce Court, upon the Queen's Proctor's intervention, Butt found the petitioner just as unbelievable: "It was impossible," he said, "to take her word against that of all the other witnesses, among whom was a daughter of her own."[115] Butt seems to have been a general skeptic when it came to party testimony; in *Willimot v. Willimot* he was similarly dismissive of the petitioner, saying that "he could not accept anything that Willimot had said."[116]

By the late 1870s and 1880s, the Queen's Proctor's office under Stephenson had clearly become skilled at preparing an incontrovertible case of adultery, judging by the number of cases in which petitioners declined to defend themselves against the Queen's Proctor's charges.[117] In *Collins v. Collins,* for example, the *Times* reported that "information reached the Queen's Proctor that the petitioner herself had not led a reputable married life, and on this becoming known to the petitioner it was intimated that she should not resist his opposition to the decree."[118] Under Stephenson, the Queen's Proctor's intervention went unopposed in well over one-half of the cases from 1879 through 1884. Another indication of the Queen's Proctor's growing ability to develop an unanswerable case can be seen in the declining number of cases he lost. During the Queen's Proctor's first decade, fifteen decrees *nisi* were made absolute in fifty-six interventions.[119] By the time of the Royal Commission in 1909, however, the King's Proctor boasted a perfect record of thirty-one decrees *nisi* rescinded in thirty-one interventions during the previous year.

The Divorce Court and the Queen's Proctor developed a procedure for voluntary withdrawal of divorce petitions rather than going through a trial. The Queen's Proctor would file a plea calling upon the petitioner to show cause why the petition should not be dismissed. If the Queen's Proctor did not receive an answer to his plea by a certain date, an assistant in the Queen's Proctor's office would swear out an affidavit testifying to the petitioner's failure to respond. The petition would subsequently be dismissed upon payment of the Queen's Proctor's costs.[120] After 1878, the Queen's Proctor could receive costs even in cases in which collusion was not alleged, and judges routinely awarded costs. Poor petitioners could arrange a payment schedule.[121] By 1892, Stephenson noted, in a "large proportion of the cases in which the Queen's Proctor takes action the parties abandon the decree *nisi* on the delivery by the Queen's Proctor of his plea, showing the grounds of his intervention, and allow the decree to be rescinded without going to trial."[122] Fewer and fewer interventions, therefore, were heard by the Divorce Court judge.

While the Queen's Proctor became skilled at presenting clear evidence of adultery, the definition of collusion had become profoundly uncertain. The current President of the Divorce Court testified in 1910 that all the King's Proctor's cases he had tried were cases of misconduct by the petitioner and that he had yet to encounter a true case of collusion.[123] The Earl of Desart supported this testimony, saying that he intervened in, at most, between one and three cases of genuine collusion yearly.[124] Lord Alverstone, however, stated, "I came to the conclusion, rightly or wrongly, early in my career as Attorney-General, that, practically speaking, the great majority of cases brought before me were collusive cases, that is to say, that the husband could not obtain a divorce according to our existing law if the facts had been known."[125] This assertion supported earlier testimony by a solicitor that "what has been held as collusion in the Divorce Court, I think, has been carried a very long way."[126] Alverstone's definition implicitly expanded the definition of collusion to include adultery by the petitioner, which, according to the Earl of Desart, made up the majority of the cases in which the Queen's Proctor intervened.[127]

In effect, the Queen's Proctor, rather than resolving the thorny dilemma of what, precisely, constituted collusion, opted for a "clean hands" doctrine derived from equity.[128] As Henry Fenn, Court Reporter at the Divorce Court for thirty-five years, wrote:

> [The King's Proctor] has his duties to fulfil, however unpleasant they may appear on the surface to the lay mind, and future petitioners ought to be fully aware of the fact that they must come into Court with what is known as "clean hands"; that is to say, their past moral conduct must bear the strictest investigation, and be fully able to bear the "fierce light," which beats on suitors in the Divorce Court. Woe betide those who have not "clean hands" and who want relief from the marriage tie![129]

At the end of his career, the Earl of Desart echoed Fenn in his testimony before the commission: "I have come to the conclusion that the principle that the petitioner must show clean hands before he or she can obtain a divorce, should be maintained."[130] While a "clean hands" doctrine may have appeared to be an attractive solution to the potentially unlimited discretion embodied in the Queen's Proctor's remit, it too had unintended consequences that would, in turn, hasten the Queen's Proctor's decline in the twentieth century.

A Double Standard?

While the Queen's Proctor's redefinition of collusion and his concomitant focus on adultery were largely unplanned responses to practical problems, they were not inconsequential. They involved a striking departure from the Queen's Proctor's original responsibility as envisioned by Parliament. The ramifications of this shift, in turn, were paradoxical: with respect to the questions of the double standard and the judge's discretion in divorce cases, the actions of the Queen's Proctor served both to defer criticism and to heighten it. By the early twentieth century, they had laid the groundwork for new criticisms of both the Queen's Proctor and the law of divorce itself.

The Queen's Proctor's turn to rooting out adultery as his primary mission served to further limit the availability of divorce, because estranged couples frequently established other relationships while still married.[131] The registry of Queen's Proctor's interventions for the 1880s contains a litany of couples discovered "acting as man and wife," having illegitimate children together, and attempting to marry.[132] Although the Queen's Proctor had been established to intervene in divorce cases in order to thwart couples who might act together to obtain a divorce they did not deserve, he now devoted his attention to marriages so definitively broken that the parties had, in many cases, set up new relationships. The typical target of the Queen's Proctor's intervention, in short, was no longer a couple working together to escape matrimony, but a pair of long-separated individuals who sought divorce in order to regularize their new unions.

The double standard in the law of divorce, which made it more difficult for wives to end their marriages than for husbands, was apparently not replicated in the interventions of the Queen's Proctor. Early on, the Queen's Proctor had been more likely to intervene in cases in which the wife petitioned for divorce, but this disparity soon subsided. During the first five years of the existence of the office, women made up only 38 percent of petitioners seeking divorce, but seventeen of the twenty-eight interventions were in cases brought by wives. During the last five years of the period studied, in contrast, interventions in cases brought by women dropped dramatically as a percentage. Of the thirty-one cases studied, only nine involved intervention into cases brought by female petitioners, while the percentage of women as petitioners overall remained roughly constant at 42 percent.[133]

Given the small sample size, it is unclear how much weight can be assigned to the earlier discrepancy. It may represent an early gender bias in divorce—many contemporaries saw divorce as "intended for the husband." This argument, however, seems to be contradicted by the fact that female petitioners at this time had equal or better luck winning decrees than their male counterparts.[134] Also, in earlier cases, there is the suggestion that "it looks more respectable for the husband to be charged with adultery than the wife."[135] Whatever the explanation for the early disparity, by 1910 Lord Alverstone did not hesitate to describe the typical case as involving a husband-petitioner: "I found in the great majority of cases where it turned out there had been collusion, the wife was the person who was charged, because the husband not unnaturally would not plead guilty to cruelty or desertion, and his adultery would not affect the object people had in trying to get a divorce; therefore, it was a very common thing for an undefended case to be a case of the wife's adultery."[136] Thus, these findings support Gail Savage's conclusion that, while the Divorce Court itself was marked by gender bias, little such explicit bias can be found in the prosecution and conduct of Queen's Proctor's cases.[137]

One of the most striking aspects of the Queen's Proctor's focus on adultery is that it was at least nominally gender neutral. Unlike the substantive law of divorce, which treated men and women differently with regard to adultery, the "clean hands" doctrine of the Queen's Proctor held both to the same standard. This practice also departed from the common judicial pattern in the United States, in which the husband's adultery, particularly with prostitutes or servants, would be treated as inconsequential.[138] Practically speaking, of course, the nominally neutral "clean hands" doctrine was superimposed on a situation in which women were doubly disadvantaged in pursuing divorces: first, by the substantive law, and second, by the socioeconomic realities that often compelled a deserted wife without a source of income to develop a new relationship outside of marriage. Victorian judges occasionally acknowledged this problem, but it was not until the Edwardian period that Divorce Court judges allowed it to weigh in their decision to grant a decree absolute despite evidence of adultery. Divorce Court judge Sir Bargrave Deane discussed this in his testimony before the Royal Commission:

> There are certain cases . . . where women come into court and pray for a divorce on the ground that their husband has been guilty of cruelty and adultery, and they have sometimes admitted that they themselves committed adultery, and pleaded extenuation, and sometimes it has been left to the King's Proctor to find out and bring it in on an Intervention. That is where the discretion of the Court comes in. If the petitioning woman has been guilty of adultery without excuse then we refuse relief, but if that woman has been driven into adultery by her husband— many cases of that sort have been proved in court—driven on to the streets, put into such a state of penury and poverty that she has been obliged to go to the protection of some other man to be supported and to live, we give her the benefit of our discretion, and give her a decree. But it is not so with men, because there is not the same temptation or compulsion exercised upon them. A man is never compelled to commit adultery, but women may be.[139]

The *Ricketts* case, in which judges had such different responses to the testimony of the parties, indicates the problems a separated wife faced. As we saw in the introduction, Harriet Ricketts petitioned for divorce on the basis of her husband William's cruelty, adultery, and desertion. William then accused her of adultery with Silas Beasly, saying that she had represented herself as Beasly's wife. Harriet responded that William had repeatedly harassed her since their separation, coming to her work and accusing her of being no better than a prostitute. When she witnessed a hit-and-run accident and had to give a statement to the police, Harriet said, she presented herself as Mrs. Beasly in order to hide from her husband.[140] One judge believed Harriet; a second did not, and her decree *nisi* was rescinded. But her testimony reflects the vulnerability of separated wives and the inclination for them to seek the security of a second marital relationship, even if illusory. Whether Harriet's story was true or not, it nonetheless resonated closely enough with expectations to be taken seriously.

Why were judges eager to apply a symmetrical standard with regard to Queen's Proctor's interventions when they consented to an asymmetrical one with regard to divorce law? The answer may have to do with the equitable origins of the "clean hands" doctrine. Equity's history as the protector of married women's property rights, even in a limited fashion, may have influenced judges to view equitable remedies as open to men and women on an equal footing.[141] Also, judges may have used the symmetry of the Queen's Proctor's intervention to assuage qualms resulting from the patent inequality of the substantive law of divorce. Significant dissent among leaders of the bar had surrounded the asymmetry of divorce from its inception.[142] As a consequence, having the highly public Queen's Proctor intervene in a more even-handed fashion may have helped ameliorate the issue for a time, until the reform of the substantive law of divorce in the twentieth century.

The question of the double standard in divorce blends into that of judicial discretion. But the dilemma of discretion was broader than just the inequality faced by women seeking divorce. Many cases, of course, never even reached a judge, as petitioners chose to withdraw their petitions rather than encounter the Queen's Proctor in court. But among those who did go to trial, few would ever receive the benefits of the discretion allowed the Divorce Court judge under the statutory laws of divorce. While the investigative efforts of the Queen's Proctor gave the judges a broad range of information to consider, and therefore the possibility of exercising discretion to craft individually tailored outcomes, Victorian judges responded by seeking simplicity and avoiding discretion.[143] The shift toward "proof" of adultery gave jurists a simple, apparently mechanistic application of law to facts. This allowed them to escape the painful and sometimes arbitrary-seeming value judgments implicated in the evaluation of narratives. Victorian judges vehemently rejected the suggestion that they should employ discretion in the Queen's Proctor's cases. In *South v. South*, petitioner's counsel asked the court to exercise discretion and allow his client to be divorced even though she admitted to committing adultery, because she had been married at age seventeen and deserted at eighteen:

> The President asked whether counsel could refer to a single case in which the Court, on the petition of the wife, had dissolved her marriage, although it had been shown that she was guilty of adultery.
>
> Mr. Sparham [petitioner's counsel] replied that he was unable to refer to such a case, but he asked the Court to exercise its discretion.
>
> The President said that this was not a matter between the petitioner and the respondent. It was an intervention by the Queen's Proctor.[144]

Similarly, in *Bloice v. Bloice,* the President doubted "whether the public had any interest in preventing the unhappy woman from getting a divorce from her worthless husband," but he refused to grant her one nonetheless, saying it was the "duty of the Queen's Proctor to act upon [the law], and therefore, whatever pity he might have for the woman in the circumstances, he must deal with the case upon the evidence as it stood."[145] By focusing on adultery, where guilt was apparently clear-cut, the Queen's Proctor allowed the judges a means of avoiding the moral ambiguities and responsibilities of discretion, clothed in the rhetoric of public interest.[146]

The Victorian compromise that obscured the questions of gender equity and the proper scope of judges' discretion under the mantle of the "clean hands" doctrine began to break down in the early twentieth century. Although popular novels are an uncertain measure of public sentiment, it is noteworthy that one of the Queen's Proctor's few literary appearances occurred in an 1887 novel in which he was faulted for his failure to take action. In Rosa Campbell-Praed's novel *The Bond of Wedlock,* the Queen's Proctor does not intervene but is presented as speaking with the voice of the community nonetheless. Ariana Lomax, the novel's heroine, is beautiful and discontented with the limited financial resources that her husband, Harvey Lomax, can command. Ariana's father schemes with his gambling partner, Sir Leopold D'Acosta, to win Ariana a divorce so that she can marry Sir Leopold. Sir Leopold, clearly modeled in part on Benjamin Disraeli, is a man-about-town, a romantic novelist, a member of Parliament, and an owner of an estate in Suffolk, a townhouse in London, and a polo ground. Traces of Jewish origin show in his visage, according to Campbell-Praed.[147] Ariana's father makes a point of showing Sir Leopold bruises on Ariana's arm, allegedly inflicted by Harvey, so that he will be able to testify to Harvey's cruelty. The only remaining problem then is to induce Harvey to commit adultery. Sir Leopold pays a friend from the demimonde to seduce Harvey, while Ariana's father turns amateur detective and spies on the two of them in a hotel in Folkestone, where they stopped on their way to Paris. With the necessary elements satisfied, Ariana braves the Divorce Court and receives a decree *nisi.*

After the decree, Harvey visits Ariana and attempts to persuade her to return to him, suggesting that Sir Leopold has paid her father to induce her to go through with the divorce. He asks Ariana whether she will marry Sir Leopold now, but Ariana refuses to answer. "I see," Harvey responds. "You are wise not to answer questions. It would be a pity if the Queen's Proctor were to intervene and spoil everything. Your father would be disappointed."[148] After a decent interval passes subsequent to the trial, the decree *nisi* is made final, and it is announced that Ariana will marry Sir Leopold: "There was much talk then. Mothers with marriageable daughters were loud in their wailings that the great part of society should become the prize of a woman who had divorced her husband and was a mere nobody. It was whispered that she and Sir Leopold had been in love with each other all along—that the Queen's Proctor should have intervened—that Harvey Lomax had been paid."[149] Ariana goes ahead with her marriage, and Harvey commits suicide on the morning of the nuptials. Shortly after their marriage, Sir Leopold loses interest in Ariana and begins an affair with Babette, the woman he hired to seduce Harvey. Also, Ariana's father confesses that it had all been arranged to pay his gambling debts.[150] The Queen's Proctor remains passive on the sidelines, and community sentiment is disappointed as a result.

By the early twentieth century, however, critics of the King's Proctor were far more likely to deplore his willingness to intervene. The 1909 Royal Commission also entertained several critics of the King's Proctor. Freke Palmer, a solicitor, boldly called for the abolition of the office: "[The King's Proctor] accomplishes no good object. His only work is to endeavour to find out that the successful party to a suit has been guilty of a matrimonial offence, in order to permanently prevent the separation of two people, who, by the very nature of what has been proved, can never live together again, and who, by his intervention, are driven to lead irregular lives."[151] Palmer was joined by George Henry Lewis, a solicitor who proposed effectively eliminating the King's Proctor's role by doing away with the six-month waiting period.[152] William Fairfax, head of the Divorce Law Reform Union, proposed substituting perjury prosecutions for the Queen's Proctor, saying that "two or three stiff sentences for perjury would do all the good the King's Proctor could do in twenty years."[153] These critics were joined by the former Queen's Proctor himself. In his memoirs, the Earl of Desart confessed "grave disquiet" that his interventions as Queen's Proctor did more harm than good by preventing incompatible couples from divorcing.[154]

These doubts about both the effectiveness of the Queen's Proctor's interventions and the wisdom of preventing divorce for those couples apparently least capable of reconciliation continued to grow, contributing to the momentum behind changing the substantive law of divorce. In the mid-1930s, collusive hotel divorces were held up to ridicule in Evelyn Waugh's *A Handful of Dust* and A. P. Herbert's *Holy Deadlock*.[155] In successive legislation in 1923 and 1937, Parliament changed many of the aspects of divorce law that made the Queen's Proctor's intervention necessary.[156] The changes ended the double standard that made divorce more difficult for wives to attain, leaving the prospect of collusion the only option open to unhappy couples. Decades of criticism of the Queen's Proctor's denial of divorce to couples who had, for all practical purposes, ended their unions finally left their mark in the form of changed substantive law of divorce. As Gail Savage notes, "during the interwar period the King's proctor became a contemptible and pathetic figure, a lightning rod for pointed satire directed at the divorce law."[157] By singling out irreconcilable spouses who had formed new unions as a—if not the—primary focus of the Queen's Proctor's interventions, Augustus Stephenson's attempt to make his office's activities more rapid and economical ultimately came to haunt his successors. Grafting an inquisitorial component onto the law of divorce, one of the most adventurous of Victorian experiments with developing engines for the production of truth had ended in public mockery.

You Can't Have Too Many Facts, Or Can You?

The shift from competing narratives of collusion to factual evidence of adultery was both predicted and satirized by Anthony Trollope in his 1868 novel *He Knew He Was Right*. Trollope, who had little sympathy with reforms in women's legal status, condemned the use of detectives to "prove" adultery.[158] *He Knew He Was Right* opens with the idyllic marriage of Emily and Louis Trevelyan, a young couple inexorably driven apart by Trevelyan's suspicions. He attempts to forbid his young wife from seeing Colonel Osborne, a friend of her father's. Insulted by the implication, Emily in turn refuses to comply, demanding instead an apology from her husband. Neither is willing to relent, and the two agree to live separately.

Trevelyan then resorts to a private detective, an ex-policeman named Bozzle, hiring him to keep watch on Emily, who has been sent to the countryside to live quietly with the mother of one of Trevelyan's friends. Bozzle was "convinced that the lady whom he was employed to watch was—no better than she ought to be. That is the usual Bozzlian language for broken vows, secrecy, intrigue, dirt and adultery."[159] Bozzle explains his method to a disgusted Trevelyan: "Any gentleman acting in our way can't be too particular,—can't have too many facts. The smallest little,—tiddly things . . . do so often turn up trumps when you get your evidence into court."[160] Boz-

zle then presents his employer with the fruits of his labors, informing him
that Colonel Osborne "was let in at the front door by Sarah French, the
housemaid, at 10:37 a.m., and was let out again by the same young woman
at 11:41 a.m."[161] While the reader is aware that nothing more scandalous
than stilted conversation occurred between Emily and the Colonel over
those sixty-four minutes, it is enough to inflame Trevelyan's suspicions.
Bozzle, meanwhile, is eager to oblige in the search for evidence: "'If there's
billy-dous going between 'em we shall nobble 'em,' said Bozzle. Trevelyan
tore his hair in despair, but believed that there would be billy-dous."[162]

Trevelyan succumbs over time to Bozzle's partial view, becoming
convinced that "no one but Bozzle would tell him facts," and he "wanted
facts, not advice. . . . Bozzle, either by fair means or foul, did get at the
truth."[163] Trevelyan's insistence on facts, rather than the advice of friends
urging reconciliation, is a signpost marking his descent into monomania.
He hires Bozzle to kidnap his own son, whom he then spirits off to a deso-
late hill-top villa in Tuscany. In Italy, Trevelyan's insanity runs its course,
stripping him of his reason, his Englishness (when Emily finds him, he has
taken up wearing Italian peasant clothes), and his masculinity. Consumed
by his madness, he at last consents to return to England as an emaciated
invalid under Emily's care. It is not a reconciliation, but merely an acknowledgment that all that is left for Trevelyan is to await his own death, which
shortly overtakes him.

As a caricature of a jealous spouse, Trollope's portrait falls flat; but as
a caricature of the Queen's Proctor, Trevelyan is uncomfortably accurate.
Trevelyan's unrelenting and disabling search for certain evidence of guilt
leaves him incapable of understanding or communication. The Queen's
Proctor, as the office developed under Stephenson, was motivated not by
madness or jealousy, but economics and efficiency. It nonetheless shared
both Trevelyan's crippling fear of delving into the complexities of competing narratives and his misguided faith in inquisitorial "facts" unmediated
by explanation.

Legal scholars have also occasionally succumbed to the romance of
facts. Scholars in this tradition have looked to continental criminal procedure, in which officers of the courts actively investigate cases, as an

alternative to the common law's reliance on party-controlled narratives.[164] The legal realist Jerome Frank, for example, eloquently expressed this anxiety about the consequences of adversarial fact-finding in his book *Courts on Trial*. Frank's fact-skepticism—the idea that judicial outcomes depend on the specific facts of the case—led him to focus on the improvement of judicial fact-finding.[165] He argued that "the just settlement of disputes demands a legal system in which courts can and do strive tirelessly to get as close as is humanly possible to the actual facts."[166] The existing adversarial system, however, did not even approach this imperfect standard. Frank famously contrasted the "fight" theory of adversarial justice with "truth" theory, and found the former lacking: "Our present trial method is . . . the equivalent of throwing pepper in the eyes of a surgeon when he is performing an operation."[167] In *Courts on Trial*, Frank suggested a number of measures to bring truth and justice closer together. Among them, he advocated adoption of Queen's Proctor–like investigators in civil cases: "Some few moves have been made in the right direction. In an English Divorce Court, an official, the King's Proctor, brings forth evidence, bearing on possible collusion, not offered by either contestant."[168] Writing in 1949, Frank was apparently unaware of (or uninterested in) moves to abolish the King's Proctor in its country of origin.

This chapter has taken Frank's suggestion seriously and used an in-depth study of this little-known experiment in English legal history to investigate the practical consequences of judicial attempts to introduce novel methods of producing truth in a context in which the usual reliance on cross-examination of party-controlled narratives seemed insufficient. Nonetheless, in the shift from untangling collusion to simply demonstrating adultery, the Queen's Proctor preserved elements of narrative interpretation. The Queen's Proctor earnestly sought out facts capable of producing "irresistible inferences" of adultery in the minds of decision makers.[169] In doing so, the Queen's Proctor endeavored to have details evoke complete narratives, confirming Robert Ferguson's observation that "trials always function through a framework of storytelling."[170] Storytelling has its dangers, however. The ways in which the Queen's Proctor appealed to habits of interpretation during the Victorian era had real human consequences.

The Queen's Proctor's decisions left intact marriages in which the parties were clearly incapable of reconciliation. In particular, as we saw in the case of the Castles at the beginning of this chapter, the hunt for adultery by the petitioner meant that where estranged couples had found new partners, the Queen's Proctor condemned all to a state of legal limbo.

The Queen's Proctor also represents the ill-perceived dangers of trying to adapt a common-law system to an inquisitorial model. While commentators from Jerome Frank on have pointed to the fact that the common-law trial develops "true" results only as a by-product of an adversarial or game-playing process,[171] few have explored what the costs would be to adopt "truth" as a direct, rather than an indirect, goal. The history of the Queen's Proctor, however, indicates that truth as a goal is likely to become simplified into a test that is easily susceptible to what is commonly agreed upon to be proof, effacing the responsibility of judges while proclaiming its mechanistic simplicity. Grafting an investigative component onto an adversarial system is likely to result in something neither fish nor fowl; neither fully investigatory, nor adequately responsive to the parties' interests. Victorian judges were unwilling to deal with the full range of possibilities presented by the Queen's Proctor's investigative capacities and instead sought to amalgamate the new element into the familiar formula of the bright-line rule. The Queen's Proctor's search for convincing evidence that would meet that bright-line test and coerce parties into withdrawing their petitions came, over time, to resemble Louis Trevelyan's monomania. Advice, discretion, and moral complexity were all neglected in the desperate search for conclusive facts.

Both the Queen's Proctor's efforts to represent the public's interest in marriages and the Indian experiment with motivating community sentiment against lying and convicted liars were unsuccessful. Neither proved to be the engine of truth for which its proponents hoped. In both cases, changing aspects of the common-law trial—through use of either shame sanctions or a third-party investigator—proved unable to manage a courtroom context thought to be dominated by willful perjury. Without a consensus on either the imposition of British rule in India or the substantive law of divorce, innovations at the level of institutions and procedure addressed

symptoms but ignored the underlying problem, which derived from social
and cultural contradictions that made jurists' visions of objective coherence impossible to realize in practice. Preconceptions about the difference
between British and "native," man and woman, upper class and lower class
inevitably made their presence felt, shaping both substantive law and trial
practice in subtle and not-so-subtle ways. In chapter 5, we look at a final instance of this revealing interaction between law reformers' aspirations and
the reality of social power: the debates that eventually led to the passage of
the 1898 Criminal Evidence Act. These debates, as we will see, were influenced in surprising ways by the pursuit of adultery cases in Divorce Court
and by the Queen's Proctor.

CHAPTER FIVE

Adultery, Sex Offenses, and the Criminal Evidence Act of 1898

ONE OF THE MORE CURIOUS ASPECTS of nineteenth-century British legal history is the long delay between the reforms permitting testimony from civil parties and those permitting it from criminal defendants. For much of the nineteenth century, Britain maintained a divided system, allowing the former testimony but not the latter. This time lag becomes less perplexing if considered in relation to the ongoing process of experimentation with the production of truth in the courtroom described in the previous chapters. The efforts to control perjury can be seen, in part at least, as largely fruitless attempts to resolve the problem of deceitful testimony in ways that could be used in the criminal courts. Despite this notable willingness to innovate, however, the gap remained until the passage of the Criminal Evidence Act of 1898, which allowed criminal defendants to testify. Given the mixed record of previous efforts to prevent witness deceit, jurists were understandably reluctant to allow testimony from those accused of criminal offenses—a group by definition strongly motivated to lie. The question, then, is what caused those jurists to change their minds. While the history of the 1898 act is complex, I argue that it can be seen in part as another in a long line of interactions between legal reason and social concerns: in this case, a revealing transformation in the nature of law reformers' arguments for systemic coherence on the one hand, and a desire to protect the reputations of respectable defendants by giving them a chance to rebut scandalous accusations on the other.

The poster child for the silenced respectable defendant was Rev. Henry Hatch, an Anglican cleric, who also figured in chapter 1 in the account of the evolution of perjury prosecutions. Hatch's career was ruined and his life disrupted by an accusation that he had sexually abused a schoolgirl in his care, Mary Eugenia Plummer, generally called Eugenia. She and her younger sister were boarding with Hatch, who was a schoolmaster. Eugenia alleged that Hatch had kissed her repeatedly, allowed her to share his bed, and molested her younger sister. Her accusation also blackened the reputation of Hatch's wife, who could hardly have failed to notice the alleged abuse, since she was in an adjoining room at the time. After a criminal trial in which neither he nor his wife could testify, Hatch was convicted of indecent conduct. He then went on to make legal history in 1860 by prosecuting Eugenia for perjury and winning a conviction. At her trial, both the Reverend Hatch and his wife Essie testified against Eugenia. The spectacle of two contradictory convictions fueled widespread interest in the case.[1]

Hatch's case was quickly seized upon as an example of the problems with a system of evidence that did not allow criminal defendants to testify. Shortly after the verdict against Eugenia Plummer, J. Pitt Taylor, the evidence scholar and treatise author, wrote to the *Times,* calling it "one of the most extraordinary cases heard in an English court of justice" and holding it up as an example of the flawed logic of the law of evidence.[2] Pitt Taylor envisioned what he described as the natural mode of procedure dictated by common sense and contrasted it with the current system: "Let the jury hear what the husband and wife have to say. . . . Examine them separately, cross-examine them astutely, and compare their statements with each other, and with the child's." But of course this could not occur. "O dear no," Pitt Taylor continued, "that will never do! They may state what is not true—they may mislead the weak jury. They must not be examined at all. The two best witnesses, next to the prosecutrix herself, are inadmissible to testify."[3] For Pitt Taylor, allowing testimony by the defendant (and his or her spouse) was the surest path toward veracity and protection of the innocent. He was not alone in that belief. For decades following the verdict, the Hatch case was a touchstone for reformers and a leading argument in the debates on both the Criminal Law Amendment Act and the Criminal Evidence Act. In 1876, it was referred to in the House of Commons as the "leading case" on the inequity of the exclusionary system of evidence.[4] In 1891, the Lord Chancellor, later Lord Halsbury, who would also shepherd the 1898 Criminal Evidence Act through Parliament, reflected on his experience as a young barrister working on the Hatch case during his introduction of an earlier version. The Lord Chancellor called Hatch's case "an illustration of the importance of such an alteration in the law as their lordships were dealing with to-night. If the clergyman had been able to give evidence at his own trial there would have been no necessity for the second performance."[5]

Hatch's case is important for us here because it had a special resonance that helps explain the eventual passage of the Criminal Evidence Act: it stood out not just for the contradictory verdicts, but also as an example of the danger the courts posed for respectable defendants accused of actions particularly repugnant to Victorian society. Hatch, while not a wealthy man, was certainly respectable. He had attended Eton College and Cambridge, had a position as chaplain at Wandsworth prison, was a teacher, and ran a household that included a governess and two other servants. His wife, Essie, also appears to have impressed journalists with her respectable behavior under trying circumstances. According to the *Times,* Mrs. Hatch "gave her evidence with very great calmness and self-possession."[6] Hatch's case may have been extraordinary, but it was also a warning call to other respectable men. The mid-Victorian era saw an increase in the possibility—both real and perceived—that a man like Hatch might face the prospect of sitting in court, forbidden to speak, as he listened to accusations that he had engaged in scandalous conduct. This chapter explores that prospect in two scenarios—adultery accusations and sexual misconduct under the Criminal Law Amendment Act—and traces how the emotion associated with enabling respectable defendants to reply, coupled with a growing trust in the power of cross-examination to ensure witness veracity, worked to undermine solicitude for the nonrespectable defendant and paved the way for the admission of testimony on oath.

A Question of Timing

As we have already seen, it took fifty years for the reform that abolished testimonial incompetence for parties in civil cases to be extended to criminal defendants. Before the mid-nineteenth century, both were barred from testifying on oath out of a concern for the credibility of those with a stake in the outcome of the case and a desire to avoid perjury. Testimonial incompetence for parties in civil cases began to unravel with the County Courts Act of 1846, which allowed testimony by parties in the new County Courts; this was followed shortly thereafter by the Evidence Amendment Act of 1851, which extended the privilege to parties in the superior courts.[7] In the United States, testimony by criminal defendants began as early as 1864, in Maine; in Britain, by contrast, criminal defendants were not allowed to testify on oath until 1898, when Parliament passed the Criminal Evidence Act. For those who look to Bentham's influence as a starting point for reform, the wait is even longer: from the 1820s, when Bentham's works were first published in English, to 1898.

This delay was not for lack of bills in Parliament. The first proposal to allow testimony by criminal defendants came as early as 1858 and was followed by many others over the next forty years. Bills to allow such testimony were almost an annual feature of the parliamentary agenda. Legal historians such as Christopher Allen, David Bentley, and Keith Smith have detailed the reform efforts and different phases of parliamentary proposals over the course of the forty years between 1858 and 1898.[8] Allen breaks this span into three periods. The first, from 1858 through 1878, saw bills introduced by private members of Parliament to remove the accused's incompetence. In Allen's second period, from 1879 through 1883, the government initiated bills that would encompass the reform in a broader codification of the criminal law. Finally, from 1884 until 1898, the government backed bills addressing testimonial incompetency as a separate measure. Despite fifteen years of government support, the measure faced delay because of Irish opposition in Parliament; after being revised to exclude Ireland, a bill finally passed.[9]

Details of the bills changed from year to year. Some made the accused both competent and compellable; others made the accused only competent. Some envisioned shielding the defendant from cross-examination; others made no distinction between the defendant and any other witness in that regard. Members debated whether cross-examination to credit should be allowed and whether character and previous convictions should be admissible into evidence. It is beyond the scope of this book to trace the outlines of each proposal. What is striking, however, is the continuity of arguments marshaled in support of the reform over its long history. From the 1850s on, reformers relied on the ideas that allowing the testimony of criminal defendants would serve the discovery of truth, that it would help safeguard the innocent, and that it would remove problematic anomalies in the law of evidence.[10]

While many of the basic arguments for the change were in place by the 1850s, Allen also identifies several broad developments that, over the course of the second half of the century, made revision of the law seem more acceptable. First, by century's end, the danger of perjury had come to appear less pressing.[11] In chapter 1, we explored how the experiment with criminal prosecution for false testimony in civil cases helped to take the sting out of the threat of perjury—and, indeed, made objections raised by opponents of the act seem less compelling than they had been before. By 1898, the problem of perjury by defendants, as we will see below, scarcely merited a second thought at the Home Office. Another change Allen has identified is the growing emphasis placed on individual responsibility in the mid-nineteenth century. Allowing testimony by the accused dovetailed with the Victorian doctrine of personal character and responsibility by insisting on accountability and by treating the accused as a fully rational agent.[12]

A third shift Allen mentions is the normalization of change—the idea that the change was no change at all. Allen calls this "the image of continuity."[13] After years of concern about the disruptive effect that allowing defendant testimony would have on trial practice, reformers gradually came to argue that extending competency would involve "no essential change in the balance of power that had already been struck between judge, counsel, and accused in a criminal trial."[14] This view was reflected in the increasingly frequent use of arguments from anomaly by those who wanted to see change in the law of evidence. This strategy was a well-established one in the rhetoric of nineteenth-century English law reform. It implied that a proposed change was not revolutionary but was instead merely a correction of lapses or a logical extension of the existing architecture of the system.

In the case of the Criminal Evidence Act, a series of incremental reforms eventually exerted a cumulative effect, making the definitive

elimination of the exclusionary system of evidence seem less like the abandonment of a time-honored precedent than a mere extension of preexisting structures to correct nagging irregularities. Each individual "anomaly"
corrected seemed like the comparatively isolated rectification of a particular problem at the time it was enacted, but the ultimate effect was to create
a situation that supported fundamental change in the law of evidence. In
the period leading up to 1898, the two most significant of these specific
reforms addressed testimony regarding adultery in the Divorce Court and
allowed for testimony by those accused of certain types of sexual abuse.
As we have seen, parties in the Divorce Court were not allowed to testify
in cases arising from adultery until 1869. The debate that led to the lifting
of that ban showed the power of the argument from anomaly to motivate
reforms that jurists had previously rejected out of a desire to avoid deceit
by parties. In 1885, the Criminal Law Amendment Act (CLAA), which
gave defendants the option of testifying when accused of a variety of sexual offenses, created a new set of anomalies that bore some revealing similarities to those addressed by the divorce reform of 1869. The CLAA was
passed as part of a larger program of new sex crime laws and was intended
to provide a safeguard against false accusation and blackmail. Once certain criminal offenses were covered by the CLAA, however, the position
of those defendants charged under older laws, who were still prohibited
from testifying, became anomalous. The need to eliminate this disparity
was one of the strongest arguments for passage of the 1898 Criminal Evidence Act.

Divorce trials and accusations of sexual offenses of the kind eventually covered by the CLAA, as we saw in the Hatch case, represented a respectable gentleman's worst nightmares. Even after the creation of the new
Divorce Court in 1857, adultery remained the basis for all divorce suits.
While the basis for divorce suits stayed the same, the gendered balance of
power did not: for the first time, more than a handful of husbands found
themselves on the receiving end of divorce petitions. Perhaps even more
disturbingly for Victorians, the evidence given in court (and also in the
resulting proceedings of the Queen's Proctor) was excruciatingly public,
recounted at great length in an ever-enthusiastic daily press. The CLAA,

for its part, covered same-sex sexual conduct and sexual abuse of children, which were associated with false accusations, blackmail, and reputation-ruining publicity if the case proceeded to court. In both of these situations, Parliament decided that the danger to respectable defendants outweighed the threat that innocent people unable to present their side of the story with eloquence or sincerity might be falsely convicted.

The roots of the Criminal Evidence Act, therefore, lay in the fear of scandal, and in particular, scandal made public in the context of a court-room. While scandal itself exists throughout history, Victorians seem to have felt its threat with particular vehemence and perhaps as a result evinced a revealing fascination with its social effects. Certainly, a preoc-cupation with the consequences of social stigma pervaded Victorian fic-tion, which, as John Kucich writes, was "structured obsessively around the very real power of lies" and the potentially damaging revelation of secrets.[15] From 1860 on, blackmail plots proliferated in popular sensation novels and works by George Eliot, William Thackeray, Charles Dickens, and Trol-lope. Alexander Welsh, in his now-classic study of George Eliot, suggests that the use of blackmail plots was not merely an attempt by elite authors to pursue popularity but also a reflection of widespread fears in mid-Victorian life.[16] The flipside of secrecy was publicity, both in the press and in the courtroom. High-profile cases were a staple of Victorian life; as Susie Steinbach points out, "Victorian culture was awash with law." These cases, as Steinbach rightly indicates, provided an opportunity for Victorians to discuss the boundaries of political and economic power, marital conduct and marital breakdown, and male homosexuality.[17] Scandal and ensuing court cases posed a keen danger to the powerful, respectable, and prosper-ous. In order to meet this threat, Parliament gave respectable defendants like Hatch and accused adulterers the opportunity to refute the scandalous accusations leveled against them.

Adultery and the Divorce Court

Even in 1851, when the parties in civil cases were made competent witnesses, and again in 1853, when the privilege was extended to spouses, two categories of cases were exempted: breach-of-promise suits and suits arising out of adultery.[18] In both situations, the temptation to lie to protect one's sexual honor was thought to be so strong that even those who shared the emerging consensus in favor of allowing party testimony took it for granted that the exceptions should be maintained. When a new Divorce Court was created in 1857, therefore, the exclusion of testimony regarding adultery remained in place.[19] Despite this element of continuity, as we will see, the introduction of the new Divorce Court had unexpected consequences for party testimony. The motives for creating the court were in many ways not particularly revolutionary; the new institution was primarily intended to address dissatisfaction with the complexity and expense of the previous procedure for obtaining a divorce, which created a situation in which very few could afford to sever their matrimonial bonds.[20] While reformers stopped short of a commitment to gender equality before the law, inequities in outcome based on the status and wealth of petitioners increasingly rankled in the mid-nineteenth century.[21] Justice William Maule's famous complaint about the expense of divorce procedure driving a hapless individual into bigamy may not have been representative, but it was widely believed to capture the heart of the problem.[22] The Divorce Court was thus at most a compromise measure, allowing a simpler procedure while maintaining most of the substance of the preexisting law.[23]

Adultery remained at the center of divorce proceedings because of the unchanged substance of the divorce law. Although a wife's adultery could serve a husband as sufficient grounds for divorce, Parliament stopped short of allowing wives to divorce their husbands for adultery alone. However, it remained a necessary part of a wife's divorce petition: to obtain a divorce, she had to prove that her husband had committed adultery and an additional "aggravating" offense—such as incest, bigamy, rape, sodomy, bestiality, cruelty, or desertion.[24] This preserved the preexisting double standard with regard to grounds for divorce; it also ensured that both husbands and wives would be alleging adultery in their cases. Adultery, as we saw in the previous chapter, would remain a centerpiece of all divorce proceedings, even though the "adultery exception" blocked parties from testifying in all suits arising out of it.

Members of Parliament might have thought that the creation of the Divorce Court was a relatively modest change, but it led to what struck many as an alarming increase in the number of cases. These cases, in turn, brought with them a pair of unanticipated and, to Victorians, disturbing results: a boom in press coverage and an important change in the balance of power between husband and wife. While the mid-Victorian rate of divorce was low by modern standards, it was dramatically high in comparison with the handful of cases that made it through the gauntlet of the pre-1858 procedure. In the first five years of the court's existence, it granted an average of 204 divorces per year; in its second five years, that average increased to 233 divorces.[25] The effect of this steady stream of cases was amplified by the publicity they received.

It had been hoped that publicity would deter couples, especially respectable ones, from obtaining divorces.[26] However, reformers had not anticipated that the Divorce Court would give rise to a new form of entertainment and become an enduring presence in the print media. Proceedings in the Divorce Court were public, unlike their parliamentary predecessors, and the doings of the new court rapidly became a popular spectacle. People flocked to the court to watch trials, and newspapers mined the cases for lurid details for their extensive stories. Parliament tried to legislate against newspapers' use of evidence in the Divorce Court, but all such attempts failed.[27] Major papers, like the *Times,* routinely covered Divorce Court proceedings, and new ones, such as the *Divorce Court Reporter,* emerged to recount the evidence presented in still greater detail. If the exhaustive coverage in the periodical press was not sufficient, a determined reader could also purchase pamphlet accounts of particularly famous trials.[28] The perception that Britain was awash in the newspaper stories generated by the Divorce Court reached into all circles of polite society. In 1868, Queen Victoria wrote the Lord Chancellor asking "whether no steps can be taken to prevent the present publicity of the proceedings before the new Divorce Court. These cases . . . fill now daily a large portion of the newspapers, and are of so scandalous a character that it makes it almost impossible for a paper to be trusted in the hands of a young lady or boy."[29] The Victorian feminist and anti–Contagious Diseases Act activist Josephine Butler felt

similarly. She commented about Divorce Court proceedings that "whatso-
ever things ye have spoken in darkness shall be heard in the light; and that
which ye have spoken in the ear in closets shall be proclaimed upon the
housetops."[30]

Publicity was not the only surprise in the new Divorce Court. For the
first time, female petitioners made up nearly half the docket, an eventuality
that likely came as a surprise to those who supported the court's creation.[31]
During its first three years and four months, 200 women and 278 men received divorces. This was a striking contrast to the history of divorce from
its inception to 1857, during which only four female petitioners received
parliamentary divorces; none of those had petitioned before 1801.[32] In the
years leading up to World War I, in contrast, wives received between 38
and 46 percent of the divorces granted.[33]

With the new court, then, divorce was transformed from an embarrassment, conducted behind closed doors and almost always at the husband's behest, into a potentially very public humiliation that a wife could
visit on a respectable husband. Although the new court expanded access to
divorce beyond the narrow circle of those who could afford the expense of
the old parliamentary process, most petitioners still tended to be from the
respectable upper-middle class.[34] The adultery exception meant that, like
the Reverend Hatch, respectable men faced the prospect of having to sit
silenced in proceedings arising from adultery, a tremendous public humiliation that the press would publicize in its every shameful detail.

Issues such as publicity and the scandals surrounding the Divorce
Court quickly prompted Parliament to make efforts to reform its procedures. The 1860 Queen's Proctor legislation, discussed in chapter 4, attempted to address the problem of collusive divorces. The problem of
the silenced spouse prevented from responding to accusations of adultery
came before Parliament several years later, in 1865. At that time, Sir Fitzroy
Edward Kelly, Queen's Counsel and former Solicitor General and Attorney
General, cited the anomalies caused by the adultery exception as reason to
eliminate it; by doing so, he and his allies began a debate that nearly led to
the abolition of all testimonial exclusions and laid the foundation for future
extensions of the right to testify.

In his attack on the adultery exception, Kelly relied heavily on the viewpoint of James P. Wilde, a Divorce Court judge. Kelly read to the House of Commons a letter he had received from Wilde regarding the effect of the adultery exception on the Divorce Court. In it, Wilde wrote that the exception "works a great anomaly and a greater still injustice."[35] Wilde focused in particular on the way the exception deprived the accused of the power to respond, which in his estimation was "a great injustice, for as the law now stands, the sayings, writings and acts of the accused are all given in evidence against him, and he is obliged to stand by and hear them without the power of one word to explain them away."[36] He called this a "grievous hardship to the individual and a great impediment to the discovery of truth."[37] To correct the wrong, Wilde supported an end to the adultery exception, with respondents made competent, but not compellable, to give evidence. Other members of Parliament agreed with Wilde in identifying the Divorce Court adultery exception as an anomaly. The Solicitor General stated that the government would not oppose the introduction of Kelly's bill, calling the "proceedings in the Divorce Court . . . an anomaly which it might be desirable to correct."[38] Mr. M'Mahon took up the argument in his support for a further proposal to allow all defendants to testify, framing it as a protection for the wrongfully accused: "At present it frequently happened that a man was convicted because he was not allowed to give evidence on his behalf, or have the evidence of his wife taken."[39] Another member decried the "gross scandal to public morals to which divorce cases gave rise" but concluded that their scandalousness was "an evil inherent in their very nature" and that the measure would not worsen the situation.[40] Kelly's more limited measure was combined with another private bill, introduced by Vincent Scully, which sought to make the accused a competent witness in all criminal cases. Although the Solicitor General had been willing to consider ending the exception for adultery cases, the government was not yet ready to allow all defendants to testify. The Attorney General promised further consideration of the question, but Parliament never returned to Kelly's and Scully's bills.[41]

Discontent with the adultery exception persisted, however. Four years later, Parliament returned to the topic with a bill introduced by

Mr. George Denman, son of Lord Thomas Denman and, like his father, an enthusiastic proponent of modernizing the law of evidence. As proposed, Denman's bill would have done away with the exceptions for testimony regarding adultery and breach-of-promise cases, as well as allowing testimony by those who would not take an oath. This became the Evidence Further Amendment Act (1869).[42] According to its provisions, testimony by parties was permitted in breach-of-promise suits, but a plaintiff had to show some corroborating evidence in order to recover damages.[43] In cases based on adultery, parties could give evidence, although they could not be asked whether they had committed adultery unless they had already given evidence to prove they had not done so.[44] Denman framed this as a logical extension of the principle of allowing testimony by parties in civil proceedings: both allowed testimony by parties with an interest in the outcome, "either morally or pecuniarily."[45]

Just as later reformers of the exclusion in criminal law would do, Denman and his supporters based their arguments against the adultery exception on its anomalous results, calling it, in Denman's words, a "monstrous anomaly amounting almost to iniquity."[46] Under the exception, the admissibility of evidence depended on whether the case arose out of adultery. In a case for restitution of conjugal rights, a wife could testify regarding her husband's adultery, but in a suit for divorce, the same testimony would not be admissible.[47] In his speech before the House of Commons, Denman listed a series of recent cases in which the decision on testimony rested on the accident of which spouse had initiated the suit. Others agreed with him, calling the anomalies "remarkable" and "plainly fortuitous" because the exception predated the establishment of the Divorce Court.[48] Divorce Court judge Wilde, now in the House of Lords as Lord Penzance, continued to reflect on the potential harm to someone accused of adultery but unable to rebut the evidence: "Was there really any reason why a petitioner or a respondent should not be allowed to get into the witness-box, and by his or her explanation get rid of the suspicion which circumstances had raised against them? For want of this power, great injustice was often done."[49] This time, the government agreed with the Attorney General, noting that "on all grounds the case appeared to be made out for admitting the evidence of parties to a suit for adultery."[50]

In his endorsement of the reform, the Attorney General went so far as to invite his colleagues to "consider whether they would like to be placed in the position" of a man accused of adultery who "knew himself to be innocent" but "was not allowed to be examined."[51] The Attorney General was not alone in imagining the principal beneficiary of the reform as a respectable gentleman, not unlike himself. Historian Allen Horstman called the 1869 law a "legislative effort to support Respectability . . . enacted so that Respectables could deny false allegations of adultery."[52] Denman himself made it clear that the parties he envisioned benefiting from his bill were from the middle and upper classes, not typical lower-class defendants, as in criminal cases. Responding to members of Parliament who objected to allowing respondents to testify in Divorce Court because the proceedings there were of a quasi-criminal nature, Denman said that the analogy did not hold. He might see an argument against allowing criminal defendants (unlike parties in divorce cases) to testify because "the prisoners were usually of a class so uneducated and so ignorant that, on examination and cross-examination, they would be almost sure to commit themselves, and to injure their own case, whether they were innocent or guilty."[53] Testimony, in his estimation, was a double-edged sword, best wielded by the educated and the intelligent.

The Criminal Law Amendment Act (1885)

The 1869 act corrected one set of anomalies, but the prohibition on testimony by criminal defendants remained in place. Ironically, what was needed to unseat the last prohibition was a new set of anomalies—a new disjuncture between the practice allowed to respectable defendants in some cases, but not in others. The CLAA would provide these anomalies, laying the foundation for the eventual decision to allow criminal defendants to testify on oath.[54] The act raised the age of consent for children to sixteen, specified penalties for sexual offenses against women and

minors, strengthened measures against prostitution, and restated criminal
sanctions against sexual conduct between men, as well as abuse of boys.[55]
It became infamous for the so-called Labouchere Amendment outlawing
acts of "gross indecency" between men, both in public and in private.[56]
Although the Labouchere Amendment and the importance of the 1885 act
in the history of criminalizing same-sex conduct has been called into question, the CLAA represented an unheralded revolution in legal procedure.[57]
Most critically for our story, the CLAA also contained a provision making
the accused, and his or her spouse, competent witnesses in the trial of any
offenses covered by the act.[58] While other anomalies had been created by
regulations passed between 1867 and 1885 allowing certain types of defendants to testify, it was those created by the CLAA that were to garner the
most attention, and also the most prosecutions.[59] If charged under the act,
the accused could speak on oath in response to charges involving prostitution, brothel-keeping, sexual abuse of children, and sexual conduct between men.

Like the 1869 act, the CLAA took shape against a backdrop of highly
public scandals. Allowing the respondent to speak in divorce cases did little to stanch the flow of Victorian scandals and their extensive coverage in
the press. As Michael Foldy notes in his history of the Oscar Wilde trials,
by the mid-1880s, newspapers were already well-practiced in purveying
the "sex scandal" story.[60] Even before the act passed, defendants charged
with the offenses it eventually covered had to fear extortion or damaging
revelation of scandal through the press from a variety of actors, including
private individuals, police officers, and even children. The scandals of the
first half of the 1880s, such as those provoked by W. T. Stead's articles in
the *Pall Mall Gazette*, "showed that the press, and even the government
itself, was ultimately not above using the techniques of the blackmailer to
disrupt public life and slander opponents."[61]

Revelation and scandal, particularly for sexual offenses, were therefore very real dangers for respectable defendants—ones that could come
from many different quarters. One of the most notable private extortionists
of the period was George Osborn, convicted and sentenced to a life term
of penal servitude for his crimes in 1886. Police described him as both a

"notorious sodomite" and an "associate of blackmailers."[62] The problem of extortion was not limited to private individuals, however; police could perpetrate it as well. Indeed, one change driving the mid-Victorian fear of blackmail was the increased (but still reluctant) involvement of the police in prosecuting sodomy and later gross indecency cases. Before the 1840s, official involvement in sodomy prosecution was uncommon, and most prosecutions, as H. G. Cocks has shown, appear to have been brought by private individuals.[63] As the police force developed during the period after 1850, its involvement in these cases grew, as did worries about police perjury.[64] Such perjury was considered to be cause for concern in a wide variety of offenses, even down to public drunkenness. As Stefan Petrow points out, in 1873, arrest of two "respectable" individuals, a barrister and an army officer, for public drunkenness touched off a controversy about the veracity of testimony by police officers. It was feared that police officers would "back each other up with the most sweeping corroboration" if a defendant resisted the charges and insisted on his or her innocence.[65] Testimony by police officers was also regarded with suspicion by members of Parliament. One member worried during the course of the debate on the CLAA that "if they put the right of search in the hands of the police . . . they might be putting an instrument in the hands of men who worked hard for extremely small salaries, and who were consequently, open to bribes."[66]

Fear of blackmail and perjury was not limited to extortionate adult witnesses, but also extended to child witnesses in sexual assault cases. Louise Jackson has demonstrated how, in the period before the CLAA, child accusers in sexual abuse cases were frequently the target of suspicion. Most of the cases involved girls, but both boys and girls were viewed as potential liars. With girls, the object of the defense's cross-examination was either to show sexual precocity or to suggest that a girl's accusation had been learned by rote and was merely recited in court. Girls' testimony had to tread a narrow path between knowledge and knowingness. Too much knowingness could open the door to accusations of sexual precocity, making the accuser a "little seductress or a minx" rather than a victim. For boys, meanwhile, accusers were portrayed as financially scheming—delinquent, streetwise youth intent on extorting money from respectable gentlemen.[67]

Certain types of child sexual abuse, in particular under-age prostitution, burst into public prominence in the 1880s. Laws against prostitution had been relatively laxly enforced during the first half of the nineteenth century, but in the early 1880s, new anxieties changed the situation. In particular, newspapers and Parliament fueled concern that there was a systematic traffic in young girls from Britain to Europe for the purpose of prostitution.[68] In 1881 and 1882, a Select Committee in the House of Lords considered the evidence, focusing on alleged sale of girls to brothels in Belgium, and also considered the broader question of juvenile prostitution in Britain. The committee discovered a system of paid agents who received a commission for each girl introduced but found little evidence that girls without "antecedent immoral lives" were involved. Once in Belgium, girls found themselves trapped by their unfamiliarity, knowing little of the local language or institutions that might help.[69] With regard to child prostitution in England, the committee found that it was "increasing to an appalling extent . . . especially in London." The increase was attributed to what Victorians considered to be typical causes of immorality: overcrowding in dwellings, lack of parental and state supervision, and the inducement of pretty dresses and a bit of money.[70] The committee recommended a number of measures to prevent under-age prostitution and to raise the age of consent for girls from thirteen to sixteen. No legislation, however, resulted from the 1882 recommendations. Bills passed by the House of Lords in 1883 and 1884 failed to gain a hearing in the lower house.[71] Parliament's inactivity triggered a reaction from social reformers. A coalition of purity reformers sought to force the government to pass anti–child prostitution legislation, which would raise the age of consent and heighten penalties for brothel-keepers. W. T. Stead, as editor of the *Pall Mall Gazette,* garnered public attention with his series "The Maiden Tribute of Modern Babylon," which purported to demonstrate the dangers of white slavery. The series was followed by a Salvation Army petition, delivered to Parliament in a wagon, and in August 1885, a mass rally in favor of the bill attracted more than a quarter of a million people.[72]

As the bill was debated, one of the primary concerns for lawmakers was the prospect of creating a new and potent temptation for blackmail and extortion. Sir Henry Holland warned that "nothing would be easier in these cases than to get the evidence of some woman, or even of a policeman, to corroborate the charge; and the unhappy man who was charged would either have to pay blackmail . . . or he would have to appear in Court." For a man with a professional reputation to maintain, he continued, the mere fact of an accusation alone could prove devastating.[73] William Harcourt noted the "considerable danger . . . of false charges being made for the purposes of extortion."[74] Liberal member Charles Hopwood echoed Holland's concern about the danger of extortion by means of false charges. Girls "steeped in depravity" between the ages of thirteen and sixteen, he asserted, would pose a great danger to both men and boys.[75]

Even younger children might make false charges. Hopwood invoked the Hatch-Plummer case of 1860, by now a hallowed classic in the annals of perjury, as a demonstration of the danger of false accusations even under the existing law of child sexual abuse, since the Plummer girls had accused the Reverend Hatch when they were eight and eleven years old.[76] Hopwood also stressed that appearances could be deceiving: in the Hatch case "the young witnesses gave the most childlike and innocent answers, which, upon subsequent inquiry, were established, beyond doubt, to be a pack of falsehoods."[77] The youthful accusers in the Hatch case were also cited by contemporary commentators on the law, who noted that even children as young as eleven had been convicted of perjury in cases growing out of sexual abuse charges.[78]

The testimony of young witnesses accusing respectable adults gave even proponents of the new measure qualms. Members pondered whether the existing practice enabling the judge to question a child witness to determine whether the child understood the nature of an oath would provide sufficient protection against falsified statements. Edward Clarke, a Conservative member of Parliament and leading barrister who would play a key role in both the scandalous Baccarat Case and the Oscar Wilde trial in the 1890s, doubted that requiring understanding would prevent fraudulent accusations. It was easy enough to coach a child to answer several typical questions, such as, "Do you know what will be done to you if you tell a lie?" Instead, Clarke suggested that cross-examination of child witnesses by legal representatives of the defendant would provide a much-needed safe-guard.[79] Clarke proposed an amendment that would allow for "the fullest opportunity of cross-examination by the prisoner or his advisers."[80] Others disagreed, wondering who "would dare to cross-examine [a] child?"[81] The final law not only placed no limit on cross-examination, it also included a proviso, in cases regarding abuse of girls younger than thirteen, rendering a witness too young to be sworn indictable for perjury nonetheless.[82] A child who did not, in the opinion of the court, understand the nature of an oath might still provide testimony as long as the court decided that he or she was possessed of sufficient intelligence and understood the duty of speaking the truth.[83]

Ensuring examination of immature witnesses and holding the threat of perjury prosecution over their heads was one safeguard envisioned in the law, but ultimately, the primary safeguard it accorded was a provision to allow the defendant to speak on oath. This measure originated with James Picton, radical member of Parliament for Leicester, who, after several months of debate on the bill, proposed that the defendant or the wife of the person charged be considered a competent witness. In introducing his amendment, he commented that testimony on an accusation of sexual abuse was similar to cases of adultery and conspiracy—these were "especially offences on which such testimony ought to be allowed."[84] The Attorney General, while not wholeheartedly embracing Picton's proposal, agreed that "of all classes of cases that dealt with in this Bill, this was the one in which the defendant should be allowed to give evidence."[85]

Not all members of Parliament were eager to tinker with allowing defendant's testimony. Picton's proposal was greeted with an array of by now familiar arguments against allowing criminal defendants to testify on oath and be cross-examined. Should the defendant be compellable? Would there be a presumption of guilt if the defendant did not take the stand? Sir William Harcourt objected to the dilemma that would result for criminal defendants: "there was no doubt that where an accused person was competent to be a witness and was not called, it raised a presumption against him. . . . [I]f he were guilty he would not appeal and if they forced a guilty man into the witness-box, whether he liked it or not, they would be subjecting him to the temptation to commit perjury, and thus rendering him liable to additional penalty attached to that offence."[86]

As in adultery cases, the danger of encouraging perjury was balanced against, and ultimately outweighed by, the potential for exoneration. Even a critic like William Harcourt agreed that "a provision like this was of the greatest value to enable a man to prove his innocence."[87] The risk posed to respectable defendants who might otherwise be silenced was important enough that a major inroad had been made in the prohibition of defendant's testimony. It was a new anomaly, and one that caused many observers at the time to look ahead to subsequent expansions. Treatise writers Frederick Mead and A. H. Bodkin, for example, called the CLAA a "somewhat bold experiment" and looked to the results to see whether the right should be extended to all criminal defendants.[88]

The importance Victorians accorded to exoneration can be seen in one of the more famous consequences of the CLAA: Oscar Wilde's multiple trials and ultimate exile. In 1895, the Marquess of Queensberry left a note for Wilde at Wilde's club, calling him a "posing Somdomite [*sic*]." In doing so, Queensberry invaded one of the privileged spaces of Victorian masculinity—the all-male club—and made public a devastating accusation.[89] Although Wilde had been advised of the risks of proceeding with a prosecution, he nonetheless went forward with libel charges against Queensberry. Edward Carson, representing Queensberry, executed one of the century's most devastating cross-examinations against Wilde. At the end of it, Carson received a note from Justice Richard Collins, saying, "I have never heard a more powerful speech nor a more searching crossXam."[90] The collapse of Wilde's libel case against Queensberry was followed quickly by a decision to prosecute Wilde under the CLAA for acts of "gross indecency."[91] He was convicted, imprisoned, and subsequently left England for a life of self-imposed exile in France. His story is well-known, but placed in its contemporary context, Wilde's tragic error—the decision to respond to Queensberry's accusation—seems less a matter of artistic temperament and more an example of the importance of refutation. Ironically, the CLAA under which Wilde was ultimately convicted also served as the institutional expression of the right to refutation.

The Criminal Evidence Act (1898)

Those interested in the legislative results of the CLAA "experiment" did not have long to wait. Once opposition to evidence reform from Irish members of Parliament was overcome, or rather, simply avoided by means of excluding Ireland from the bill, the path was cleared for the CLAA's anomalies to be generalized and transformed into the new normal in criminal law.[92] And, once again, the anomalies of the current state of law would be personified by the Reverend Henry Hatch. Nearly forty years after his trial, Hatch was still invoked in arguments supporting testimony by defendants. In 1897, during a House of Commons debate on what would become the Criminal Evidence Act, Edward Clarke retold Hatch's story and argued that "standing alone, [the Hatch case] should be sufficient to satisfy any Member of the House as to the absolute necessity of this alteration of the law."[93] Hatch's story was clearly a familiar one. Clarke's recitation of the multiple trials of the Reverend Hatch and his declaration that despite all the proceedings "the question of his guilt or innocence was never tried in a case in which all persons could be heard" was greeted with cheers in the House. Interestingly, perhaps out of his own concern for the reputation of a fellow respectable, Clarke did not identify Hatch by name. Instead, he referred to a "clergyman" who was "convicted of a shameful offence because his mouth and that of his wife were closed," a shorthand that members readily understood. Hatch remained the symbol for respectability silenced in the face of scandal.[94]

Debate on the criminal evidence bill largely followed the outlines of debate in previous years. Earlier exceptions to the rule against testimonial incompetence, such as admission of testimony regarding adultery in the Divorce Court after 1869 and the CLAA, were cited in support of the measure. "In the Divorce Court, where the issues were often as serious, painful, and disastrous as in the criminal Courts, the parties were available as witnesses in their own defence," one member reminded the House.[95] The Attorney General began his lengthy argument for the bill with a list of anomalies, including the one created by the CLAA: "a man charged under the Criminal Law Amendment Act with a criminal assault could give evidence, while a man charged with a common assault could not give evidence."[96] Other members of Parliament followed suit. Edward Clarke pointed to the difference in treatment between defendants accused of stealing a woman's purse and those accused of committing a sexual assault on a woman.[97] After reporting on the debates, the *Times* concluded that "we have [an] exceptionally anomalous state of things" and that the "anomalies have vexed the souls of theorists."[98]

Judges and supporters argued that the CLAA's admission of testimony by defendants was now an exception to be embraced. More than a decade's experience with the CLAA had convinced most reformers, if not necessarily the most ardent letter writers in the *Times,* that extending competence to the accused would be relatively unproblematic.[99] Justice Henry Lopes, for example, recalled trying the very first case brought under the CLAA, involving the abduction of a young girl. It worked "admirably," in his recollection, and in 1897, he was happy to advocate extending the principle to other criminal cases.[100] Lord Herschell, himself a previous Lord Chancellor, said that he was pleased by the operation of the CLAA.[101] Crucially, the CLAA allowed defendants to refute charges against them. Reformers and government officials supporting the bill argued that the first instinct of innocent defendants was to speak in their own defense. A. C. Plowden assured the *Times* that "the average innocent man . . . would prefer to fall under the fire of cross-examination rather than wither in silence in the dock. The first instinct of such a man would be to speak, to repel the accusation, to face his foes and challenge them in the proof."[102] Both current and previous Lord Chancellors in 1898 framed the importance of the law in terms of allowing a defendant, generally referred to as "a man," the right to tell his own story.[103]

Telling one's own story, however, had profound class implications for the bill's opponents. In the House of Commons, Mr. E. H. Pickersgill observed that any advantage to an innocent defendant would depend on his coolness and self-possession, which "were largely associated with education and therefore the Bill would give to the educated man an advantage over the uneducated man."[104] Uneducated men, even when innocent, "had a great tendency to tell lies about comparatively immaterial facts."[105] Pickersgill later amplified his complaint, saying that the proposed measure would tend to "establish the most odious of all distinctions—a class distinction."[106] Others agreed, attempting to remind the House that it was also "legislating for the poor, the miserable, the ignorant, the confused—almost the dumb, you may say—who are driven into a Criminal Court and have, probably for the first time in their lives, to endeavour to string together a few sentences against more or less skilled opponents."[107] John Morley tried, ineffectually, to persuade his fellow members that they were not making laws for themselves—"all of us are more or less educated persons, more or less able to take care of ourselves in cross-examination, but this is a change which will not affect, speaking generally, persons in our position but humble and ignorant persons."[108]

Morley and Pickersgill, however, were very much in the minority in 1898. In general, members of Parliament were much less sympathetic to poor defendants who might seal their fates with verbal blunders. In this indifference they were typical of their era. A willingness to take measures that would restrict the liberties of those who were habitually on the wrong side of the legal process, such as drunkards or the mentally disabled, united both Conservative social reformers and the socially activist New Liberals in the 1890s. New Liberalism saw an increased role for the state in furthering moral reform and policing the unruly "residuum" of the population.[109] Parliament's collective shrug when confronted with the fate of poor defendants coincided with a broader insistence on responsibility at the expense of liberty.

Few denied that the law had a potentially greater effect on poor defendants. It was not just liberal members of Parliament who believed that poor defendants could make costly errors, and even commit perjury, in the process of defending themselves. The Home Office noted, in an 1897 memo, that "even innocent [defendants] at present are prone to believe in the virtues of an alibi when the true defence is (e.g.) that the identification is not satisfactory."[110] The poverty of many criminal defendants made the Home Office uneasy, as shown in another 1897 memo, about the wisdom of equating civil and criminal proceedings. Civil proceedings were likely to take place between people sufficiently well-to-do to engage counsel, whereas most criminal defendants were unlikely to have the benefit of counsel, except perhaps at the trial itself. If criminal proceedings were evaluated as credibility contests between two sides, rather than as tests of the prosecution's case, "the defendant, unless he happened to be a well-to-do man, would be likely to suffer great injustice."[111] Despite these qualms about the potential effect on poor defendants, the Home Office supported the measure.

Indifference to poor defendants was motivated in part by anxiety regarding the fate of well-educated defendants. The other side of the class division was put forward in Parliament with striking frankness by Sir R. Reid. "Let us see what is sought to be prevented," he began.

> I will take the case of myself or any other gentleman. We are all liable to have false accusations brought against us. Suppose we happen to walk along the street, or into a railway carriage, or some other place in which there are only two or three others, apparently of a respectable character, who have formed a conspiracy to accuse us of an offence. It is possible that gentlemen who are wealthy are more exposed to that danger and more liable to be the object of such a conspiracy than others. I want to put it to any gentleman to just think what his position and feelings would be when he was approaching his trial when he knew he would not be allowed to go into the witness box and give a solemn denial to the charge on oath; and not only so, but to give himself an opportunity of having his testimony corroborated by cross-examination.[112]

Members of Parliament were willing to see themselves in Hatch's position, or the position of defendants facing charges under the CLAA. In a similar vein, "An Old Cross-Examiner" asked readers of the *Times* whether they would like to have the "old rule preserved if [they] had the bad luck to face a blackmailing or mistaken indictment, or a groundless suit in the Divorce Court?"[113] A. C. Plowden stated flatly in his letter to the *Times* that "there is no one of us who may not some fine day find himself accused of some hideous crime or another—the victim of a malicious set of circumstances all setting in the same direction."[114]

Reid's suggestion that his colleagues should contemplate the possibility that they might find themselves in the position of the unjustly accused defendant was by no means isolated. The Recorder of Gravesend wrote the Home Office in support of allowing testimony on a similar measure in 1891. It was, he wrote, the plight of a "gentleman" who had been placed in "extreme peril" as a result of a larceny accusation concocted by two pawnbrokers that prompted him to share his feelings with the Home Office.[115] The Recorder suggested extending the CLAA's provisions for defense testimony to all criminal charges, stating his belief that many innocent people had greatly benefited from the CLAA's Section 20. George Pitt-Lewis also wrote to the Home Secretary in 1893 arguing that extending the right to testify to all criminal defendants would cut down on what he called "vexatious prosecutions": "Take, for instance a prosecution for rape. A girl, supposed to be of good character is (after the usual course of events in such cases) surprised in flagrante delicto with a man. Of course she prosecutes for rape. He is acquitted, after giving evidence, & then he indicts her for perjury." Moreover, he hastened to add, this was no imaginary case; he had worked with similar ones.[116] Harry Bodkin Poland reminded *Times* readers in 1897 about the recent case of an Oxford undergraduate convicted for assault on the basis of what the student said was perjured testimony by a local policeman, to which he was unable to respond in court. Poland asked readers to imagine themselves in the shoes of the undergraduate, arguing, "I would ask any candid reader to say, [after reading the undergraduate's letter to the *Times*] whether the law which excludes a defendant in such a case can be a just law."[117]

The government did not entirely disregard the dilemma of poor defendants, however, but the extent of that concern was strictly limited to *innocent* poor defendants. In preparation for the 1898 session, the government made concerted efforts to refute long-time critic Herbert Stephen's argument that the bill would result in the conviction of innocent defendants. Stephen, who worked on the Northern Circuit, claimed that "somewhere between five and ten innocent prisoners are convicted each year through

giving their own evidence. The prisoners who can give evidence are between one-fourth and one-fifth of the whole number at assizes." Passing
the bill, Stephen estimated, would result in thirty erroneous convictions
on the Northern Circuit alone, and untold more on the eight other circuits.[118] Kenneth Muir Mackenzie, the Lord Chancellor's undersecretary,
requested that the Home Office research Stephen's accusation, though his
request belied his disbelief: "If there have been such cases, you probably
let the poor things out: and you will have formed an opinion as to whether
their conviction was due to their having given evidence."[119]

The Home Office concluded that no requests for pardon had been
made on that basis: "the S. of S. cannot recall a single instance in which such
a plea has been made a ground for advising a total or partial remission of
sentence." Going back to CLAA convictions in 1894 and 1895 (in order to
ensure that there had been adequate time to file petitions), the Home Office
reported that in "no case did the prisoner allege that he had been injured
by giving evidence himself." Instead, the Home Office singled out a case in
which a prisoner had been invited to give evidence, refused because he felt
confused, and then later regretted that decision.[120] The memo concluded
that Stephen's statement was "baseless."[121] Another Home Office memo
noted that the percentage of acquittals was higher in CLAA cases (between
31 and 50 percent) than in the ordinary run of cases heard at the assizes.
Requests for pardons on the ground of innocence were more common in
CLAA cases, but the Home Office memo attributed that to the he said/she
said nature of many rape cases, which made "shaky" convictions more likely.
As with credibility contests in rape cases, more "shaky" convictions might
result from giving the defendant the right to testify, but the memo found that
potential danger would likely be "counterbalanced by the number of innocent defendants who would be enabled to demonstrate their innocence."[122]

Learning to Live with the Lie

Compared with the beginning of our story, when perjury prosecutions were contemplated in all instances of false testimony, the landscape
of legal thought looked quite different by 1898. Perjury, it was broadly

acknowledged, would still happen in the courtroom. Women's testimony, in particular, was expected to be unreliable. In that way, little had changed. But, crucially, legislators decided that eradicating or discouraging perjury would no longer be a government priority. Rather than structuring the law in order to avoid perjury, they were content to rely on cross-examination to expose it. In a measure of how sensitivity to the threat of perjury by defendants had changed by the end of the century, the Home Office dismissed the problem in an 1897 memo. Changing the law of evidence would be the cause of a "large amount of perjury," the Home Office acknowledged. But perjury by a prisoner "is perhaps not a very serious matter: if a man has committed a burglary it is not a very serious matter that he should also commit perjury to escape the consequence of it."[123]

The Home Office memo in 1897 also expressed concern about the prospect of perjury committed by wives of male defendants. It combined a recognition of women's economic dependence on their husbands with a sweeping disregard for married women's truthfulness. Arguing that "it is a matter of common experience that women are able to believe in the innocence of an accused friend or relative in the face of evidence sufficient to convince any man," the Home Office noted the petitions "that come from women and especially prisoners' wives are especially marked by a disinclination to accept the logic of facts." Moreover, such lying female relatives operated without social sanction ("the opinion of her own class would applaud rather than condemn her") and without practical legal recourse ("the prosecution of a wife for evidence given on behalf of her husband would be so painful a business that it would probably be rare"). In the face of such "commonsense" knowledge about women, extending the right to testify to the male defendant's spouse "deserved more discussion than it has yet received."[124] The Home Office stopped short, however, of recommending any change to the proposed bill.

In 1898, another Home Office memo worried that juries favor rape plaintiffs: "once a jury take to comparing the story a woman tells with the story a man tells, the man is likely to have but little chance." Once again relying on popular "wisdom" rather than legal precedent, the memo fretted that "it is common knowledge that women are more able to lie with vraisemblance and conviction than men do: for instance the whole success of the 'The Liars' at the Criterion now arises from this."[125] "The Liars" was a comedy by Henry Arthur Jones that ran at the Criterion Theatre from 6 October 1897 until November 1898.[126] A farce revolving around an apparent (but unconsummated) incidence of unfaithfulness and an uneaten French dinner, "The Liars" is a curious source for the Home Office. It does, however, feature many jokes about women's inability to tell the truth when a lie could do:

> SIR C: Let us go over the various possibilities of the case. There are only two.
>
> LADY J: What are they?
>
> SIR C: Possibility number one—get out of it by telling fibs. Possibility number two—get out of it by telling the truth. Why not possibility two?
>
> LADY J: Oh, couldn't!
>
> . . .
>
> SIR C: On possibility number one, tell a fib. I put that possibility first out of natural deference and chivalry towards ladies. The objection I have to telling fibs is that you get found out.
>
> LADY J: Oh, not always! I mean, if you arrange things not perhaps as they were, but as they ought to have been.
>
> SIR C: I see. In that way a lie becomes a sort of idealized and essential truth—
>
> LADY J: Yes. Yes—
>
> SIR C: I'm not a good hand at—idealizing.
>
> LADY J: Ah, but then you're a man! No, I can't tell the truth. Gilbert would never believe me.[127]

Skepticism about women's testimony was alive and well in the Home Office during the 1890s, but it played a comparatively minor role in the debate on the Criminal Evidence Act of 1898. Again, while some officials apparently believed that women were irrepressible liars, no one was motivated to alter proposed legislation. One potential explanation for the Home Office's willingness to overlook the issue was mentioned in a memo the previous year: the paucity of female criminal defendants. One memo noted that of the prisoners committed for trial in 1895, only one-seventh were women.[128] Women might often be liars, but they would make infrequent appearances in the dock.

The final passage of the Criminal Evidence Act also represented a concluding episode in the history of reconciliation with cross-examination described in chapter 2. It is testament to the general level of comfort that had been achieved with cross-examination that the final version of the bill was passed without an extensive limitation on it. In previous years, pro-posed bills had restricted cross-examination with respect to character, but the final version did not.[129] Because the fear of perjury now concentrated on the hardened criminal, the extent of cross-examination became the bone of contention in the debate over allowing the sworn testimony of criminal defendants. In particular, opinions differed on whether defendants should be subject to cross-examination as to character and prior convictions. While some argued that allowing cross-examination as to prior convictions amounted to cruelty to defendants, others maintained that "we need not shed many tears over the habitual criminal."[130] Even Herbert Stephen, a steadfast opponent of the measure, rejected the idea that criminal defen-dants be shielded from cross-examination as to past convictions.[131]

The Attorney General defended this omission of any form of protec-tion from cross-examination, noting that he had asked many judges whether they thought cross-examination had done a disservice to defendants; all of them said it had not. Furthermore, "It seemed better to have one uniform and simple code of law; and, speaking for those Courts of which he had a long experience, he did not believe our Judges would ever allow the posi-tion of a prisoner to be prejudiced or the license of counsel to go too far in the matter of examination or cross-examination of prisoners."[132] Edward Clarke went further, suggesting that an overreaching cross-examination would work in defendants' favor by making it seem they were being treated unfairly.[133] Edward Cox's arguments in favor of the barrister's probity and the ultimate wisdom of allowing the legal profession a central role in the production of truth in the courtroom had become common sense.

In the end, a slight concession was made to critics of cross-examination. The version of the act that passed in 1898 contained a limited restriction: if defendants attacked the characters of prosecutors or their witnesses, they could be cross-examined as to their own credit.[134] This fell far short, however, of the previous demand that the characters of defendants be entirely off-limits in cross-examination. Practically speaking, defendants faced a tight constraint: either do nothing to discredit the witnesses on the other side, or face cross-examination as to their own credit.

In addition to Parliament's unwillingness to limit cross-examination, we can also gauge the extent of cross-examination's victory by its reception in the press. During the years before 1898, the *Times* had published a rash of letters criticizing the abuse of cross-examination and exploring alternatives for its limitations such as Stephen's Indian Evidence Act. If anyone knew the arguments against unlimited cross-examination, it was the editors of the *Times*. Nonetheless, the newspaper embraced Parliament's decision to leave regulation of cross-examination to the consciences of counsel. In its leader in support of the new law, the *Times* opined that "we do not for a moment believe" that it might lead to abuse of cross-examination: "Not only the British spirit of fair play, but all the traditions of our Bench and Bar afford securities against such a danger more effective than any that could be put into an Act of Parliament."[135]

The rise of cross-examination to its current status as main guarantor of truth, if not perhaps the greatest legal engine ever invented, had now received the imprimatur of Parliament. The license of counsel that had appeared so ferocious in the person of Mr. Chaffanbrass now seemed a routine part of adversarial procedure. Out of the welter of experimentation during the Victorian period, cross-examination lasted the longest. Other potential engines of truth—including criminal prosecution, shame sanctions, and the inquisitorial pursuit of perjurers—lay by the wayside. With the extension of the right to testify to the criminal defendant, and the incorporation of cross-examination as the quid pro quo for that right, the modern Anglo-American trial took the form we still recognize today.

Notes

Introduction

1. Kentish *Observer,* 6 Aug. 1850, 6; Maidstone and Southeastern *Gazette,* 1 Aug. 1850, 3.
2. "Ricketts v. Ricketts," in the *Times* (London), 21 Mar. 1885, 4; 9 July 1885, 3.
3. James Oldham, "Truth-telling in the Eighteenth-Century English Courtroom," in *Law and History Review* 12 (1994): 94–121.
4. Public Record Office, Kew, HO 45/9784/B2907M.
5. Oldham, "Truth-telling," 94.
6. Samuel Smiles, *Self-Help, with Illustrations of Character and Conduct* (London: John Murray, 1866), 387. On Smiles, see Asa Briggs, *Victorian People* (London: Penguin, 1954), 124–47. Sincerity, of course, has more meanings than simple truthfulness. But here I use it in the sense of "freedom from dissimulation or duplicity; honesty; straightforwardness." See *A New English Dictionary on Historical Principles* (Oxford: Clarendon, 1918), 9:73.
7. Walter E. Houghton, *The Victorian Frame of Mind* (New Haven, CT: Yale University Press, 1957), 218.
8. Ibid., 220–21.
9. Ibid., 218–19.
10. Ibid., 425–26.
11. John Kucich, *The Power of Lies: Transgression in Victorian Fiction* (Ithaca, NY: Cornell University Press, 1994).
12. Wilde was not alone in his ironic lament about the decline of lying. Elliot Browne asked: "Now that public interest in the Spelling Bees has so greatly diminished, why not institute the Lying Bee? We commend this suggestion to the consideration of the School Boards." C. Elliot Browne, "The Art of Lying," in *New Quarterly Magazine* 8 (1877): 185.
13. For the development of muscular Christianity, see David Newsome, *Godliness and Good Learning* (London: John Murray, 1961); Norman Vance, *The Sinews of the Spirit: The Ideal of Christian Manliness in Victorian Literature and Religious Thought* (Cambridge: Cambridge University Press, 1985);

J. Springhall, "Building the Character of the British Boy," in J. A. Mangan and James Walvin, eds., *Manliness and Morality: Middleclass Masculinity in Britain and America, 1800–1940* (New York: St. Martin's Press, 1987), 52–74.

14. Jonathan H. Grossman, *The Art of Alibi: English Law Courts and the Novel* (Baltimore: Johns Hopkins University Press, 2002), 7–8.

15. Ibid., 19–20.

16. Ibid., 137–63.

17. Allyson N. May, *The Bar and the Old Bailey, 1750–1850* (Chapel Hill: University of North Carolina Press, 2003), 217–18.

18. Albany Fonblanque, Edward Barrington de Fonblanque, ed., *The Life and Labours of Albany Fonblanque* (London: R. Bentley and Son, 1874), 340. On the development of adversarial ethics, see generally David Cairns, *Advocacy and the Making of the Adversarial Criminal Trial, 1800–1865* (Oxford: Clarendon, 1998).

19. Martin J. Wiener, "Domesticity: A Legal Discipline for Men?," in Martin Hewitt, ed., *An Age of Equipoise? Reassessing Mid-Victorian Britain* (Aldershot: Ashgate, 2000), 156.

20. W. L. Burn, *Age of Equipoise* (New York: Norton, 1965), 8.

21. Martin J. Wiener, *Men of Blood: Violence, Manliness and Criminal Justice in Victorian England* (Cambridge: Cambridge University Press, 2004), 13–14.

22. Martin J. Wiener, *An Empire on Trial: Race, Murder, and Justice under British Rule, 1870–1935* (Cambridge: Cambridge University Press, 2009), 231–33.

23. Martin J. Wiener, *Reconstructing the Criminal: Culture, Law and Policy in England, 1830–1914* (Cambridge: Cambridge University Press, 1990), 53.

24. Ibid., 54–55.

25. Ibid., 63.

26. On bankruptcy reforms, see V. Markham Lester, *Victorian Insolvency: Bankruptcy, Imprisonment for Debt, and Company Winding-Up in Nineteenth-Century England* (Oxford: Clarendon, 1995). Similar trends can be seen in debt litigation more broadly. Examining personal debt litigation in the nineteenth century, Margot Finn finds that modernization of trade tended to reinforce traditional notions of personal morality and character. Despite the progress of the cash economy, courts and theorists still tried to distinguish "innocent" debtors from criminals. Status, class, gender, and reputation still continued to matter in a growing capitalist economy, despite Sir Henry Maine's characterization of a transition from status to contract. Margot C.

Finn, *The Character of Credit: Personal Debt in English Culture, 1740–1914* (Cambridge: Cambridge University Press, 2003), ch. 7, 320, 327. Yet another parallel may be found in the enthusiasm to combat commercial fraud in the form of adulteration. The campaign against adulteration of food prompted parliamentary investigation in the mid-1850s and legislation in 1860. See Harold Perkin, *The Origins of Modern English Society, 1780–1880* (London: Routledge & Kegan Paul, 1969), 440–41.

27. Barbara Weiss, *The Hell of the English: Bankruptcy and the Victorian Novel* (Lewisburg, PA: Bucknell University Press, 1986), 44–45; Wiener, *Reconstructing the Criminal,* 69.

28. Lester, *Victorian Insolvency,* 68.

29. John Henry Wigmore, *A Treatise on the System of Evidence in Trials at Common Law,* vol. 2 (Boston: Little, Brown, 1904), 1697–98 (Sec. 1367).

30. William Twining, *Theories of Evidence: Bentham and Wigmore* (Stanford, CA: Stanford University Press, 1985), 110.

31. See *California v. Green,* 399 U.S. 149, 158 (1970), *White v. Illinois,* 502 U.S. 346 (1992), *Lilly v. Virginia,* 526 U.S. 116 (1999), and *U.S. v. Salerno,* 505 U.S. 317 (1992) (Stevens, J., dissenting).

32. Robert P. Burns, "A Wistful Retrospective on Wigmore and His Prescriptions for Illinois Evidence Law," in *Northwestern University Law Review* 100 (2006): 131–50, 135.

33. Wigmore, *Treatise,* 1699.

34. John H. Langbein, *The Origins of Adversary Criminal Trial* (Oxford: Oxford University Press, 2003).

35. May, *Bar and the Old Bailey;* Cairns, *Advocacy;* Thomas P. Gallanis, Jr., "The Rise of Modern Evidence Law," in *Iowa Law Review* 84 (1999): 499.

36. Christopher Allen, *The Law of Evidence in Victorian England* (Cambridge: Cambridge University Press, 1997).

37. William Cornish, Stuart Anderson, Ray Cocks, Michael Lobban, Patrick Polden, and Keith Smith, eds., *The Oxford History of the Law of England,* vols. XI–XIII (Oxford: Oxford University Press, 2010).

38. Jan-Melissa Schramm, *Testimony and Advocacy in Victorian Law, Literature and Theology* (Cambridge: Cambridge University Press, 2000), 71.

39. Catherine Hall, *Civilising Subjects: Metropole and Colony in the English Imagination, 1830–1867* (Chicago: University of Chicago Press, 2002), 9.

40. Several notable exceptions to this rule are Rande Kostal, *A Jurisprudence of Power: Victorian Empire and the Rule of Law* (Oxford: Oxford University Press, 2005); Wiener, *Empire on Trial;* and Douglas Hay and Paul Craven,

eds., *Masters, Servants and Magistrates in Britain & the Empire, 1562–1955* (Chapel Hill: University of North Carolina Press, 2004).

41. On the disciplinary boundaries separating legal and other forms of historical scholarship, see Margot Finn, "Victorian Law, Literature and History," in *Journal of Victorian Culture* 7 (2002): 134.

Chapter One. The Rise and Fall of Perjury Prosecutions

1. The 1851 act to allow parties to testify was the most dramatic in a series of initiatives that abolished disqualification for interest piece by piece. In 1843, the first major inroad came with the admission of interested nonparty witnesses. See Evidence Act 1843 (6 & 7 Vict., c. 85). It was followed by the establishment of the County Courts, in which civil parties were allowed to testify, County Courts Act 1846 (9 & 10 Vict., c. 95); the privilege of testifying was extended to the spouses of parties in civil actions in the Evidence Amendment Act 1853 (16 & 17 Vict., c. 83). Criminal defendants, however, would have to wait forty-five years before being allowed to testify on oath by the Criminal Evidence Act 1898 (61 & 62 Vict., c. 36).

2. See Evidence Act 1851 (14 & 15 Vict., c. 99). On the legislative history of these reforms, see C. J. W. Allen, *The Law of Evidence in Victorian England* (Cambridge: Cambridge University Press, 1997); Keith Smith, "The Trial: Adversarial Characteristics and Responsibilities," in William Cornish, Stuart Anderson, Ray Cocks, Michael Lobban, Patrick Polden, and Keith Smith, eds., *The Oxford History of the Laws of England: 1820–1914,* vol. XIII (Oxford: Oxford University Press, 2010), 92–107; Joel N. Bodansky, "The Abolition of the Party-Witness Disqualification: An Historical Survey," in *Kentucky Law Journal* 70 (1981–82): 91; C. Jackson, "Irish Political Opposition to the Passage of Criminal Evidence Reform at Westminster," in J. F. McEldowney and Paul O'Higgins, eds., *The Common Law Tradition: Essays in Irish Legal History* (Dublin: Irish Academic Press, 1990), 185; David Johnson, "Trial by Jury in Ireland 1860–1914," in *Legal History* 17 (1996): 270, 276; Graham Parker, "The Prisoner in the Box—The Making of the Criminal Evidence Act, 1898," in John A. Guy and H. G. Beale, eds., *Law and Social Change in British History* (London: Royal Historical Society, 1984), 156.

3. Comment, "Perjury: The Forgotten Offense," in *Journal of Criminal Law & Criminology* 65 (1974), 361–72. One brief treatment of the history of perjury in England exists: T. Humphrey, "The History of Perjury," in *Quarterly Review* 292 (1954): 294–301. For other historical discussions, see Stuart P. Green, "Lying, Misleading and Falsely Denying: How Moral Concepts In-

form the Law of Perjury, Fraud, and False Statements," in *Hastings Law Journal* 53 (2001): 182–91; Richard H. Underwood, "False Witness: A Lawyer's History of the Law of Perjury," in *Arizona Journal of International and Comparative Law* 10 (1993): 215; "Perjury: An Anthology," in *Arizona Journal of International and Comparative Law* 13 (1996): 307; and "Perjury! The Charges and the Defenses," in *Duquesne Law Review* 26 (1998): 715.

4. Jeremy Bentham, *Rationale of Judicial Evidence,* 5 vols. (London: Hunt and Clarke, 1827), 1:201–9; 277–85, 305; 306–40. For his theory of sanctions, see Jeremy Bentham, J. H. Burns, and H. L. A. Hart, eds., *An Introduction to the Principles of Morals and Legislation* (Oxford: Oxford University Press, 1996).

5. Evidence Act 1843 (6 & 7 Vict., c. 85).

6. County Courts Act 1846 (9 & 10 Vict., c. 95).

7. *Parl. Deb.,* 3rd ser., 116 (11 Apr. 1851): 4. On Brougham's law reform efforts generally, see Michael Lobban, "Henry Brougham and Law Reform," in *The English Historical Review* 115 (2000): 1184.

8. *Parl. Deb.,* 3rd ser., 116 (11 Apr. 1851): 5.

9. "Answers of the County Court Judges upon the Examination of Parties," in *House of Lords Sessions Papers,* 1851, vol. 16, p. 329, reprinted as "Evidence of Parties," in *Law Review* 13 (1850–51): 395.

10. *Parl. Deb.,* 3rd ser., 116 (11 Apr. 1851): 13.

11. "Answers of the County Court Judges," p. 402.

12. *Parl. Deb.,* 3rd ser., 116 (11 Apr. 1851): 14.

13. *Parl. Deb.,* 3rd ser., 118 (16 July 1851): 840–42.

14. See, e.g., ibid., 843.

15. Criminal Procedure Act 1851 (14 & 15 Vict., c. 100). See Patrick Polden, "The Courts of Law," in Cornish et al., eds., *Oxford History of the Law of England,* vol. XI, 616–17.

16. *Parl. Deb.,* 3rd ser., 61 (8 Mar. 1842): 215–16.

17. On the Georgian Perjury Act, see "Memoranda for Magistrates," in *Law Times* 1 (12 Apr. 1843): 486–87; on private prosecutors, see *Law Times* 21 (28 May 1853): 85.

18. *Law Times* 15 (1 June 1850): 212.

19. *Law Times,* 3rd ser., 18 (23 July 1851): 1371.

20. "Indictments for Perjury," in the *Times* (London), 6 Nov. 1851, 5, col. d.

21. Letter to H. Brougham dated 19 July 1851, attached to letter from H. Brougham to W. Brougham dated 22 July 1851, in the Brougham Collection, University College, London (hereafter Brougham Collection).

22. Letter to H. Brougham dated 16 Feb. 1852, Brougham Collection MS. 17,260.

23. Letter to H. Brougham dated 26 Nov. 1851, Brougham Collection MS. 26,394.

24. Letter to H. Brougham dated 20 Nov. 1851, Brougham Collection MS. 13,271.

25. "Law Amendment and the Judges of the Superior Courts," in *Law Review* 15 (1851–52): 365, 370–71.

26. The *Times* (London), 19 Mar. 1858, 6, col. b.

27. F. Safford, "The Present State of the Law of Perjury," in *Law Magazine & Review*, 3rd ser., 2 (1873): 912, 915.

28. Martin J. Wiener, *Reconstructing the Criminal: Culture, Law, and Policy in England, 1830–1914* (Cambridge: Cambridge University Press, 1990), 258.

29. *R. v. Potts*, 1845, the *Times* (London), 5 Mar. 1845, 8; *Central Criminal Court Sessions Papers* (hereafter CCCSP), 5th Sess., 1844–45, 637 (directed verdict in a suit brought to revenge verdict in civil case); *R. v. Meeks*, 1840, Gloucestershire *Chronicle*, 29 Aug. 1840, 4 (acquittal in a prosecution for perjury in a perjury case arising from a debt case).

30. *R. v. Mumford*, 1835, CCCSP, 5th Sess., 1835, 695–703; *R. v. Brown*, 1835, Nottingham *Review*, 31 July 1835, 4.

31. The *Times* (London), 15 Sept. 1840, 7.

32. *R. v. Ostle, Allison, & Allison*, 1835, Carlisle *Journal*, 15 Aug. 1835, 3; the *Times* (London), 10 Aug. 1835, 13; Carlisle *Journal*, 15 Aug. 1835, 3.

33. F. G. Bailey, *The Prevalence of Deceit* (Ithaca, NY: Cornell University Press, 1991), 67–75; J. A Barnes, *A Pack of Lies: Towards a Sociology of Lying* (New York: Cambridge University Press, 1994), 83–84.

34. Edmund Head, *Report on the Law of Bastardy* (London: Her Majesty's Stationery Offices, 1840); Thomas William Saunders, *The Law and Practice of Orders of Affiliation* (London: Law Times Office, 1848); A. R. Higginbotham, "'Sin of the Age': Infanticide and Illegitimacy in Victorian London," in *Victorian Studies* 32 (1989): 319–37.

35. U. R. Q. Henriques, "Bastardy and the New Poor Law," in *Past & Present* 37 (1967): 106.

36. Bastardy Act 1845 (8 & 9 Vict., c. 10); Poor Law Amendment Act 1844 (7 & 8 Vict., c. 101, s. 2).

37. Saunders, *Law and Practice*, 12–20.

38. *Law Times* 60 (8 Apr. 1876): 417.

39. *R. v. Berry, Law Times Reports* 32 (1859): 324; Saunders, *Law and Practice*, 7th ed. (London: Law Times Office, 1878), 75.

40. *Law Times* 11 (10 June 1848): 233.

41. "The Amendment of the Law of Evidence," in *Law Times* 99 (1 June 1895): 103, 105.

42. J. E. Archer, *"By a Flash and a Scare": Arson, Animal Maiming, and Poaching in East Anglia, 1815–1879* (Oxford: Oxford University Press, 1990); Barrister, *Clarke's New Game Laws* (London, 1843); J. E. Archer, "'A Reckless Spirit of Enterprise': Game-Preserving and Poaching in Nineteenth-Century Lancashire," in D. W. Howell and K. O. Morgan, eds., *Crime, Protest and Police in Modern British Society: Essays in Memory of David J. V. Jones* (Cardiff: University of Wales Press, 1999) 149–75; D. Jones, "Rural Crime and Protest," in G. E. Mingay, ed., *The Victorian Countryside* (London: Routledge, 1981), 2: 566–79; F. M. L. Thompson, "Landowners and the Rural Community," ibid., 2: 457–74.

43. Jones, "Rural Crime and Protest," 2:566.

44. Gloucestershire *Chronicle*, 2 Apr. 1870, 5.

45. On licensing laws and the Victorian culture of drink, see Mark Girouard, *Victorian Pubs* (New Haven, CT: Yale University Press, 1975); Brian H. Harrison, *Drink and the Victorians: The Temperance Question in England, 1815–1872* (Pittsburgh: University of Pittsburgh Press, 1971); and F. M. L. Thompson, *The Rise of Respectable Society* (Cambridge: Cambridge University Press, 1988), 308–22.

46. "Discussion of 'Evidence in Criminal Cases,'" in *Transactions of the National Association for Promotion of the Social Sciences* 1882 (London, 1883), 248, 255.

47. *R. v. Coles*, 1865, Hampshire *Chronicle*, 3 Mar. 1865, 3.

48. V. M. Lester, *Victorian Insolvency* (Oxford: Oxford University Press, 1995).

49. John Pitt Taylor, "On the Expediency of Passing an Act to Permit Defendants in Criminal Courts, and their Wives or Husbands, to Testify on Oath," *Law Times* 36 (13 Apr. 1861): 290.

50. *Solicitors' Journal* 12 (1 Aug. 1868): 820.

51. Allen, *Law of Evidence*, 123–80; Rosemary Pattenden, *English Criminal Appeals, 1844–1994* (Oxford: Clarendon, 1996), 5–33.

52. J. Roland Philips, "Appeal in Criminal Cases," in *Law Magazine & Review*, 3rd ser., 1 (1872): 132, 134; see also "New Trials in the County Courts," *Law Times* 68 (13 Nov. 1869): 2.

53. David J. Bentley, *English Criminal Justice in the Nineteenth Century* (London: Hambledon, 1998), 162–64.

54. *Law Times* 39 (19 Mar. 1864): 227.

55. On the Hatch case, see "Law of Evidence—'Incompetency' of Witnesses," in *Solicitors' Journal* 4 (2 June 1860): 597; the *Times* (London), 6 Apr. 1860, 9; 10 May 1860, 11; 11 May 1860, 11; 12 May 1860, 11; 14 May 1860, 11; 16 May 1860, 12; 4 June 1860, 11; and CCCSP, 7th Sess., 1859 (No. 425), 59.

56. *Law Times* 40 (30 Sept. 1865): 573; see also "Discussion on 'Is it expedient to Remove any and what of the remaining Restrictions on the Admissibility of Evidence in Civil and Criminal Cases?,'" in G. Hastings, ed., *Transactions of the National Association for the Promotion of Social Science 1865* (London: Longman, 1866), 239–40; *Law Times* 60 (19 Mar. 1864): 227; *Law Times* 39 (20 Feb. 1864): 182; "Law of Evidence Bill," in *Law Times* 35 (7 July 1860): 193.

57. *Jackson's Oxford Journal*, 24 July 1852, 5; the *Times* (London), 20 July 1852, 7.

58. Pattenden, *English Criminal Appeals*, 13; *Solicitors' Journal* 11 (23 Feb. 1867): 385; "Evidence of Parties in Criminal Cases," *Solicitors' Journal* 4 (7 July 1860): 696, 697; *Law Times* 39 (19 Mar. 1864): 227; *Law Times* 39 (20 Feb. 1864): 182; and "Law of Evidence Bill," in *Law Times* 35 (7 July 1860): 193.

59. *Solicitors' Journal* 25 (14 May 1881): 523.

60. Ibid.

61. J. Ll. J. Edwards, *The Law Officers of the Crown* (London: Sweet and Maxwell, 1964); Philip B. Kurland and D. W. M. Waters, "Public Prosecutions in England, 1854–79: An Essay in English Legislative History," in *Duke Law Journal* (1959): 493.

62. For the relevant legislation, see the Prosecution of Offenses Act 1879 (42 & 43 Vict., c. 22); the Prosecution of Offenses Act 1884 (47 & 48 Vict., c. 58). On the Director of Public Prosecutions, see "The Office of Public Prosecutor," in *Law Journal* 19 (14 June 1884): 358; *Law Journal* 29 (10 Nov. 1894): 641.

63. Quoted in Kurland and Waters, "Public Prosecutions," 514.

64. Ibid., 516.

65. Bristol *Gazette,* 12 Aug. 1852, 2.

66. Somerset County *Gazette,* 14 Aug. 1852, 2.

67. Somerset County *Herald,* 14 Aug. 1852, 4; see also *R. v. Atkinson,* 1855, Westmorland *Gazette* and Kendall *Advertiser,* 24 Feb. 1855, 5 (complaining about inadequate time to investigate a case of perjury suddenly indicted at assizes).

68. "The Amendment of the Law of Evidence in Criminal Cases," in *Law Times* 99 (1 June 1895): 103, 105.

69. For successive prosecutions, see, e.g., "Stowell-Kennett case. Charge of Perjury Against a Solicitor," in *Solicitors' Journal* 2 (12 Dec. 1858): 84. For dismissal of a vindictive case, see, e.g., *R. v. Wilkes*, 1852, Worcestershire *Chronicle*, 10 Mar. 1852, 8; the *Times* (London), 11 Mar. 1852, 7. For extortion, see, e.g., *R. v. Samuel*, 1852, the *Times* (London), 26 Oct. 1852, 6; *CCCSP*, 12th Sess., 1851–52 (No. 978), n.p.

70. See the Vexatious Indictments Act 1859 (22 & 23 Vict., c. 17). On the prominent case and related discussion, see "The Law and the Lawyers," *Law Times* 31 (3 July 1853): 181; *Law Times* 31 (10 July 1858): 189; and *Law Times* 33 (20 Aug. 1859): 273.

71. Maidstone and Kentish *Journal*, 13 July 1885, 5.

72. *R. v. Mowbray*, 1865, Sussex *Advertiser*, 12 Oct. 1864, 4; 25 Mar. 1865, 3; the *Times*, 25 Mar. 1865, 14. The jury in this case insisted on convicting the defendant, despite repeated instructions by the judge to the contrary.

73. James Fitzjames Stephen, *A General View of the Criminal Law of England* (London: Macmillan, 1863), 279.

74. See, e.g., *R. v. Taylor*, 1885, Essex *Standard*, 7 Nov. 1885, 6; *R. v. Silles*, 1885, Norfolk *Chronicle* and Norwich *Gazette*, 4 Nov. 1885, 7; *R. v. Howlett*, 1885, Norfolk *Chronicle* and Norwich *Gazette*, 4 Nov. 1885, 7; *R. v. Hodgkinson*, 1885, Chester *Chronicle*, 7 Feb. 1885, 3.

75. *R. v. Silles*, 1885, Norfolk *Chronicle* and Norwich *Gazette*, 4 Nov. 1885, 7.

76. *R. v. Drake*, 1870, Dorset County *Chronicle*, 10 Mar. 1870, 3, 4, 7.

77. *R. v. Warne*, 1880, Durham County *Advertiser*, 23 Jan. 1880, 3.

78. Cornwall *Royal Gazette*, 14 Nov. 1895, 2.

79. "Perjury in County Courts," 6 *Law Journal*, 22 Sept. 1871, at 648.

80. On York, see Yorkshire *Gazette, Supplement*, 17 Mar. 1855, 1; the *Times* (London), 15 Mar. 1855, 9. On Leicester, see Leicester *Journal*, 19 Mar. 1852, 1. On the 1865 cases, see Gloucester *Chronicle, Supplement*, 8 Apr. 1865, 2; the *Times* (London), 6 Apr. 1865, 13.

81. "The Office of the Public Prosecutor," *Law Journal* 29 (10 Nov. 1894): 641.

82. *Law Journal* 27 (4 June 1892): 359–60.

83. House of Commons, C. B. Stuart-Wortley, "Prosecutions of Offences Acts, 1879 and 1884," Apr. 1892, *Parliamentary Papers*, 1892 LXV, 192.

84. House of Commons, "Prosecution of Offences Acts, 1879 and 1884," *Parliamentary Papers*, 1896 LXIX, 259.

85. On complaints regarding perjury cases, see "The Office of the Public Prosecutor," *Law Journal* 29 (10 Nov. 1894): 641. On the summoning of the director to Parliament, see House of Commons, *Parliamentary Papers*, 1890 LIX, 213; 1897 LXIII, 59–60.

86. "The Plague of Perjury," in the *Globe* (London), 13 Mar. 1893, reprinted in House of Commons, *Parliamentary Papers*, 1894 LXXI, 266.

87. "The 'Perjury Plague,'" in *Law Journal* 28 (18 Mar. 1893): 191; Letter from A. Barrister to the Editor of the St. James *Gazette*, Mar. 14, 1892, reprinted in House of Commons, *Parliamentary Papers*, 1894 LXXI, 266.

88. *Law Journal* 29 (26 May 1894): 319.

89. "Plague of Perjury," 266.

90. Humphrey, "History of Perjury," 294–301; see also *Parl. Deb.*, 3rd scr., 155 (1859): 149.

91. Thomas Edward Crispe, *Reminiscences of a K.C.* (London: Methuen, 1909), 154; Henry Edwin Fenn, *Thirty-Five Years in the Divorce Court* (London: T. Werner Laurie, 1910), 139.

92. *Law Times* 40 (24 June 1865): 407.

93. On the Campbell case, see Barbara Leckie, *Culture and Adultery: The Novel, the Newspaper, and the Law, 1857–1914* (Philadelphia: University of Pennsylvania Press, 1999), 79–92. On the Russell case, see A. S. Holmes, "'Don't Frighten the Horses': The Russell Divorce Case," in G. Robb and N. Erber, eds., *Disorder in the Court: Trials and Sexual Conflict at the Turn of the Century* (New York: New York University Press, 1999), 140.

94. Text of Bill, No. 328, House of Commons, *Parl. Deb.*, 3rd ser., 328 (1888): 1237; "Perjury in Divorce Cases," the *Times* (London), 27 July 1888, 13, col. c. Darling withdrew his bill within two weeks of introducing it; unfortunately, no debate on its merits has been preserved. See *Parl. Deb.*, 3rd ser., 329 (1888): 179.

95. C. B. Stuart-Wortley, "Prosecution of Offences Acts, 1879 and 1884," April 1890, in House of Commons, *Parliamentary Papers*, 1890, LIX, 214.

96. Ibid., 187–88. The director singled out *R. v. Taplin and Owen* as a rare example of a divorce case in which public prosecution was merited. In *Taplin*, the petitioner for divorce and the co-respondent (the individual he accused of committing adultery with his wife) had claimed not to know each other; evidence was produced showing not only that they were old friends, but also that they had boasted publicly about their plot to stage the petitioner's discovery of the co-respondent in his wife's bedroom. The director noted that "this sort of evidence is seldom procurable," however.

97. Stuart-Wortley, "Prosecution of Offences Acts, 1879 and 1884," 213.

98. G. W. E. Russell, "Prosecution of Offences Acts, 1879 and 1884," Apr. 1894, in House of Commons, *Parliamentary Papers*, 1894 LXXI, 264.

99. Letter from C. P. Butt, late President of the Probate Division, to A. Stephenson, Director of Public Prosecutions, 15 Apr. 1892, in House of Commons, *Parliamentary Papers*, 1893–94 LXXIV, Pt. 1, 681.

100. C. B. Stuart-Wortley, "Prosecution of Offences Acts, 1879 and 1884," April 1892, in House of Commons, *Parliamentary Papers,* 1892 LXV, 190–92.

101. "The Perjury Plague," *Law Journal* 28 (18 Mar. 1893): 191. On worries about the excessive power of judges, see, e.g., Letter from R. Couch, late Chief Justice of the High Court, Calcutta, to A. Stephenson, Director of Public Prosecutions, 18 Apr. 1892, in *Parliamentary Papers,* 1893–94 LXXIV, Pt. 1, 681 ("I should not like to give the Court, before which the false swearing took place, the power to punish it. In many cases a hasty and erroneous view might be taken of the evidence"). Stephenson appears to have solicited Couch's views because his proposal resembled a provision in the Indian Code of Civil Procedure.

102. Extract from the Manchester *Guardian,* 15 May 1893, reprinted in *Parliamentary Papers,* 1894 LXXI, 371.

103. Criminal Evidence Act 1898 (61 & 62 Vict., c. 36).

104. Allen, *Law of Evidence,* 140–44, 167–71. See also Jackson, "Irish Political Opposition"; and Johnson, "Trial by Jury in Ireland," 264.

105. "Mr. Justice Hawkins on the Evidence of Prisoners," in *Law Journal* 33 (7 May 1898): 238.

106. "Evidence in Criminal Cases Bill," in *Law Journal* 33 (5 Mar. 1898): 114.

107. *Solicitors' Journal* 41 (24 Apr. 1897): 434.

108. "Criminal Evidence Bill," in *Solicitors' Journal* 40 (13 June 1896): 561, 562.

109. "The Amendment of the Law of Evidence," in *Law Times* 99 (1 June 1895): 103, 105; "The Criminal Evidence Act," in *Law Journal* 34 (14 Jan. 1899): 20–21.

110. "The Judges and the Criminal Evidence Act," in *Law Journal* 33 (24 Dec. 1898): 638.

111. "The Criminal Evidence Act," in *Law Journal* 33 (19 Nov. 1898): 561.

112. "The Criminal Evidence Act," in *Law Journal* 33 (5 Nov. 1898): 532; "Sir Forrest Fulton on the Criminal Evidence Act," in *Law Journal* 33 (22 Oct. 1898): 519–20.

113. *Solicitors' Journal* 43 (5 Aug. 1899): 684.

114. *Solicitors' Journal* 43 (18 Feb. 1899): 254; *Solicitors' Journal* 44 (28 July 1900): 638.

115. *Solicitors' Journal* 22 (19 Oct. 1878): 941.

Chapter Two. The Gentlemanly Art of Cross-examination

1. Anthony Trollope, *The Three Clerks* (Oxford: Oxford University Press, 1989 [1857]), 469.

2. James Fitzjames Stephen, *A General View of the Criminal Law of England* (London: Macmillan, 1863), 297.

3. See David J. Cairns, *Advocacy and the Making of the Criminal Trial, 1800–1865* (Oxford: Oxford University Press, 1998); John H. Langbein, *The Origins of Adversary Criminal Trial* (Oxford: Oxford University Press, 2003); Stephan Landsman, "The Rise of the Contentious Spirit: Adversary Procedure in Eighteenth-Century England," in *Cornell Law Review* 75 (1990): 497.

4. Landsman, "Rise of the Contentious Spirit," 501.

5. On the Courvoisier case, see David Mellinkoff, *The Conscience of a Lawyer* (St. Paul, MN: West, 1973).

6. Raymond Cocks, *The Foundations of the Modern Bar* (London: Sweet and Maxwell, 1983), 5, 8.

7. On Brougham, see Mellinkoff, *Conscience of a Lawyer,* 188–89.

8. Langbein, *Origins,* 246.

9. James Fitzjames Stephen, "The Morality of Advocacy," in *Cornhill Magazine* 3 (1861): 455.

10. *Law Times* 92 (2 Jan. 1892): 138.

11. Mark Osiel, "Lawyers as Monopolists, Aristocrats, and Entrepreneurs," in *Harvard Law Review* 103 (1990): 2023.

12. The rule was laid down for contentious cases in 1888 and for noncontentious ones in 1897. See Brian Abel-Smith and Robert Stevens, *Lawyers and the Courts* (Cambridge, MA: Harvard University Press, 1967), 222.

13. Baron Farrer Herschell, *The Rights and Duties of an Advocate* (Glasgow: Wm. Hodge, 1890), 20.

14. See Richard L. Abel, "American Lawyers," in Richard L. Abel, ed., *Lawyers: A Critical Reader* (New York: New Press, 1997), 117–31.

15. See, e.g., W. J. Reader, *Professional Men* (New York: Basic Books, 1966), 2; Cocks, *Foundations of the Modern Bar,* 177–94.

16. Osiel, "Lawyers as Monopolists," 2046.

17. The Prisoners' Counsel Act 1836 (6 & 7 Will. IV, c. 114); Cairns, *Advocacy,* 25–36.

18. Quoted in Langbein, *Origins,* 254–55.

19. Landsman, "Rise of the Contentious Spirit," 540–49.

20. Langbein, *Origins,* 295–96.

21. See Allyson May, *The Bar and the Old Bailey, 1750–1850* (Chapel Hill: University of North Carolina Press, 2003), 133–36, 140.

22. Quoted in J. R. Lewis, *The Victorian Bar* (London: Robert Hale, 1982), 24.

23. Sir Henry Hawkins, *Reminiscences of Sir Henry Hawkins,* ed. Richard Harris (London: Edward Arnold, 1904), 1:80.

24. Cocks, *Foundations of the Modern Bar,* 20–22.

25. See Lansdman, "Rise of the Contentious Spirit," 536; May, *Bar and the Old Bailey*, 126.

26. Quoted in Landsman, "Rise of the Contentious Spirit," 536.

27. May, *Bar and the Old Bailey*, 114–17.

28. Thomas Hague, *A Letter to William Garrow, Esq., in which the Conduct of Counsel in the Cross-Examination of Witnesses, and Commenting on Their Testimony, is Fully Discussed, and the Licentiousness of the Bar Exposed* (London: R. McDonald, 1808), 3, 18.

29. John Beattie, "Garrow for the Defence," in *History Today* 41 (1991): 49, 53.

30. Landsman, "Rise of the Contentious Spirit," 458.

31. Ibid., 554.

32. John Cordy Jeaffreson, *A Book about Lawyers*, 2nd ed. (London: Hurst and Blackett, 1867), 2:184.

33. On other Victorian novelists critical of the bar, see Bege Bowers Neel, "Lawyers on Trial: Attitudes toward the Lawyer's Use and Abuse of Rhetoric in Nineteenth-Century England" (Ph.D. diss., University of Tennessee, 1984), 150–93.

34. Trollope, *Three Clerks*, 469.

35. Anthony Trollope, *Orley Farm* (New York: Dover, 1981 [1862]), 2:245.

36. Quoted in R. D. McMaster, *Trollope and the Law* (New York: St. Martin's Press, 1986), 54.

37. See N. John Hall, *Trollope: A Biography* (Oxford: Oxford University Press, 1993), 106–8.

38. Quoted in McMaster, *Trollope and the Law*, 57–58.

39. Anthony Trollope, *The New Zealander*, ed. N. John Hall (Oxford: Clarendon, 1972), 56.

40. "Contemporary Literature," in *Home and Foreign Review* 2 (Jan. 1863): 291.

41. Trollope, *Orley Farm*, 2:165.

42. Trollope, *New Zealander*, 58.

43. Anthony Trollope, *Phineas Redux* (Oxford: Oxford University Press, 2000 [1874]) 2:236–37.

44. Trollope, *Orley Farm*, 2:359, 129.

45. Trollope, *Three Clerks*, 469.

46. See James Turner, *Reckoning with the Beast: Animals, Pain and Humanity in the Victorian Mind* (Baltimore: Johns Hopkins University Press, 1980), 40, 44; Harriet Ritvo, *The Animal Estate: The English and Other Creatures in the Victorian Age* (Cambridge, MA: Harvard University Press, 1987), 144–48, 160–66.

47. Eliza Acton, *Modern Cookery in All its Branches: Reduced to a System of Easy Practice for the Use of Private Families* (Philadelphia: Lea and Blanchard, 1845 [rpt. of 2nd London ed.]), 61.

48. Trollope, *Three Clerks,* 469, 610.

49. William Forsyth, *Hortensius: An Historical Essay on the Office and Duties of an Advocate,* 3rd ed. (London: John Murray, 1879), 410.

50. Archer Polson, *Law and Lawyers* (London: Longman, 1840) 1:180.

51. Marc Galanter, *Lowering the Bar: Lawyer Jokes and Legal Culture* (Madison: University of Wisconsin Press, 2005), 35, 37.

52. See Neel, "Lawyers on Trial," 163.

53. Polson, *Law and Lawyers,* 1:182.

54. Ibid., 1:181.

55. Langbein, *Origins,* 233, 245–47.

56. Thomas Starkie, *A Practical Treatise on the Law of Evidence,* 2nd ed. (London: J. W. and T. Clarke, 1833) 1:160.

57. Daniel Duman, *The English and Colonial Bars in the Nineteenth Century* (London: Croom Helm, 1983), 8. Population growth over the same fifty-year period was approximately 80 percent. Drawing on census data, Penelope Corfield has noted an increase in the number of barristers in England and Wales from approximately 290 in 1780 to 2,816 in 1851. See Corfield, *Power and the Professions in Britain, 1700–1850* (London: Routledge, 1995), 91.

58. W. Wesley Pue, "Guild Training vs. Professional Education: The Committee on Legal Education and the Law Department of Queen's College in Birmingham in the 1850s," in *American Journal of Legal History* 33 (1989): 241, 243–46.

59. [James Stephen], "Professional Etiquette," in *Cornhill Magazine* 8 (July–Dec. 1863): 101–11, 105.

60. See Duman, *English and Colonial Bars,* 9; W. Wesley Pue, "Rebels at the Bar: English Barristers and the County Courts in the 1850s," in *Anglo-American Law Review* 16 (1987): 303.

61. Patrick Polden, *A History of the County Court, 1846–1971* (Cambridge: Cambridge University Press, 1999), 60.

62. Patrick Polden, "The Education of Lawyers," in William Cornish, Stuart Anderson, Ray Cocks, Michael Lobban, Patrick Polden, and Keith Smith, eds., *The Oxford History of the Laws of England,* vol. XI (Oxford: Oxford University Press, 2010), 1178–79.

63. Christopher W. Brooks and Michael Lobban, "Apprenticeship or Academy? The Idea of a Law University, 1830–1860," in Jonathan A. Bush and Alain

Wijfells, eds., *Learning the Law: Teaching and the Transmission of English Law, 1150–1900* (London: Hambledon, 1999), 353, 370, 382.

64. Pue, "Guild Training vs. Professional Education," 247, 250–51.

65. Quoted in Cocks, *Foundations of the Modern Bar,* 187.

66. Evidence Act 1851 (14 & 15 Vict., c. 99).

67. On Cox's career, see Cocks, *Foundations of the Modern Bar,* 64–71.

68. Neel, "Lawyers on Trial," 88.

69. Cocks, *Foundations of the Modern Bar,* 72.

70. "The Position of the Advocate," in *Law Magazine,* new ser. 48 (1852): 17, 223, 226.

71. Edward W. Cox, *The Advocate: His Training, Practice, Rights and Duties* (London: Law Times, 1852), 391, 375, 380–81, 377, emphasis in original.

72. Ibid., 392, emphasis in original.

73. See, e.g., W. T. S. Daniel, "On Advocacy as Connected with the Administration of Justice," in *Papers Read before the Juridical Society* 1 (12 Jan. 1859): 306; "License of Counsel," in *Law Magazine* 39 (1848): 55–56.

74. Cox, *Advocate,* 383–84, emphasis in original.

75. Ibid., 383–84, 398.

76. "The Moral Code of the Bar," in *Law Times* 40 (30 Sept. 1865): 575. See also "The Profession of Advocacy," in *Cornhill Magazine* 105 (1865): 110–11; T. N. Talfourd, "On the Principle of Advocacy as Developed in the Practice of the Bar," in *Law Magazine and Review,* new ser. 4 (1846): 12–13.

77. Cox, *Advocate,* 385, 390.

78. Cox, in *Law Times* 1 (1843): 15, quoted in Cocks, *Foundations of the Modern Bar,* 67.

79. Cox, *Advocate,* 392.

80. See Howard C. Warren, *A History of the Association Psychology* (New York: Charles Scribner's, 1921), 7; Robert M. Young, *Mind, Brain and Adaptation in the Nineteenth Century* (Oxford: Oxford University Press, 1970), 95.

81. David Hartley, *Observations on Man* (Gainesville, FL: Scholars' Facsimiles, 1966 [1749]), 374.

82. Alexander Bain, *The Senses and the Intellect,* 3rd ed. (New York: Appleton, 1874), 327; William Hamilton, *Lectures on Metaphysics and Logic,* 2nd ed. (Edinburgh: Blackwood and Sons, 1841), 2:231.

83. On the connection between pain and memory, see Alexander Bain, *On the Study of Character* (London: Parker and Sons, 1861), 264; on the connection between pain and lying, see Bain, *Mental and Moral Science* (London: Longmans, 1884 [1868]), 274; Thomas Brown, *Lectures on the Philosophy of the Mind* (Edinburgh: William Tait, 1840), 569.

84. Alexander Bain, *The Emotions and the Will*, 3rd ed. (New York: Appleton, 1888), 218.

85. James Ram, *A Treatise on Facts*, 3rd American ed. (New York: Baker, Voorhis, 1873 [1861]), 50, 50–51, 60–61, 141–42, 142.

86. William Wills, *Essay on the Principles of Circumstantial Evidence* (Philadelphia: T. and J. W. Johnson, 1853 [1838]), 248.

87. Ram, *Treatise on Facts*, 206–7, 169.

88. Ibid., 157, 158, 229.

89. See Alexander Welsh, *Strong Representations: Narrative and Circumstantial Evidence in England* (Baltimore: Johns Hopkins University Press, 1992), 15.

90. Starkie, *Practical Treatise of the Law of Evidence*, 1:160.

91. James Fitzjames Stephen, *A History of the Criminal Law of England* (New York: Franklin, 1964 [1883]), 1:401.

92. [James Fitzjames Stephen], "Oaths," in *Cornhill Magazine* 7 (1863): 527.

93. Wills, *Essay on the Principles of Circumstantial Evidence*, 31.

94. Richard Harris, *Hints on Advocacy*, 4th ed. (London: Waterlow, 1880), 84.

95. On relations between Chancery and common-law bars, see Joshua Getzler, "Chancery Reform and Law Reform," in *Law and History Review* 22 (2004): 601–8; Michael Lobban, "Preparing for Fusion: Reforming the Nineteenth-Century Court of Chancery, Part II" and "Forum Response: The Chancellor, the Chancery, and the History of Law Reform," in *Law and History Review* 22 (2004): 565–99 and 615–17; Patrick Polden, "Mingling the Waters: Personalities, Politics and the Making of the Supreme Court of Judicature," in *Cambridge Law Journal* 61 (2002): 575–611.

96. See, e.g., W. F. Finlason, "Illustrations of Our Judicial System," in *Law Magazine and Review*, 3rd ser. (1874): 180–88.

97. W. Wesley Pue, "Lawyers and Political Liberalism in Eighteenth- and Nineteenth-Century England," in Terence C. Halliday and Lucien Karpik, eds., *Lawyers and the Rise of Western Political Liberalism* (Oxford: Clarendon, 1997), 197, 199.

98. Stephen, "Professional Etiquette," 103.

99. A. V. Dicey, "Legal Etiquette," in *Fortnightly Review* 8 (July–Dec. 1867): 174.

100. "Disbarment of Edwin J. James, Q.C.," in *Law Magazine and Review* 12 (1862): 279, 268.

101. Lewis, *Victorian Bar*, 94–95; W. Wesley Pue, "Moral Panic at the English Bar," in *Law and Social Inquiry* 15 (1990): 49–118, see esp. 75–86.

102. On the suit against Thesiger and Cresswell, see Pue, "Moral Panic," 60–75. For a survey of Kennedy's career, see W. Wesley Pue, "Exorcising Profes-

sional Demons: Charles Rann Kennedy and the Transition to the Modern Bar," in *Law and History Review* 4 (1987): 152–72.

103. *Pall Mall Gazette* (London), 17 May 1867, 4.

104. *Law Journal* 2 (16 Aug. 1867): 371.

105. Cocks, *Foundations of the Modern Bar*, 219–20.

106. Francis Parker, "The Profession of Advocacy," in *Cornhill Magazine* 12 (1865): 110–11.

107. For a celebration of the prosecution's cross-examination in the criminal trial, see Richard Harris, *Illustrations in Advocacy* (London: Waterlow, 1884 [1879]) 227–48.

108. This account of the Claimant's story largely follows Frederick Herbert Maugham, *The Tichborne Case* (London: Hodder and Stoughton, 1936). For an excellent political history of the Tichborne movement, see Rohan McWilliam, *The Tichborne Claimant: A Victorian Sensation* (London: Continuum, 2007).

109. See, e.g., J. B. Atlay, *Famous Trials of the Century* (London: Grant Richards, 1899), 230; Serjeant Ballantine, *Some Experiences of a Barrister's Life* (New York: Henry Holt, 1882), 409; Hawkins, *Reminiscences*, 2: 307–8.

110. Lewis, *Victorian Bar*, 64.

111. See, e.g., *Daily Times* (London), 2 July 1874, in the Yale Tichborne Clipping File, 3:154, Special Collections, Yale Law Library, New Haven, CT (hereafter Yale Tichborne Clipping File).

112. For the full text of Kenealy's cross-examination of Roger Bellew, see *Daily Telegraph* (London), 6 June 1873, in Yale Tichborne Clipping File, 1:103.

113. "The License and the Punishment of Counsel," in *Law Times* 56 (7 Mar. 1874): 321.

114. Manchester *Guardian*, 3 Mar. 1874, in Yale Tichborne Clipping File, 4:809.

115. *Pall Mall Gazette* (London), reprinted in *Law Times* 56 (7 Mar. 1874): 332.

116. *Pall Mall Gazette* (London), reprinted in *Law Times* 56 (14 Mar. 1874): 352.

117. "License and Punishment of Counsel," 321.

118. Ibid.

119. "Dr. Kenealy," in *Law Journal* 9 (11 Apr. 1874): 200.

120. Ibid.

121. *Solicitors' Journal* 18 (21 Mar. 1874): 373.

122. "Dr. Kenealy," in *Law Journal* 9 (14 Mar. 1874): 139.

123. Ibid., 140.

124. "Dr. Kenealy" (11 Apr. 1874): 200.

125. "Dr. Kenealy and Gray's Inn," in *Law Journal* 9 (21 Mar. 1874): 157.

126. "Dr. Kenealy" (11 Apr. 1874): 200.

127. "Dr. Kenealy and the Bar of the Oxford Circuit," in *Solicitors' Journal* 18 (11 Apr. 1874): 439.

128. *Law Times* 56 (11 Apr. 1874): 409.

129. *Solicitors' Journal* 18 (9 May 1874): 516.

130. Michael Roe, *Kenealy and the Tichborne Cause* (Melbourne: Melbourne University Press, 1974), 72.

131. *Law Times* 57 (8 Aug. 1874): 274.

132. "Dr. Kenealy," *Solicitors' Journal* 19 (28 Nov. 1874): 64.

133. *Law Times* 58 (5 Dec. 1874): 84.

134. Harris, *Illustrations in Advocacy,* 89.

135. Harris, *Hints on Advocacy,* 88–89.

136. *Parl. Deb.*, 3rd ser., 328 (4 July 1888): 345.

137. Ibid., 352.

138. Herschell, *Rights and Duties of an Advocate,* 18.

139. "Cross-examination," in *Law Times* 102 (16 Jan. 1897): 239.

140. James Fitzjames Stephen, *A Digest of the Law of Evidence,* 2nd ed. (St. Louis: F. H. Thomas, 1879), 145.

141. Ibid.

142. Baron Bramwell, "Cross-examination," in *Nineteenth Century* 31 (Feb. 1892): 186.

143. Ram, *Treatise on Facts,* 227–28.

144. Herschell, *Rights and Duties of an Advocate,* 20.

145. *Munster v. Lamb* (1883), 11 Q.B.D. 588.

146. *Munster v. Lamb,* 596.

147. Lewis Sturge, *Basic Rules of the Supreme Court* (London: Butterworths, 1961), 90.

148. See *Law Journal* 18 (14 July 1883): 383; "The New Rules of Court," in *Solicitors' Journal* 27 (23 Aug. 1883): 691.

149. *Solicitors' Journal* 31 (27 Nov. 1886): 71.

150. Gail Savage, "'. . . Equality from the Masculine Point of View . . .': The 2nd Earl Russell and Divorce Law Reform in England," in *Russell: The Journal of the Bertrand Russell Archives,* new ser. 16 (summer 1996): 67–84.

151. This account of the Russell divorce case has been reconstructed from the extensive reports published in the *Times*. See the *Times* (London), 2 Dec. 1891, 3–4; 3 Dec. 1891, 13–14; 4 Dec. 1891, 13–14; 5 Dec. 1891, 7.

152. The *Times* (London), 3 Dec. 1891, 13. On prosecutions for homosexual sodomy during the Victorian period, see H. G. Cocks, *Nameless Offences: Homosexual Desire in the 19th Century* (London: I. B. Tauris, 2003).

153. The *Times* (London), 3 Dec. 1891, 14.

154. The *Times* (London), 4 Dec. 1891, 14.

155. The *Times* (London), 5 Dec. 1891, 7.

156. The *Times* (London), 4 Dec. 1891, 14.

157. The *Times* (London), 5 Dec. 1891, 7.

158. This account of *Osborne v. Hargreave & Wife* has been reconstructed from the extensive reports published in The *Times*. See the *Times* (London), 12 Dec. 1891; 16 Dec. 1891, 3–4; 18 Dec. 1891, 14; 21 Dec. 1891, 13–14; 22 Dec. 1891, 4; 23 Dec. 1891, 4, 7; 28 Dec. 1891, 9; 29 Dec. 1891, 5; 6 Feb. 1892, 9; 10 Mar. 1892, 3; 23 Mar. 1892, 11; 29 Mar. 1892, 11; 14 Apr. 1892, 4.

159. The *Times* (London), 16 Dec. 1891, 3.

160. Ibid.

161. The *Times* (London), 20 Oct. 1891, 13; 3 Nov. 1891, 5.

162. The *Times* (London), 23 Dec. 1891, 4.

163. Ibid., 7.

164. The *Times* (London), 28 Dec. 1891, 9; 29 Dec. 1891, 5.

165. The *Times* (London) 6 Feb. 1892, 9.

166. See M. E. Rodgers, "Gendered Assumptions—Madness, Pregnancy and Childbirth," in Judith Rowbotham and Kim Stevenson, eds., *Behaving Badly: Social Panic and Moral Outrage* (London: Ashgate, 2003), 211; Sally Shuttleworth, *Charlotte Brontë and Victorian Psychiatry* (Cambridge: Cambridge University Press, 1996), 71–98.

167. Quoted in *Law Journal* 27 (9 Jan. 1892): 16. The *Law Journal* angrily rejected the notion of class justice. While conceding that the sufferings of elite convicts might be greater, they found this consideration was "outweighed by the fact that the refined inherit a stronger power of resisting punishment."

168. The *Times* (London), 23 Dec. 1891, 7.

169. Edward Manson, "Cross-examination: A Socratic Fragment," in *Law Quarterly Review* 8 (1892): 160–61.

170. Letter from Counsel, The *Times* (London), 31 Dec. 1891, 12.

171. Lewis, *Victorian Bar*, 34.

172. Letter from Witness Box, the *Times* (London), 30 Dec. 1891, 10.

173. Editorial, the *Times* (London), 2 Jan. 1892, 7.

174. James Q. Whitman, *Harsh Justice: Criminal Punishment and the Widening Divide between America and Europe* (Oxford: Oxford University Press, 2003), 7.

175. On the Prince of Wales's involvement with a case, see W. Teignmouth Shore, ed., *The Baccarat Case* (Toronto: Canada Law Book, 1932), 75–80. The prince was called upon to testify in a slander case involving the accusation that the plaintiff had cheated at cards.

176. Letter from Huxham and Browns, the *Times* (London), 6 Jan. 1892, 3.

177. Letter from J.H.P., the *Times* (London), 29 Dec. 1891, 10.

178. Letter from J.P., the *Times* (London), 30 Dec. 1891, 10; Letter from Temple Bar to E.C., the *Times* (London), 31 Dec. 1891, 12.

179. Letter from An Equity QC, the *Times* (London), 2 Jan. 1892, 10.

180. Letter from R. St. J. Corbet, the *Times* (London), 28 Dec. 1891, 9.

181. Letter from A Barrister of 17 Years' Standing, the *Times* (London), 29 Dec. 1891, 10.

182. Letter from Counsel, the *Times* (London), 31 Dec. 1891, 12.

183. "Cross-examination as a Forensic Art," in *Law Times* 92 (2 Jan. 1892): 138.

184. *Solicitors' Journal* 36 (9 Jan. 1892): 159.

185. *Law Journal* 27 (2 Jan. 1892): 1. The rule in question: R.S.C. ord. 36, R 38.

186. *Solicitors' Journal* 36 (2 Jan. 1892): 146; (9 Jan. 1892): 158.

187. *Law Journal* 26 (19 Dec. 1891): 783–84.

188. Letter from W. T. Dooner, Lt. Col., Royal Inniskilling Fusiliers, the *Times* (London), 1 Jan. 1892, 5.

189. Bramwell, "Cross-examination," 184.

190. Letter from R.A.M., the *Times* (London), 6 Jan. 1892, 3.

191. Letter from W.L.B., the *Times* (London), 2 Jan. 1892, 10.

192. Letter from A Good Witness, the *Times* (London), 31 Dec. 1891, 12.

193. "Cross-examination as a Forensic Art," in *Law Times* 92 (2 Jan. 1892): 138.

194. Bramwell, "Cross-examination," 183.

195. Letter from A Barrister of Twelve Years' Standing, the *Times* (London), 30 Dec. 1891, 10.

196. Letter from A Barrister of Twelve Years' Standing, the *Times* (London), 1 Jan. 1892, 5.

197. Letter from King's Bench Walk, the *Times* (London), 2 Jan. 1892, 10.

198. *Law Journal* 27 (9 Jan. 1892): 16.

199. Letter from R.A.M., the *Times* (London), 6 Jan. 1892, 3.

200. *Law Journal* 26 (12 Dec. 1891): 769.

201. Letter from Russell to Santayana dated 19 Dec. 1891, quoted in Savage, "Equality from the Masculine Point of View," 81.

202. Herschell, *Rights and Duties of an Advocate*, 14.

203. Ibid., 20.

204. Harris, *Illustrations in Advocacy*, 244.

205. On the ambiguity of the rules governing cross-examination in the eighteenth and earlier nineteenth century, see Langbein, *Origins*, 283–84.

206. Bramwell, "Cross-examination," 186.

207. Thomas Starkie, *A Practical Treatise of the Law of Evidence* (London: J. & W. T. Clarke, 1824), 1:137.

208. S. March Phillipps, *A Treatise on the Law of Evidence,* 4th ed. (London: A. Stahan, 1820), 1:293–94.

209. S. March Phillipps, *A Treatise on the Law of Evidence,* 8th ed. (London: Saunders and Benning, 1838) 917–20.

210. *Parl. Deb.,* 3rd ser., 124 (10 Mar. 1853), 1367–68.

211. John Pitt Taylor, *A Treatise on the Law of Evidence,* 2nd ed. (London: W. Maxwell, 1855), 2:1136–37.

212. "Cross-examination to Credit," in *Pall Mall Gazette* (17 June 1873), 1.

213. William Oldnall Russell, *A Treatise on Crimes and Misdemeanors* (London: T & J. W. Johnson, 1877), 2:541.

214. See, e.g., *Solicitors' Journal* 20 (2 Sept. 1876): 855–56.

215. Ernest Bowen-Rowlands, "Examination and Cross-examination as to Character," in *Law Quarterly Review* 11 (1895): 23.

216. *Solicitors' Journal* 23 (8 Feb. 1879): 270.

217. "Cross-examination as to Character," in *Law Journal* 8 (6 Dec. 1873), 718.

218. "Cross-examining Witnesses," in *Law Journal* 8 (30 Aug. 1873): 504.

219. "Cross-examination as to Character," in *Law Journal* 8 (6 Dec. 1873): 718.

220. "Cross-examination to Credit," in *Law Journal* 11 (23 Sept. 1876): 532.

221. "The Use and Abuse of Cross-examination," in *Solicitors' Journal* 23 (1878): 523.

222. *Solicitors' Journal* 20 (2 Sept. 1876): 855–56.

223. *Solicitors' Journal* 36 (9 Jan. 1892): 158–59.

224. "Cross-examination to Credit," in *Law Journal* 11 (23 Sept. 1876): 531.

Chapter Three. Perjury and Prevarication in British India

1. India Political Department, Foreign Letter, 25 May 1858, No. 9 of 1858, India Office Records, Oriental and India Office Collections, British Library (hereafter IOR), F/4/2723.

2. Ibid.

3. Perjury, suggestion to defile natives accused of, 30 Aug. 1858, draft No. 53 of 1858, IOR E/4/854.

4. Diane Kirkby and Catherine Coleborne, "Introduction," in Diane Kirkby and Catherine Coleborne, eds., *Law, History, Colonialism: The Reach of Empire* (Manchester: Manchester University Press, 2001), 3.

5. Peter Fitzpatrick, *The Mythology of Modern Law* (London: Routledge, 1992), 107.

6. Thomas R. Metcalf, *Ideologies of the Raj: The New Cambridge History of India, Vol. 3* (Cambridge: Cambridge University Press, 1995), 39.
7. Martin Chanock, "Criminological Science and the Criminal Law on the Colonial Periphery," in *Law and Social Inquiry* 20 (1995): 938.
8. See, e.g., John L. Comaroff, "Images of Empire, Contests of Conscience," in Frederick Cooper and Ann Laura Stoler, eds., *Tensions of Empire: Colonial Cultures in a Bourgeois World* (Berkeley: University of California Press, 1997), 165; Markus Dirk Dubber, *The Police Power: Patriarchy and the Foundations of American Government* (New York: Columbia University Press, 2005), 91.
9. House of Commons, "Answers of the Judges of Circuit to Interrogatories," *Parliamentary Papers,* 1812–13, X, 250.
10. John L. Comaroff, "Colonialism, Culture, and the Law: A Foreword," in *Law and Social Inquiry* 26 (2001): 311.
11. Metcalf, *Ideologies of the Raj,* 24.
12. James Mill, *The History of British India,* 4th ed. (London: James Madden, 1848), 5:613.
13. On ideas about native chicanery, see Ranajit Guha, *An Indian Historiography of India: A Nineteenth-Century Agenda and Its Implications* (Calcutta: K. P. Bagchi, 1988), 10.
14. Metcalf, *Ideologies of the Raj,* 12.
15. Thomas D. Morris, *Southern Slavery and the Law, 1619–1860* (Chapel Hill: University of North Carolina Press, 1996), 233.
16. Nicholas Dirks, "Foreword," in Bernard S. Cohn, *Colonialism and Its Forms of Knowledge: The British in India* (Princeton, NJ: Princeton University Press, 1996), ix.
17. Cohn, ibid., 4.
18. C. A. Bayly, *Empire and Information: Intelligence Gathering and Social Communication in India, 1780–1870* (Cambridge: Cambridge University Press, 1996), 167–68.
19. See ibid., 151–54; C. A. Bayly, "Knowing the Country: Empire and Transformation in India," in *Modern Asian Studies* 27 (1993): 38; Radhika Singha, "'Providential Circumstances': The Thuggee Campaign of the 1830s and Legal Innovation," in *Modern Asian Studies* 27 (1993): 83.
20. Joachim Hayward Stocqueler, *The Hand-Book of India, A Guide to the Stranger and the Traveller, and a Companion to the Resident* (London, 1845), 142.
21. George Hadley, *A Compendious Grammar of the Current Corrupt Dialect of the Jargon of Hindostan* (London: J. Sewell, 1801), 231, 236, quoted in Bayly, "Knowing the Country," 288.

22. J. Statham, *Indian Recollections* (London: Samuel Bagster, 1832), 127.

23. William Buyers, *Recollections of Northern India* (London: John Snow, 1848), 505.

24. William Henry Sleeman, *Rambles and Recollections of an Indian Official* (London: J. Hatchard and Son, 1844), 2:109–45.

25. Metcalf, *Ideologies of the Raj*, 41.

26. Cohn, *Colonialism and Its Forms of Knowledge*, 66; J. Duncan M. Derrett, *Religion, Law and the State in India* (New York: Free Press, 1968).

27. Tapas Kumar Banerjee, *Background to Indian Criminal Law* (Bombay: Orient Longmans, 1963), 40; George Claus Rankin, *Background to Indian Law* (Cambridge: Cambridge University Press, 1946), 164–65.

28. Niharkana Majumdar, *Justice and Police in Bengal, 1756–1793: A Study of the Nizamat in Decline* (Calcutta: K. L. Mukhopadhyay, 1960), 326 (appendix F).

29. Satya Prakash Sangar, *Crime and Punishment in Mughal India* (New Delhi: Reliance Publishing House, 1967), 37–38.

30. Charles Hamilton, *The Hedaya or Guide, A Commentary on the Mussulman Laws* (New Delhi: Kitab Bhavan, 1982 [1791]), 372.

31. Derrett, *Religion, Law and the State in India*, 239–41.

32. Rankin, *Background to Indian Law*, 190.

33. Nathaniel Brassey Halhed, *A Code of Gentoo Laws, or, Ordinations of the Pundits, From a Persian Translation, Made from the Original, written in the Shanscrit Language* (London, 1776), 127.

34. Ibid., 128.

35. Douglas Haynes and Gyan Prakash, "Introduction: The Entanglement of Power and Resistance," in Douglas Haynes and Gyan Prakash, eds., *Contesting Power: Resistance and Everyday Social Relations in South Asia* (Berkeley: University of California Press, 1991), 2. On resistance and the study of colonial legal institutions, see also Sally Engle Merry, "Resistance and the Cultural Power of Law," in *Law and Society Review* 29 (1995): 11.

36. John D. Rogers, "Cultural and Social Resistance: Gambling in Colonial Sri Lanka," in Haynes and Prakash, *Contesting Power*, 194.

37. See "Government v. Degumbur Gowallah and Others," in *Nizamut Adawlut Reports* 4 (4 Feb. 1831): 10; "Government v. Haro Mochee," in *Nizamut Adawlut Reports* 4 (19 Dec. 1831): 99; "Government v. Sumbhoo, Aged 23," in *Nizamut Adawlut Reports* 4 (5 Oct. 1835): 259; "Case of Sopannah bin Kalljee," in *Reports of Cases in the Court of Sudder Foujdaree Adawlut* 1 (15 Sept. 1841): 144.

38. "Government v. Soomut Rajpoot," in *Nizamut Adawlut Reports* 2 (16 Jan. 1824): 313.

39. "Government v. Mahommed Alee," in *Nizamut Adawlut Reports* 2 (17 Sept. 1822): 204.

40. "Government v. Ramsoondur Bhagul," in *Nizamut Adawlut Reports* 2 (21 Feb. 1825): 363; "Case of Luxiah bin Budiah Bheel," in *Reports of Cases in the Court of Sudder Foujdaree Adawlut* 1 (31 July 1837): 116.

41. "Government v. Sheeboo Doss Byragee," in *Nizamut Adawlut Reports* 5 (12 Oct. 1839): 144.

42. Mahabir Prashad Jain, *Outlines of Indian Legal History* (Bombay: N. M. Tripathi, 1952), 70–130, 143–99.

43. Ibid., 154.

44. Orby Mootham, *The East India Company's Sadar Courts, 1801–1834* (Bombay: N. M. Tripathi, 1983).

45. Jain, *Outlines of Indian Legal History*, 154–58, 197.

46. Mootham, *East Indian Company's Sadar Courts*, 23, 47.

47. Jain, *Outlines of Indian Legal History*, 152, 397–402.

48. Jörg Fisch, *Cheap Lives and Dear Limbs: The British Transformation of the Bengal Criminal Law* (Wiesbaden: F. Steiner, 1983).

49. Letter from the Third Judge, Circuit Court, Dacca Division, to the Register of the Nizamut Adawlut, 10 Oct. 1797, in Bengal Proceedings, 24 Nov. 1797, No. 24, IOR P/128/34.

50. Resolution of the Court, Nizamut Adawlut, in Bengal Proceedings, 24 Nov. 1797, No. 24, IOR P/128/34.

51. Clare Anderson, *Legible Bodies: Race, Criminality and Colonialism in South Asia* (London: Bloomsbury Academic Press, 2004), 16.

52. Extract from the Proceedings of the Nizamut Adawlut, 8 Nov. 1797, in Bengal Proceedings, 24 Nov. 1797, No. 24, IOR P/128/34.

53. Letter from the Deputy Register of the Nizamut Adawlut to G. H. Burlow, Secretary to Government, Bengal, 22 Nov. 1797, in Bengal Proceedings, 24 Nov. 1797, No. 18, IOR P/128/34.

54. Regulation XVII of 1797, Sec. 3.

55. Ibid.

56. Ibid., Sec. 2.

57. Radhika Singha, *A Despotism of Law: Crime and Justice in Early Colonial India* (Oxford: Oxford University Press, 1998), 245.

58. Anderson, *Legible Bodies*, 19.

59. House of Commons, "Answers of the Judges of Circuit to Interrogatories of Government, New System of Revenue and of Judicial Administration 1801," *Parliamentary Papers* 1812–13, IX, Jessore, 16; Juanpore, 33; Hooghly, 45; Nuddea, 55; Burdwan, 67, 24; Pergunnas, 74; Sylhet, 131; Sarun, 240.

60. Ibid., Backergunge, 117; Tipperah, 124; Moorshedabad, 179; Patna, 232; Benares, 276.

61. Ibid., 226–27.

62. Ibid., 56–57.

63. Ibid., 149, 164, 257, 287, 196.

64. Ibid., 251.

65. Letter from J. Lumsden, Register to the Nizamut Adawlut, to Henry St. George Tucker, Secretary to Government in the Revenue and Judicial Departments, Bengal, in Bengal Proceedings, 19 Mar. 1801, IOR P/128/54. My thanks to Ray Cocks for directing me to this source.

66. Regulation III of 1801, Sec. 1.

67. F. L. Beaufort, *A Digest of the Criminal Law of the Presidency of Fort William* (Calcutta: Thacker, Spink, 1850), 655–56.

68. Regulation III of 1801, Sec. 2.

69. Jain, *Outlines of Indian Legal History,* 185–87; Samuel Schmitthener, "A Sketch of the Development of the Legal Profession in India," *Law and Society Review* 3 (1968–69): 349–55.

70. Regulation III of 1801, Sec. 1.

71. Letter from W. B. Bayley, Secretary to Government, to Register, Nizamat Adawlut, 16 Feb. 1817, in Bengal Criminal Consultation, 16 Feb. 1817, IOR P/132/64.

72. Regulation XVII of 1817, Sec. IV.

73. Regulation II of 1807, Sec. II, Cl. 2.

74. Regulation XVII of 1817, Sec. XIV, Cl. 4.

75. Fisch, *Cheap Lives and Dear Limbs,* 84.

76. Regulation VIII of 1793, Sec. LXII.

77. Regulation II of 1819, Sec. XIX, Cl. 2; Regulation VII of 1822, Sec. XIX, Cl. 2.

78. See, e.g., Bombay Regulations II of 1812, Sec. VIII; IV of 1819, Sec. XIII; X of 1827, Sec. IX.

79. Henry Strachey Papers, Folder 190, in Strachey Papers, IOR MSS Eur F 128.

80. Henry Strachey, "On the moral character of the Hindoos as described in Mill's British India, with some general reflexions on the evidence of national character," Henry Strachey Papers, Folder 218, in Strachey Papers, IOR MSS Eur F 128.

81. House of Commons, "Criminal Offenders (Committals Statistics)," *Parliamentary Papers* 1835, XLV, 21. In 1830, there were nine convictions out of eighteen committals.

82. Rankin, *Background to Indian Law,* 183.

83. Regulation VII of 1802, Sec. XL, Cl. 2, Cl. 1.

84. For prohibition of prosecution of parties, see Regulation I of 1810 and Extract from the Proceedings of the Foujdaree Adawlut, 14 Mar. 1809, in Madras Proceedings, 27 Mar. 1810, IOR P/322/45; for the reenactment, see Regulation IX of 1816; for extension to criminal cases, see Regulation II of 1822; for extension to all tribunals, see Regulation VIII of 1829.

85. Regulation VI of 1811. See also Judicial Consultation, Madras, 23 Apr. 1811, IOR P/322/56.

86. C.O. 31 Jan. 1814, in Circular Orders of the Court of Foujdaree Udalut, from 1803 to 30th June 1834, at 4, 3, 5 (Madras, 1835), IOR V/27/144/48.

87. C.O. 3 May 1821, in Circular Orders of the Court of Foujdaree Udalut, from 1803 to 30th June 1834, at 47–48 (Madras, 1835), IOR V/27/144/48.

88. Letter from Thomas Warden, Esq., Second Judge on Circuit, Western Division, to the Register of the Foujdarry Adawlut, 20 Nov. 1822, in Board Collections, Judicial Letter, 31 Dec. 1823, No. 22906, IOR F/4/867.

89. Extract from the Proceedings of the Foujdarry Adawlut, 30 Dec. 1822, in Board Collections, Judicial Letter, 31 Dec. 1823, No. 22906, IOR F/4/867.

90. Ibid.; Letter from D. Hill, Secretary to Government, to Board for Preparing Regulation, 18 Apr. 1823, in Board Collections, Judicial Letter, 31 Dec. 1823, No. 22906, IOR F/4/867; Letter from W. Oliver, Register of the Foujdarry Adawlut, to D. Hill, Secretary to Government, 9 July 1823, in Board Collections, Judicial Letter, 31 Dec. 1823, No. 22906, IOR F/4/867.

91. Letter from R. Clarke, Secretary to Regulation Board, to D. Hill, Secretary to Government, 18 Dec. 1823, in Board Collections, Judicial Letter, 31 Dec. 1823, No. 22906, IOR F/4/867.

92. Letter from W. Hudleston, Register of the Foujdarry Adawlut, to D. Hill, Secretary to Government, 30 Jan. 1823, in Board Collections, Judicial Letter, 31 Dec. 1823, No. 22906, IOR F/4/867.

93. Note that this is a description of procedure in Bengal; Madras was somewhat different, in that more of the local level policing remained in the hands of traditional officials.

94. George Campbell, *Modern India: A Sketch of the System of Civil Government* (London: John Murray, 1852), 459.

95. Lt. Col. Archibald Galloway, *Observations on the Law and Constitution, and Present Government of India*, 2nd. ed. (London, 1832), 349. See also Judicial Letter to Madras, 29 Apr. 1814, in *Selections of Papers from the Records at the East-India House, Relating to the Revenue, Police and Civil and Criminal Justice, Under the Company's Government in India*, Vol. II (London, 1820), 240.

96. Letter from C. M. Lushington, Second Judge of Circuit, Southern Division,

to W. Hudleston, Register to the Foujdarry Adawlut, 17 Aug. 1825, in Judicial Letter, 23 Jan. 1827, Board Collection No. 28516, IOR F/4/1035.

97. Proceedings of the Foujdarry Adawlut, 16 Dec. 1825, in Judicial Letter, 23 Jan. 1827, Board Collection No. 28516, IOR F/4/1035.

98. Letter from J. M. McLeod, Secretary to Government, to Herbert Compton, Advocate General, 24 Feb. 1826, in Judicial Letter, 23 Jan. 1827, Board Collection No. 28516, IOR F/4/1035.

99. Letter from Herbert Compton, Advocate-General, to D. Mill, Chief Secretary to Government, 6 Mar. 1826, in Judicial Letter, 23 Jan. 1827, Board Collection No. 28516, IOR F/4/1035.

100. Letter from J. M. McLeod, Secretary to Government, Judicial Department, to W. Hudleston, Register of the Foujdarry Adawlut, 17 Mar. 1826, in Judicial Letter, 23 Jan. 1827, Board Collection No. 28516, IOR F/4/1035.

101. Proceedings of the Foujdarry Adawlut, 21 June 1826, in Judicial Letter, 23 Jan. 1827, Board Collection No. 28516, IOR F/4/1035.

102. For the government's advocacy of change, see Letter from J. M. McLeod, Secretary to Government, Judicial Department, to G. J. Casamajor, Register of the Foujdarry Adawlut, 18 July 1826, in Judicial Letter, 23 Jan. 1827, Board Collection No. 28516, IOR F/4/1035; for the court's agreement, see Letter from G. J. Casamajor, Register of the Foujdarry Adawlut, to J. M. McLeod, Secretary to Government, Judicial Department, 28 Aug. 1826, in Judicial Letter, 23 Jan. 1827, Board Collection No. 28516, IOR F/4/1035.

103. Regulation III of 1826.

104. Letter from G. J. Casamajor, Register of the Foujdarry Adawlut, to J. M. McLeod, Secretary to Government, Judicial Department, 28 Aug. 1826, in Judicial Letter, 23 Jan. 1827, Board Collection No. 28516, IOR F/4/1035.

105. Regulation III of 1826, Sec. 3.

106. Ibid., Sec. 2., Cl. 2.

107. C.O. 23 Nov. 1826, in Circular Orders of the Court of Foujdaree Udalut, from 1803 to 30th June 1834, at 141–42 (Madras, 1835), IOR V/27/144/48.

108. Regulation XIII of 1832.

109. Indian Law Commissioners, *Second Report on the Indian Penal Code* (Calcutta, 1847), IOR V/26/100/6, 60.

110. Letter from G. J. Casamajor, Register of the Foujdarry Adawlut, to the Acting Secretary to Government, 27 Feb. 1827, in Judicial Letter, 20 Mar. 1833, Board Collection No. 52893, IOR F/4/1336.

111. Letter from W. Lavie, Assistant Criminal Judge, Combaconum, to the Register of the Provincial Court of Circuit, Southern District, 22 Feb. 1827, in Judicial Letter, 20 Mar. 1833, Board Collection No. 52893, IOR F/4/1336.

112. Letter from J. Monro, Magistrate of Tinnevelly, to Register of the Court of Circuit, Southern Division, 21 Feb. 1827, in Judicial Letter, 20 Mar. 1833, Board Collection No. 52893, IOR F/4/1336.

113. Letter from A. Sinclair, Acting Magistrate, Tanjore, to Register of the Court of Circuit, Southern Division, 21 Feb. 1827, in Judicial Letter, 20 Mar. 1833, Board Collection No. 52893, IOR F/4/1336.

114. Letter from S. Nicholls, Criminal Judge of Madura, to Register of the Court of Circuit, Southern Division, 21 Feb. 1827, in Judicial Letter, 20 Mar. 1833, Board Collection No. 52893, IOR F/4/1336.

115. For fines, see Letter from W. Lavie, Assistant Criminal Judge, Combaconum, to the Register of the Provincial Court of Circuit, Southern District, 22 Feb. 1827, in Judicial Letter, 20 Mar. 1833, Board Collection No. 52893, IOR F/4/1336; for degrading punishment, see Minute of James Taylor, First Judge, Trichinopoly, 17 Mar. 1827, in Judicial Letter, 20 Mar. 1833, Board Collection No. 52893, IOR F/4/1336; for imprisonment and fines, see Minute of John Bird, Third Judge, Trichinopoly, 12 Mar. 1827, in Judicial Letter, 20 Mar. 1833, Board Collection No. 52893, IOR F/4/1336; for lashings, see Letter from H. Dickinson, Magistrate, Trichinopoly, to the Register of the Court of Circuit, Southern Division, 2 Mar. 1827, and Letter from J. Sullivan, Magistrate, Coimbatore, to the Register of the Court of Circuit, Southern Division, 22 Feb. 1827, in Judicial Letter, 20 Mar. 1833, Board Collection No. 52893, IOR F/4/1336.

116. Letter from E. Smalley, Magistrate, Nellore, to Register of the Court of Circuit, Northern Division, 22 Feb. 1827, in Judicial Letter, 20 Mar. 1833, Board Collection No. 52893, IOR F/4/1336.

117. Letter from R. Bayard, Magistrate, Ganjam, to Register of the Court of Circuit, Northern Division, 8 Mar. 1827, in Judicial Letter, 20 Mar. 1833, Board Collection No. 52893, IOR F/4/1336.

118. Draft Regulation for better prosecution and punishment of false and wilfully malicious accusations of heinous crimes, in Judicial Letter, 20 Mar. 1833, Board Collection No. 52893, IOR F/4/1336.

119. Regulation IX of 1832, Sec. II.

120. "Bhola Pandeh v. Sumbhoo Rajpoot," in *Nizamut Adawlut Reports* 1 (16 Aug. 1813): 284. See also "Government v. Mussummaut Kukha," in *Nizamut Adawlut Reports* 1 (27 Sept. 1815): 314.

121. C.O. No. 126, 18 July 1841, in C. G. Cheap, ed., *Circular Orders Passed by the Nizamut Adawlut for the Lower and Western Provinces and Communicated to the Criminal Authorities in the Bengal and Agra Provinces by the Registers of those Courts, from 1796 to 1844 Inclusive* (Calcutta, 1846), 375.

122. Letter from J. Hawkins, Register, Nizamut Adawlut, to F. J. Halliday, Secretary to the Government of Bengal, Judicial Department, 22 July 1842, in Legislative Letter, 17 Mar. 1843, Board Collection No. 90255, IOR F/4/2016.

123. Construction No. 656, 2 Sept. 1831, in *Constructions by the Courts of the Sudder Dewanny & Nizamut Adawlut of the Regulations and Laws, for the Civil Government of the Whole of the Territories under the Presidency of Fort William in Bengal* (Calcutta: F. Carbury, 1833), 2:21–22.

124. Ibid., 2:22–23.

125. C.O. No. 34, 4 Mar. 1850, in J. Carrau, ed., *Circular Orders of the Court of Nizamut Adawlut, Communicated to the Criminal Authorities, from 1796 to 1853 inclusive* (Calcutta: Thacker, Spink, 1855), 439.

126. Motilal Chimanlal Setalvad, *The Common Law in India*, 2nd ed. (Bombay: N. M. Tripathi, 1970), 126.

127. Rankin, *Background to Indian Law*, 200–201.

128. John Clive, *Macaulay: The Shaping of the Historian* (Cambridge, MA: Belknap Press, 1973), 295–96; George Otto Trevelyan, *The Life and Letters of Lord Macaulay* (London: Longmans, 1876), 1:378–80.

129. Trevelyan, *Life and Letters*, 1:379.

130. Ibid., 1:380.

131. Clive, *Macaulay*, 427; David Skuy, "Macaulay and the Indian Penal Code of 1862: The Myth of the Inherent Superiority and Modernity of the English Legal System Compared to India's Legal System in the Nineteenth Century," in *Modern Asian Studies* 32 (1998): 517.

132. Letter from T. B. Macaulay to Lord Auckland, Governor-General, 14 Oct. 1837, reprinted in Whitely Stokes, *The Anglo-Indian Codes* (Oxford: Clarendon, 1892), 1:2 n.3. See also "Letter from the Indian Law Commissioners, 2 May 1837," in C. D. Dharker, ed., *Lord Macaulay's Legislative Minutes* (Oxford: Oxford University Press, 1946), 260–61.

133. Letter from Macaulay to Auckland, in Stokes, *Anglo-Indian Codes*, 1:2 n.3.

134. Macaulay, "Legislative Minute No. 28, n.d.," in Dharker, ed., *Lord Macaulay's Legislative Minutes*, 256.

135. Clive, *Macaulay*, 442–43.

136. *A Penal Code Prepared by the Indian Law Commissioner and Published by Command of the Governor General of India in Council*, ¶¶ 188–200 (Calcutta, 1837), IOR W935.

137. Ibid., ¶ 188.

138. Ibid., ¶ 189.

139. Ibid., ¶¶ 191, 192.

140. "Notes on the Indian Penal Code," reprinted in Thomas Babington Macaulay, *Miscellaneous Works of Lord Macaulay,* ed. Lady Trevelyan, vol. 4 (New York: Harper and Brothers, 1880), 194–95.

141. For the Benthamite debate on universal versus local legislation, see Kartik Kalyan Raman, "Utilitarianism and the Criminal Law in Colonial India: A Study of the Practical Limits of Utilitarian Jurisprudence," in *Modern Asian Studies* 28 (1994): 739.

142. "Notes on the Indian Penal Code," 238.

143. Ibid., 240–42.

144. Indian Law Commissioners, *Second Report,* 52, 55.

145. Ibid., 57, 61, 60.

146. Act XLV of 1860.

147. Walter Morgan and Arthur George MacPherson, *The Indian Penal Code (Act XLV, of 1860) with Notes* (Calcutta: G. C. Hay, 1863), §§ 193, 205.

148. India Legislative Consultations, 27 Feb. 1840, IOR P/207/9.

149. Letter from P. Willoughby, Secretary to the Government of Bombay, to the Officiating Secretary to the Government of India in the Legislative Department, 21 Dec. 1839, in India Legislative Consultations, 27 Feb. 1840, IOR P/207/9.

150. Letter from T. H. Davidson, Acting Register, Sudr Adawlut, to the Secretary to Government, 9 Dec. 1839, in India Legislative Consultations, 27 Feb. 1840, IOR P/207/9.

151. Letter from the Judges of the Madras Sudr Adawlut, to the Indian Law Commissioners, 28 June 1836, in India Legislative Consultations, 27 Feb. 1840, IOR P/207/9.

152. Minute of the Acting Puisne Judge, 26 June 1836, in India Legislative Consultations, 27 Feb. 1840, IOR P/207/9.

153. Letter from Hawkins, Register, to F. J. Halliday, Secretary to the Government in the Judicial Department, Bengal, 29 Nov. 1839, in India Legislative Consultations, 27 Feb. 1840, IOR P/207/9.

154. Letter from N. V. Smith, Officiating Register, Sadr Adawlut, NWP, to J. Davidson, Officiating Secretary to Government, NWP, 27 Dec. 1839, in India Legislative Consultations, 27 Feb. 1840, IOR P/207/9.

155. Letter from Sutherland, Secretary to the Indian Law Commission, to J. P. Grant, Officiating Secretary to the Government of India, Legislative Department, 3 Feb. 1840, in India Legislative Consultations, 27 Feb. 1840, IOR P/207/9.

156. Minute by A. Amos, n.d., in India Legislative Consultations, 27 Feb. 1840, IOR P/207/9.

157. Act V of 1840, Sec. I.

158. For all statistics, see Despatch from Government of India, to the Court of Directors in the Home Department, 13 Nov. 1847, in Legislative Letter, 13 Nov. 1847, Board Collection No. 113843, IOR F/4/2255.

159. Judicial Department, 18 July 1849, IOR E/4/1088.

160. Letter from A. Shakespear, Assistant Secretary to Government, 26 Feb. 1847, in Legislative Letter, 13 Nov. 1847, Board Collection No. 113843, IOR F/4/2255.

161. Bombay Judicial Letter, 15 Nov. 1851, Board Collection No. 137551, IOR F/4/2466.

162. Letter from M. Larken, Register, Bombay Sudr Foujdaree, to J. G. Lumsden, Secretary to Government, Bombay, 4 June 1850, in Bombay Judicial Letter, 15 Nov. 1851, Board Collection No. 137551, IOR F/4/2466.

163. Letter from M. Larken, Register, Sudr Foujdaree Adawlut, to J. G. Lumsden, Secretary to Government, Bombay, 4 July 1850, in Bombay Judicial Letter, 15 Nov. 1851, Board Collection No. 137551, IOR F/4/2466.

164. Letter from A. Elphinston, Magistrate, Khandesh, to M. Larken, Register, Sudr Foujdaree Adawlut, 9 Jan. 1850, in Bombay Judicial Letter, 15 Nov. 1851, Board Collection No. 137551, IOR F/4/2466.

165. Letter from M. Larken, Register, Sudr Foujdaree Adawlut, to J. G. Lumsden, Secretary to Government, Bombay, 4 July 1850, in Bombay Judicial Letter, 15 Nov. 1851, Board Collection No. 137551, IOR F/4/2466.

166. Indian Law Commissioners, *Second Report*, 57.

167. Lata Mani, *Contentious Traditions: The Debate on Sati in British India* (Berkeley: University of California Press, 1998).

168. C. R. Baynes, *The Criminal Law of the Madras Presidency as Contained in the Existing Regulations and Acts* (Madras: Pharoah and Co., Athenaeum, 1848), 52.

169. Extract of a General Letter from the Government of India to the Honourable Court of Directors in the Legislative Department, 22 Apr. 1839, in Board Collection No. 7804, IOR F/4/1815.

170. Letter from J. Hawkins, Officiating Registrar of the Nizamut Adawlut, to F. J. Halliday, Officiating Secretary to the Government of Bengal in the Judicial Department, 15 Dec. 1837, in Board Collection No. 7804, IOR F/4/1815.

171. Letter from R. D. Mangles, Officiating Secretary, Government of India, to W. H. Macnaghten, Secretary to the Government of India, 27 Feb. 1838, in Board Collection No. 7804, IOR F/4/1815.

172. Ibid.; Letter from R. D. Mangles, Officiating Secretary to the Government of India, Legislative Department, to F. J. Halliday, Officiating Secretary to the

Government of Bengal, 16 Apr. 1838, in Board Collection No. 78257, IOR F/4/1836.

173. See, e.g., Letter from H. B. Harington, Registrar of the Nizamut Adawlut North-Western Provinces, to J. Thomason, Officiating Secretary to the Governor General in the Judicial Department, North-Western Provinces, 8 June 1838, in Board Collection No. 7804, IOR F/4/1815.

174. Extract from the Proceedings of the President of the Council of India in Council in the Legislative Department, Letter from W. H. Macnaghten, Secretary to the Government of India with the Governor General, to F. H. Maddock, Officiating Secretary to the Government of India, 20 Aug. 1838, in Board Collection No. 7804, IOR F/4/1815.

175. For the expansion of the judge's power to order transportation, see Act XXVIII of 1838.

176. Minute by the Right Honourable the Governor General, 12 July 1848, in India Legislative Consultations, 27 Jan. 1849, IOR P/257/52.

177. For support of Dalhousie's proposal, see, e.g., Letter from the Registrar of the Nizamut Adawlut, to F. J. Halliday, Secretary to the Government of Bengal, 9 June 1848, in India Legislative Consultations, 27 Jan. 1849, IOR P/257/52; for "scanty clothing," see Letter from T. H. Davidson, Registrar to the Foujdaree Adawlut, to H. G. Montgomery, Bart., Secretary to the Government, Fort St. George, 13 June 1848, in India Legislative Consultations, 27 Jan. 1849, IOR P/257/52.

178. Act II of 1849.

179. Letter from M. Larken, Register to Bombay Sudder Foujdaree Adawlut, to J. G. Lumsden, Secretary to the Judicial Department, 6 Nov. 1848, in India Legislative Consultations, 27 Jan. 1849, IOR P/257/52.

180. Letter from F. J. Halliday, Officiating Secretary to the Government of India, to H. M. Elliot, Secretary to the Government of India with the Governor General, 16 Dec. 1848, in India Legislative Consultations, 27 Jan. 1849, IOR P/257/52.

181. Letter from Sir Matthew Sausse, Chief Justice of Bombay, to the Judicial Committee, 4 July 1859, in Judicial Home Correspondence, IOR L/PJ/2/200/69.

182. P. B. Vachha, *Famous Judges, Lawyers and Cases of Bombay: A Judicial History of Bombay during the British Period* (Bombay: N. M. Tripathi, 1962), 55, 59.

183. Letter from Sir Matthew Sausse, Chief Justice of Bombay, to the Judicial Committee, 4 July 1859, in Judicial Home Correspondence, IOR L/PJ/2/200/69.

184. William Twining, *Rethinking Evidence* (Evanston, IL: Northwestern University Press, 2004), 53.

185. Quoted ibid., 54.

186. *Solicitors' Journal* 15 (28 Oct. 1871): 910.

187. See ibid., 911; John J. Paul, *The Legal Profession in Colonial South India* (Mumbai: Oxford University Press, 1991).

188. *Solicitors' Journal* 16 (2 Mar. 1872): 320.

189. *Solicitors' Journal* 15 (28 Oct. 1871): 911.

190. *Solicitors' Journal* 16 (29 June 1872): 652–53.

191. Stephen, *Digest,* 199–200.

192. K. J. M. Smith, *James Fitzjames Stephen: Portrait of a Victorian Rationalist* (Cambridge: Cambridge University Press, 1988), 76.

193. David Bentley, *English Criminal Justice in the Nineteenth Century* (London: Hambledon, 1998), 174.

194. Smith, *James Fitzjames Stephen,* 79.

195. Stephen, Letter to the Lord Chancellor, 11 Nov. 1886, in Public Record Office, Kew, LCO 1/42.

196. Harry Bodkin Poland, Letter to the Lord Chancellor, 6 Oct. 1886, in Public Record Office, Kew LCO 1/42.

197. Stephen, *Digest,* 198.

198. Letter to the Editor, the *Times* (London), 24 Apr. 1897, 13.

199. B.C.S., Letter to the Editor, the *Times* (London), 9 Apr. 1898, 10.

Chapter Four. The Queen's Proctor

1. "Castle v. Castle and Wombwell," in the *Times* (London), 31 Jan. 1881, 4.

2. "Castle v. Castle and Wombwell, The Queen's Proctor Intervening," in the *Times* (London), 9 Nov. 1881, 4.

3. "Castle v. Castle and Wombwell—The Queen's Proctor Intervening," in the *Times* (London), 8 Feb. 1882, 4.

4. Public Record Office, Kew (hereafter PRO), J77/249/7149. The J77 series contains records of divorce cases.

5. See Carole Pateman, *The Sexual Contract* (Oxford: Polity, 1988), 154–88.

6. Austin Sarat and William L. F. Felstiner, "Law and Strategy in the Divorce Lawyer's Office," in *Law and Society Review* 20 (1986): 108, 117–25.

7. Norma Basch, *Framing American Divorce: From the Revolutionary Generation to the Victorians* (Berkeley: University of California Press), 6, 103.

8. Hendrik Hartog, *Man and Wife in America: A History* (Cambridge, MA: Harvard University Press, 2000), 27, 67.

9. Henry Edwin Fenn, *Thirty-Five Years in the Divorce Court* (London: Werner Laurie, 1910), 139.

10. *Parl. Deb.*, 3rd ser., 155 (1859): 149. See also Travers Humphrey, "The History of Perjury," in *Quarterly Review* 292 (1954): 294–301.

11. Gail L. Savage, "The Divorce Court and the Queen's/King's Proctor: Legal Patriarchy and the Sanctimony of Marriage in England, 1861–1937," in *The Canadian Historical Association, Historical Papers* (1989): 210–28. On the creation of the Queen's Proctor's responsibility in divorce cases, see Stephen Cretney, *Family Law in the Twentieth Century: A History* (Oxford: Oxford University Press, 2002), 178–81; William Cornish, "Marital Breakdown: Separation and the Coming of Judicial Divorce," in William Cornish, Stuart Anderson, Ray Cocks, Michael Lobban, Patrick Polden, and Keith Smith, eds., *The Oxford History of the Laws of England*, Vol. XIII (Oxford: Oxford University Press, 2010), 794–97; and Patrick Polden, "The Civilian Courts and the Probate, Divorce and Admiralty Division," in Cornish et al., eds., *Oxford History*, Vol. XI, 752–54.

12. Unfortunately, the exact figure is not known because the roster of cases for one year—1873—is incomplete. The total figure is probably between 220 and 240.

13. On the history of divorce in England, see A. James Hammerton, *Cruelty and Companionship: Conflict in Nineteenth-Century Married Life* (London: Routledge, 1992); Janice Hubbard Harris, *Edwardian Stories of Divorce* (New Brunswick, NJ: Rutgers University Press, 1996); Lee Holcombe, *Wives and Property: Reform of the Married Women's Property Law in Nineteenth-Century England* (Toronto: University of Toronto Press, 1983), 88–110; Allen Horstman, *Victorian Divorce* (London: Croom Helm, 1985); Mary Lyndon Shanley, *Feminism, Marriage and the Law in Victorian England* (Princeton, NJ: Princeton University Press, 1989), 22–48; Lawrence Stone, *Road to Divorce: A History of the Making and Breaking of Marriage in England* (Oxford: Oxford University Press, 1995); Olive Anderson, "State, Civil Society and Separation in Victorian Marriage," in *Past and Present* 163 (1999): 161–201; Ann Sumner Holmes, "The Double Standard in the English Divorce Laws, 1857–1923," in *Law and Social Inquiry* 20 (1995): 601; Gail L. Savage, "'Intended Only for the Husband': Gender, Class, and the Provision for Divorce in England, 1858–1868," in Kristine Ottesen Garrigan, ed., *Victorian Scandals: Representations of Gender and Class* (Athens: Ohio University Press, 1992), 11–42; Gail L. Savage, "Divorce and the Law in England and France Prior to the First World War," in *Journal of Social History* 21 (Spring 1988): 499–513; Gail L. Savage, "Operation of the 1857

Divorce Act, 1860–1910: A Research Note," in *Journal of Social History* 16 (Summer 1983): 103–10; Margaret K. Woodhouse, "The Marriage and Divorce Bill of 1857," in *American Journal of Legal History* 3 (1959): 260.

14. Matrimonial Causes Act 1857 (20 & 21 Vict., c. 85).

15. See Barbara Leckie, *Culture and Adultery: The Novel, the Newspaper and the Law* (Philadelphia: University of Pennsylvania Press, 1999); and Savage, "Divorce Court and the King's/Queen's Proctor," 210–27.

16. *Parl. Deb.*, 3rd ser., 155 (1859): 510.

17. Ibid., 1377.

18. *Law Times* 33 (9 July 1859): 202.

19. *Parl. Deb.*, 3rd ser., 157 (1860): 1876–79.

20. *Parl. Deb.*, 3rd ser., 158 (1860): 133.

21. Matrimonial Causes Act 1860 (23 & 24 Vict., c. 144, Sec. VII). The act also granted the Judge Ordinary power to condemn the petitioners for the Queen's Proctor's costs.

22. *Parl. Deb.*, 3rd ser., 160 (1860): 1750, 1831.

23. *Parl. Deb.*, 3rd ser., 155 (1859): 993.

24. *Parl. Deb.*, 3rd ser., 155 (1859): 146.

25. See, e.g., Lord Redesdale's testimony in *Parl. Deb.*, 3rd ser., 157 (1860): 1882.

26. "The Divorce Court," in *Law Magazine and Review* 7 (1859): 167.

27. "Decrees Nisi in Divorce," in *Law Magazine and Review* 13 (1862): 156.

28. See John Pemble, *Venice Rediscovered* (Oxford: Oxford University Press, 1996), 86–90.

29. "The New Divorce Bill and the Queen's Proctor," in *Solicitors' Journal* 4 (14 Apr. 1860): 443–44.

30. Henry Brougham, "Remarks on Certain Defects in the Procedure of the Divorce Court," in *Law Magazine and Review* 6 (1858–59): 383–84. On Brougham's law reform efforts generally, see Michael Lobban, "Henry Brougham and Law Reform," in *English Historical Review* 115 (2000): 1184–215.

31. "Decrees Nisi in Divorce," in *Law Magazine and Review* 13 (1862): 154–56.

32. "The Practice of the Divorce Court," in *Law Magazine and Review* 3, 3rd ser. (1874): 776.

33. George Browne, *A Treatise on the Principles and Practice of the Court for Divorce and Matrimonial Causes*, 4th ed. (London: Henry Sweet, 1880), 112.

34. On the varieties of collusion, see Cretney, *Family Law,* 186–88.

35. Matrimonial Causes Act 1866 (29 & 30 Vict., c. 32).

36. Matrimonial Causes Act 1873 (36 & 37 Vict., c. 31).

37. Matrimonial Causes Act 1878 (41 & 42 Vict., c. 19); *Parl. Deb.*, 3rd ser., 238 (1878): 1136–37.

38. For the text of the bill, see *Parl. Deb.*, 3rd ser., 328 (1888): 1237; for its withdrawal, see *Parl. Deb.*, 3rd ser., 329 (1888): 179.

39. Evidence Act 1851 (14 & 15 Vict., c. 99, Sec. 4); Evidence Amendment Act 1853 (16 & 17 Vict., c. 83, Sec. 2).

40. "Law Evidence Amendment Bill," in *Solicitors' Journal* 10 (10 Mar. 1866): 443.

41. *Solicitors' Journal* 13 (1 May 1869): 515; Robert J. Phillimore, "On Jurisprudence and Amendment of the Law," in George Hastings, ed., *Transactions of the National Association for Promotion of the Social Sciences* (London: Longman, 1866), 29.

42. On the judges' frustration, see *Solicitors' Journal* 10 (25 Aug. 1866): 1026; for the statute, see Evidence Further Amendment Act 1869 (32 & 33 Vict., c. 68). Originally, the proposed bill had made parties both competent and compellable, but it was amended during debate. See *Solicitors' Journal* 13 (7 Aug. 1869): 827.

43. See Harris, *Edwardian Stories of Divorce*, 65–103; Holmes, "Double Standard."

44. For the published records, see Royal Commission on Divorce and Matrimonial Causes, *Minutes of Evidence Taken before the Royal Commission on Divorce and Matrimonial Causes*, 3 vols. (London: His Majesty's Stationery Office, 1912). A registry of the cases in which the Queen's Proctor intervened between 1875 and 188 is preserved at Kew. See PRO TS 29/2. It contains information on the source of the Queen's Proctor's information, the location of investigation, its cost, and the eventual outcome of the case. In total, it lists some 210 cases, suggesting that a much greater number investigated, but not intervened in, have gone unrecorded.

45. *Minutes Taken*, 1:149.

46. Ibid., 1:69.

47. Ibid., 2:137.

48. Ibid., 1:39, 126.

49. See, e.g., ibid., 1:40; 2:124, 137.

50. Ibid., 2:144.

51. PRO TS 29/2.

52. PRO TS 29/1, 421.

53. PRO TS 29/1, 317, 323, 355, 385.

54. PRO TS 29/1, 145, 31, 1.

55. For examples of such contestation, see "Shewell v. Shewell and Fox, the Queen's Proctor Intervening," in the *Times* (London), 24 Apr. 1869, 11; and "St. Paul v. St. Paul and Farquhar, the Queen's Proctor Intervening," in *Law Reports: Courts of Probate and Divorce* 1 (1869): 743.

56. This story became mythologized as the reason for the Queen's Proctor's establishment. See the Judge Ordinary's comments reported in "Drummond, Commonly Called Viscountess Forth, v. Drummond, Commonly Called Viscount Forth, and the Queen's Proctor," in the *Times* (London), 19 Apr. 1861, 11.

57. For affidavits, see PRO TS 29/1, 151; for photographs, see PRO TS 29/3, 231.

58. "Director of Public Prosecutions," in *Law Journal* 19 (21 June 1884): 395.

59. PRO TS 29/1, 207.

60. House of Commons, "Divorce Suits (Intervention of the Queen's Proctor)," *Parliamentary Papers* 1873, LIV, 185.

61. PRO TS 29/1, 99, 243, 273.

62. *Minutes Taken*, 2:145.

63. House of Commons, "Divorce Suits (Intervention of the Queen's Proctor)," *Parliamentary Papers* 1873, LIV, 185; 1877, LXIX, 287, 289.

64. For cases brought by the Judge Ordinary, see PRO TS 29/1, 169, 305; by outraged aunts, see ibid., 311; by other relations, see ibid., 37, 79; by anonymous letters, see ibid., 80, 81; by discontented losing parties, see ibid., 67, 99.

65. See, e.g., PRO TS 29/1, 225, 79; 29/3, 231.

66. PRO TS 29/1, 243.

67. PRO TS 29/1, 251, 257.

68. "Barnes v. Barnes and Power, alias de la Poer," in the *Times* (London), 31 July 1868, 11.

69. *Minutes Taken*, 2:120.

70. "Mr. Francis Hart Dyke," in *Solicitors' Journal* 20 (22 July 1876): 748.

71. J. Ll. J. Edwards, *The Law Officers of the Crown* (London: Sweet and Maxwell, 1964), 376, 368.

72. "Gethin v. Gethin and the Queen's Proctor (Intervening)," in the *Times* (London), 23 Dec. 1861, 9.

73. "The Queen's Proctor," in *Law Journal* 10 (28 Aug. 1875): 501.

74. Browne, *Treatise*, 320–21; see also "Howarth v. Howarth," in *Law Reports: Probate Division* 9 (1884): 218, 223; "Bowen v. Bowen and Evans (the Queen's Proctor Intervening)," in *English Reports* 164 (Mat. 1864): 1381.

75. "Cox v. Cox and the Queen's Proctor (Intervening)," in the *Times* (London), 22 Jan. 1861, 9; 2 May 1861, 11; 1 June 1861, 11; "Cox v. Cox and her Majesty's

Proctor Intervening," in *Law Journal Reports: Probate, Matrimonial and Admiralty,* new ser. 30 (1861): 255.

76. "Poore v. Poore and Lake (the Queen's Proctor Intervening)," in the *Times* (London), 17 Jan. 1876, 11.

77. "Gavaron v. Gavaron and Cauchois, the Queen's Proctor Intervening," in the *Times* (London), 27 Nov. 1865, 11.

78. "Barnes v. Barnes and Grimwade, the Queen's Proctor Intervening," in *Law Reports: Courts of Probate and Divorce* 1 (1867): 505.

79. See "Joyce v. Joyce, the Queen's Proctor Intervening," in the *Times* (London), 6 Feb. 1864, 11; 13 Feb. 1864, 11; 28 Apr. 1864, 13; 6 July 1864, 13; 27 July 1864, 11; 8 June 1865, 13; "Brenchley v. Brenchley, The Queen's Proctor Intervening," in the *Times* (London), 16 July 1866, 11; "Gavaron v. Gavaron and Cauchois, the Queen's Proctor Intervening," in the *Times* (London), 9 Feb. 1865, 11; 3 May 1865, 11; 27 Nov. 1865, 11; "Harding v. Harding and Lance, the Queen's Proctor Intervening," in the *Times* (London), 4 May 1863, 11; 7 May 1863, 13; 4 May 1864, 13; 11 May 1865, 12; 12 May 1865, 11; 13 May 1865, 11; 15 May 1865, 13; 5 July 1865, 13; "Harding v. Harding and Lance, the Queen's Proctor Intervening," in *Law Journal Reports: Probate, Matrimonial and Admiralty,* new ser. 34 (1865): 110; "Harper v. Harper, the Queen's Proctor Intervening," in the *Times* (London), 10 Feb. 1865, 11; 5 Mar. 1866, 11.

80. "Poore v. Poore and Lake (the Queen's Proctor Intervening)," in the *Times* (London), 11 June 1874, 11; 17 Jan. 1876, 11; "Rayner v. Rayner and Masters," in the *Times* (London), 28 Jan. 1875, 11; 20 May 1876, 13; 22 May 1876, 13; 25 May 1876, 11; 26 May 1876, 11; "Van Reable v. Van Reable (the Queen's Proctor Intervening), in the *Times* (London), 12 July 1875, 11; 15 July 1875, 11; 16 July 1875, 11; 17 July 1875, 13.

81. "Ravenscroft v. Ravenscroft, Smith and Whitney (the Queen's Proctor Intervening)," in the *Times* (London), 9 Feb. 1872, 11; see also 2 July 1870, 11; 8 Feb. 1872, 12; 21 Feb. 1872, 11.

82. "The Queen's Proctor," in *Law Journal* 10 (28 Aug. 1875): 501.

83. PRO J77/1/140/3050.

84. "Van Reable v. Van Reable (the Queen's Proctor Intervening)," in the *Times* (London), 16 July 1875, 11.

85. "Van Reable v. Van Reable (the Queen's Proctor Intervening)," in the *Times* (London), 17 July 1875, 13; see also 12 July 1875, 11; 15 July 1875, 11.

86. "Gladstone v. Gladstone," in the *Times* (London), 20 July 1874, 11; 31 July 1874, 11; 1 Aug. 1874, 11; 3 Aug. 1874, 10; 6 Aug. 1874, 11; 7 Aug. 1874, 11; 22 Apr. 1875, 13; 27 May 1875, 13; 26 July 1875, 11; 29 July 1875, 11; 30 July 1875, 11; 6 Aug. 1875, 12; 7 Aug. 1875, 11; 12 Jan. 1876, 11; 24 May 1876, 13; 20 Dec. 1876,

11; *Law Journal Reports: Probate and Matrimonial*, new ser. 44 (1875): 46; 45 (1876): 82; *Law Review: Probate and Divorce* 3 (1875): 260.

87. "The Queen's Proctor," in *Law Journal* 10 (28 Aug. 1875): 501.

88. *Solicitors' Journal* 20 (19 Aug. 1876): 824.

89. Edwards, *Law Officers of the Crown*, 376–77.

90. See, e.g., PRO J77/248/7092.

91. "Drummond (commonly called Viscountess Forth) v. Drummond (commonly called Viscount Forth), and the Queen's Proctor Intervening," in *English Reports*, 164 (Mat. 1861): 998.

92. "Soper v. Soper, the Queen's Proctor Intervening," in the *Times* (London), 13 May 1871, 12. For discussion of evidence taken as proof of adultery, see Cretney, *Family Law*, 169–75.

93. Elaine Showalter, "Family Secrets and Domestic Subversion," in Anthony Wohl, ed., *The Victorian Family: Structure and Stresses* (London: Croom Helm, 1978), 106–14.

94. Leckie, *Culture and Adultery*, 130–34.

95. "Masters v. Masters, the Queen's Proctor Intervening," in the *Times* (London), 12 Dec. 1863, 10; 30 Apr. 1864, 13; 25 July 1864, 10.

96. "Gray v. Gray and the Queen's Proctor (Intervening)," in the *Times* (London), 27 Nov. 1861, 9; 24 Feb. 1862, 11; 26 Feb. 1862, 11; 15 Mar. 1862, 13; 18 Jan. 1861, 11; 21 Mar. 1861, 11; 18 Apr. 1861, 11; 23 May 1861, 11; 5 June 1861, 11; 13 June 1861, 11.

97. "Brenchley v. Brenchley, The Queen's Proctor Intervening," in the *Times* (London), 16 July 1866, 11; "Mulvogue v. Mulvogue (The Queen's Proctor Showing Cause)," in the *Times* (London), 2 May 1877, 13; 25 Feb. 1878, 11; "Robinson v. Robinson (Queen's Proctor Intervening)," in the *Times* (London), 23 Nov. 1880, 4; 10 Feb. 1881, 4; "Mawford v. Mawford, the Queen's Proctor Intervening," in the *Times* (London), 7 Nov. 1866, 11; 19 Nov. 1866, 9; 10 Feb. 1868, 11.

98. "Sparks v. Sparks, the Queen's Proctor Intervening," in the *Times* (London), 27 June 1884, 3.

99. "Whitmore v. Whitmore, The Queen's Proctor Intervening," in the *Times* (London), 17 Jan. 1866, 11; 31 Jan. 1866, 11.

100. "Bowen v. Bowen and Evans and the Queen's Proctor (Intervening)," in the *Times*, 14 Nov. 1863, 11; 24 Feb. 1864, 11; 4 May 1864, 13; "Bowen v. Bowen and Evans (the Queen's Proctor Intervening)," in *Law Journal Reports: Probate, Matrimonial and Admiralty*, new ser. 33 (1864): 129.

101. *Baxter*, 1883, in PRO J77/285/8413.

102. Holmes, "Double Standard," 119.

103. *Favell,* 1883, in PRO J77/283/8339; *Paraschides,* 1880, in PRO J77/241/6857; *Blezard,* 1881, in PRO J77/267/7796.

104. *Stacey,* 1865, in PRO J77/53/216; *Soper,* 1871, in PRO J77/97/1326.

105. "Goodman v. Goodman, the Queen's Proctor Intervening," in the *Times* (London), 10 June 1870, 11; 26 Apr. 1869, 11; "Hampson v. Hampson, the Queen's Proctor Intervening," in the *Times* (London), 18 Jan. 1867, 9; 31 Jan. 1868, 9.

106. "Holt v. Holt and Davis, the Queen's Proctor Intervening," in the *Times* (London), 22 Jan. 1869, 11; 19 Nov. 1869, 9; 20 Nov. 1869, 11.

107. "Stocker v. Stocker and Gidding, the Queen's Proctor Intervening," in the *Times* (London), 1 Apr. 1870, 11.

108. "Willimot v. Willimot—The Queen's Proctor Showing Cause," in the *Times* (London), 8 June 1883, 4; "Gethin v. Gethin and the Queen's Proctor (Intervening)," in the *Times* (London), 23 Dec. 1861, 9; 22 Jan. 1862, 11; "Gethin v. Gethin and the Queen's Proctor," *Law Journal Reports: Probate, Matrimonial and Admiralty,* new ser. 31 (1862): 58; "Walpole v. Walpole and Pyne, the Queen's Proctor Intervening," in the *Times* (London), 6 Feb. 1871, 11; 3 Feb. 1872, 11; 16 Feb. 1872, 10.

109. "Hulse v. Hulse and Tavernor, the Queen's Proctor Intervening," *Law Reports: Courts of Probate and Divorce* 2 (1871): 357.

110. "Wilson v. Wilson, The Queen's Proctor Intervening," in the *Times* (London), 2 June 1866, 11; 15 June 1866, 11; 20 June 1866, 11.

111. "Marris v. Marris and Burke and the Queen's Proctor Intervening," in the *Times* (London), 1 Feb. 1862, 11 (emphasis in original); "Marris v. Marris and Burke, and the Queen's Proctor," *Law Journal Reports: Probate, Matrimonial and Admiralty,* new ser. 31 (1862): 69.

112. *Mayes,* 1875, in PRO J77/154/3601.

113. "Boardman v. Boardman, The Queen's Proctor Intervening," in the *Times* (London), 26 July 1866, 11.

114. "Ricketts v. Ricketts," in the *Times* (London), 21 Mar. 1885, 4; see also "Hebblethwaite v. Hebblethwaite, the Queen's Proctor Intervening," in the *Times* (London), 20 Dec. 1869, 11; 21 Dec. 1869, 11.

115. "Ricketts v. Ricketts, The Queen's Proctor Intervening," in the *Times* (London), 9 July 1885, 3.

116. "Willimot v. Willimot—The Queen's Proctor Showing Cause," in the *Times* (London), 8 June 1883, 4.

117. "Castle v. Castle and Wombwell—The Queen's Proctor Intervening," in the *Times* (London), 31 Jan. 1881, 4; 9 Nov. 1881, 4; 8 Feb. 1882, 4; "Collins

v. Collins (The Queen's Proctor Showing Cause)," in the *Times* (London), 21 July 1880, 4; 30 July 1880, 4; 10 Nov. 1880, 4; "Cox v. Cox, The Queen's Proctor Intervening," in the *Times* (London), 19 Feb. 1883, 4; "Forrest v. Forrest (The Queen's Proctor Intervening)," in the *Times* (London), 28 Jan. 1876, 11; 26 Nov. 1877, 11; "Green v. Green and Armstrong—The Queen's Proctor Showing Cause," in the *Times* (London), 4 Mar. 1885, 4; "Lamb v. Lamb and Norvell—The Queen's Proctor Showing Cause," in the *Times* (London), 16 Jan. 1884, 4; "Maskell v. Maskell (The Queen's Proctor Intervening)," in the *Times* (London), 7 Mar. 1879, 4; 3 May 1880, 6; "Mayes v. Mayes (The Queen's Proctor Intervening)," in the *Times* (London), 4 June 1875, 5; 7 Dec. 1876, 11; "Moore v. Moore, Paul and Mead—The Queen's Proctor Showing Cause," in the *Times* (London), 12 Dec. 1883, 4; "Strickland v. Strickland—The Queen's Proctor Showing Cause," in the *Times* (London), 7 Mar. 1883, 4; "Whisken v. Whisken and Godfrey—The Queen's Proctor Intervening," in the *Times* (London), 4 Mar. 1885, 4.

118. "Collins v. Collins (The Queen's Proctor Showing Cause)," in the *Times* (London), 10 Nov. 1880, 4.

119. House of Commons, "Divorce Suits (Intervention of the Queen's Proctor)," Parliamentary Papers, LIV, 1873, 185.

120. PRO J77/307/9163.

121. Browne, *Treatise*, 373.

122. *Prosecution of Offences Acts, 1879 and 1884. Return to an address of the Honourable House of Commons, dated 7 March 1892.* Parliamentary Papers, LXV 163 (1892), 187.

123. *Minutes Taken*, 1:40.

124. Ibid., 2:145.

125. Ibid., 2:126.

126. Ibid., 1:152.

127. Ibid., 2:143.

128. On the "clean hands" doctrine in divorce law, see Cretney, *Family Law*, 176–77.

129. Fenn, *Thirty-Five Years in the Divorce Court*, 226.

130. *Minutes Taken*, 2:141.

131. Anderson, "State, Civil Society and Separation," 160; Holmes, "Double Standard," 98.

132. PRO TS 29/3, 243, 275, 291, 299, 303, 313, 317, 321, 327, 335, 337, 341, 349.

133. Savage, "Divorce Court and the King's/Queen's Proctor," table 1.

134. Savage, "Intended Only for the Husband," 26–27.

135. "Gray v. Gray and the Queen's Proctor (Intervening)," in the *Times* (London), 13 June 1861, 10; for additional coverage of *Gray v. Gray,* the first case with a Queen's Proctor intervention to come to trial, see the *Times* (London), 18 Jan. 1861, 11; 21 Mar. 1861, 11; 18 Apr. 1861, 11; 23 May 1861, 11; 5 June 1861, 11; 27 Nov. 1861; 24 Feb. 1862, 11; 26 Feb. 1862, 11; 15 Mar. 1862, 13.

136. *Minutes Taken,* 2:120.

137. Savage, "Divorce Court and the King's/Queen's Proctor," 223.

138. Basch, *Framing American Divorce,* 165–68.

139. *Minutes Taken,* 1:58.

140. PRO J77/309/9215.

141. On this aspect of equity, see Susan Staves, *Married Women's Separate Property in England* (Cambridge, MA: Harvard University Press, 1990); Eileen Spring, *Law, Land and Family: Aristocratic Inheritance in England, 1300–1800* (Chapel Hill: University of North Carolina Press, 1993), 114–22; Amy Louise Erickson, *Women and Property in Early Modern England* (London: Routledge, 1993), 114–28.

142. Lord Lyndhurst, for example, was a steadfast critic of the double standard. See O. R. McGregor, *Divorce in England: A Centenary Study* (London: William Heinemann, 1957), 19–21. On other critics, see Savage, "Intended Only for the Husband," 15–18.

143. J. G. Beamer, "The Doctrine of Recrimination in Divorce Proceedings," in *University of Kansas City Law Review* 10 (1942): 236 n.108.

144. "South v. South, The Queen's Proctor Intervening," in the *Times* (London), 23 Jan. 1884, 4.

145. "Bloice v. Bloice (The Queen's Proctor Intervening)," in the *Times* (London), 18 Feb. 1878, 11; see also 6 Nov. 1876, 11.

146. Victorian judges had chosen "only to exercise the discretion to grant a divorce to a petitioner guilty of adultery in the most exceptional circumstances"; Cretney, *Family Law,* 269–70.

147. Rosa Campbell-Praed, *The Bond of Wedlock: A Tale of London Life* (London: F. V. White, 1887), 1:61.

148. Ibid., 2:183.

149. Ibid., 2:193.

150. Ironically, Ariana's father's confession would not have entitled the Queen's Proctor to intervene: collusion by the relations of parties was perfectly permissible, as long as the parties themselves did not come to an agreement. See "Saxty v. Saxty and Saxty (The Queen's Proctor Intervening)," in the *Times* (London), 15 Apr. 1878, 11; 2 May 1877, 13, in which a brother's efforts to bring about his sister's divorce are not considered collusive.

151. *Minutes Taken,* 2:98–99.

152. Ibid., 1:84.

153. Ibid., 1:211. Others, however, argued that perjury prosecutions were not a solution, because no jury would convict an alleged perjurer under these circumstances. See ibid., 1:153.

154. Earl Desart and Sybil Lubbock, *A Page from the Past: The Memoirs of the Earl of Desart* (London: Jonathan Cape, 1936), 164.

155. Cretney, *Family Law,* 229–33.

156. Matrimonial Causes Act 1923 (13 & 14 Geo. 5, c. 19), Matrimonial Causes Act 1937 (1 Edw. 8 & 1 Geo. 6, c. 12).

157. Savage, "Divorce Court and the King's/Queen's Proctor," 216.

158. R. D. McMaster, *Trollope and the Law* (London: Macmillan, 1986), 23–29.

159. Anthony Trollope, *He Knew He Was Right* (Brisbane: University of Queensland Press, 1974 [1868]), 1:263.

160. Ibid., 1:183.

161. Ibid., 1:184.

162. Ibid., 1:301–2.

163. Ibid., 1:301, 211.

164. Mirjan R. Damaška, *The Faces of Justice and State Authority: A Comparative Approach to the Legal Process* (New Haven, CT: Yale University Press, 1986), 119–25.

165. Neil Duxbury, "Jerome Frank and the Legacy of Legal Realism," in *Journal of Law and Society* 18 (1991): 185–86.

166. Jerome Frank, *Courts on Trial: Myths and Reality in American Justice* (New York: Atheneum, 1963 [1949]), 102.

167. Ibid., 85.

168. Ibid., 97.

169. "Gethin v. Gethin (the Queen's Proctor Intervening)," in *English Reports* 164 (Mat. 1862): 1114. In this case the fact was the testimony of landladies who said they heard the creak of a bed when the petitioner was visited by a male friend and saw rumpled bedcovers afterwards. The Queen's Proctor applied for a new trial when the jury resisted the supposedly irresistible inference and found for the petitioner.

170. Robert A. Ferguson, "Untold Stories in the Law," in Peter Brooks and Paul Gewirtz, eds., *Law's Stories: Narrative and Rhetoric in the Law* (New Haven, CT: Yale University Press, 1996), 84, 85.

171. Frank, *Courts on Trial,* 80–102.

Chapter Five. Adultery, Sex Offenses, and
the Criminal Evidence Act of 1898

1. "The Case of The Rev. Mr. Hatch," in the *Times* (London), 10 May 1860, 11.

2. J. Pitt Taylor, "Letter to the Editor," in the *Times* (London), 18 May 1860, 12.

3. Ibid.

4. *Parl. Deb.*, 3rd ser. 229 (25 May 1876): 1184.

5. The *Times* (London), 27 May 1891, 6.

6. The *Times* (London), 10 May 1860, 11.

7. County Courts Act 1846 (9 & 10 Vict., c. 95, s. 83); Evidence Act 1851 (14 & 15 Vict., c. 99).

8. Christopher J. W. Allen, *The Law of Evidence in Victorian England* (Cambridge: Cambridge University Press, 1997); David Bentley, *English Criminal Justice in the Nineteenth Century* (London: Hambledon, 1998); Keith Smith, "The Trial: Adversarial Characteristics and Responsibilities," in William Cornish, Stuart Anderson, Ray Cocks, Michael Lobban, Patrick Polden, and Keith Smith, eds., *The Oxford History of the Laws of England: Vol. XIII 1820–1914* (Oxford: Oxford University Press, 2010), 58–121.

9. C. Jackson, "Irish Political Opposition to the Passage of Criminal Evidence Reform at Westminster," in J. F. McEldowney and Paul O'Higgins, eds., *The Common Law Tradition: Essays in Irish Legal History* (Dublin: Irish Academic Press, 1990), 185; Graham Parker, "The Prisoner in the Box— The Making of the Criminal Evidence Act, 1898," in John A. Guy and H. G. Beale, eds., *Law and Social Change in British History* (London: Royal Historical Society, 1984), 156.

10. Allen, *Law of Evidence*, 161.

11. Ibid., 167–71.

12. Ibid., 173–75.

13. Ibid., 171–73.

14. Ibid., 152.

15. John Kucich, *The Power of Lies: Transgression in Victorian Fiction* (Ithaca, NY: Cornell University Press, 1994), 38.

16. Alexander Welsh, *George Eliot and Blackmail* (Cambridge, MA: Harvard University Press, 1985), 4.

17. Susie L. Steinbach, *Understanding the Victorians* (London: Routledge, 2012), 160, 171.

18. Evidence Act 1851 (14 & 15 Vict., c. 99, s. 4); Evidence Amendment Act 1853 (16 & 17 Vict., c. 83, s. 2).

19. Divorce and Matrimonial Causes Act 1857 (20 & 21 Vict., c. 85, s. 43).

20. William Cornish, "Matrimonial Breakdown: Separation and the Coming of Judicial Divorce," in Cornish et al., eds., *Oxford History of the Laws of England,* 784–92.

21. Mary Lyndon Shanley, *Feminism, Marriage, and the Law in Victorian England, 1850–1895* (Princeton, NJ: Princeton University Press, 1989), ch. 2.

22. Cornish, "Matrimonial Breakdown," 782.

23. Allen Horstman, *Victorian Divorce* (London: Croom Helm, 1985), 79; Cornish, "Matrimonial Breakdown," 785.

24. Divorce and Matrimonial Causes Act 1857 (20 & 21 Vict., c. 85, s. 27).

25. Gail L. Savage, "The Operation of the 1857 Divorce Act, 1860–1910: A Research Note," in *Journal of Social History* 16 (1982–83): 104.

26. Horstman, *Victorian Divorce,* 83, 99.

27. Stephen Cretney, *Law, Law Reform and the Family* (Oxford: Oxford University Press, 1998), 95.

28. Barbara Leckie, *Culture and Adultery: The Novel, the Newspaper and the Law, 1857–1914* (Philadelphia: University of Pennsylvania Press, 1999), 64–69.

29. Quoted ibid., 93.

30. Quoted ibid., 110.

31. Gail L. Savage, "'Intended Only for the Husband': Gender, Class, and the Provision for Divorce in England, 1858–1868," in Kristine Otteson Garrigan, ed., *Victorian Scandals* (Athens: Ohio University Press, 1992), 27.

32. Danaya C. Wright, "Untying the Knot: An Analysis of the English Divorce and Matrimonial Causes Court Records, 1858–1866," in *University of Richmond Law Review* 38 (2004): 921; Cornish, "Matrimonial Breakdowns," 779.

33. Cornish, "Matrimonial Breakdowns," 787.

34. Savage, "Intended Only for the Husband," 21.

35. *Parl. Deb.,* 3rd ser., 180 (14 Feb. 1865): 258.

36. Ibid.

37. Ibid.

38. Ibid., 261.

39. *Parl. Deb.,* 3rd ser., 177 (1 Mar. 1865): 943.

40. *Parl. Deb.,* 3rd ser., 180 (15 June 1865): 318.

41. Bentley, *English Criminal Justice,* 162.

42. Evidence Further Amendment Act 1869 (32 & 33 Vict., c. 68).

43. Ibid., s. 2.

44. Ibid., s. 3.

45. *Parl. Deb.,* 3rd ser., 177 (28 Apr. 1869): 1799.

46. Ibid.

47. Ibid., 1800.

48. Ibid., 1810; *Parl. Deb.*, 3rd ser., 180 (26 July 1869): 671.

49. Ibid., 673.

50. *Parl. Deb.*, 3rd ser., 177 (28 Apr. 1869): 1809.

51. Ibid.

52. Horstman, *Victorian Divorce*, 145.

53. *Parl. Deb.*, 3rd ser., 177 (28 Apr. 1869): 1813.

54. Criminal Law Amendment Act 1885 (48 & 49 Vict., c. 69).

55. Frederick Mead and A. H. Bodkin, *The Criminal Law Amendment Act, 1885* (London: Shaw & Sons, 1885); Keith Smith, "Offences against the Person," in Cornish et al., eds., *Oxford History of the Laws of England*, 404–9.

56. H. G. Cocks, *Nameless Offences: Homosexual Desire in the Nineteenth Century* (London: I. B. Tauris, 2010), 17.

57. Steinbach, *Understanding*, 205.

58. Criminal Law Amendment Act 1885 (48 & 49 Vict., c. 69, s. 20).

59. Allen, *Victorian Law of Evidence*, 142 n.66. Complete list in Mead and Bodkin, *Criminal Law Amendment Act*, 117–18.

60. Michael S. Foldy, *The Trials of Oscar Wilde: Deviance, Morality, and Late-Victorian Society* (New Haven, CT: Yale University Press, 1997), 50.

61. Cocks, *Nameless Offences*, 200.

62. Ibid., 92.

63. Ibid., 39.

64. Ibid., 61.

65. Stefan Petrow, *Policing Morals: The Metropolitan Police and the Home Office, 1870–1914* (Oxford: Clarendon, 1994), 217.

66. *Parl. Deb.*, 3rd ser., 300 (3 Aug. 1885): 873.

67. Louise A. Jackson, *Child Sexual Abuse in Victorian England* (London: Routledge, 2000), ch. 5; see also Jackson, "The Child's Word in Court: Cases of Sexual Abuse in London, 1870–1914," in Margaret L. Arnot and Cornelie Usborne, eds., *Gender and Crime in Modern Europe* (London: UCL Press, 1999), 222–37.

68. Mead and Bodkin, *Criminal Law Amendment Act*, 11.

69. Ibid.

70. Ibid., 11–12.

71. Ibid., 14.

72. Frank Mort, *Dangerous Sexualities: Medico-Moral Politics in England since 1830* (London: Routledge, 2000), 81–82.

73. *Parl. Deb.*, 299 (22 May 1885): 1185.

74. *Parl. Deb.*, 300 (31 July 1885): 758.

75. *Parl. Deb.*, 300 (30 July 1885): 582.

76. Ibid., 584.

77. *Parl. Deb.*, 300 (31 July 1885): 759.

78. Mead and Bodkin, *Criminal Law Amendment Act,* 15.

79. *Parl. Deb.*, 300 (31 July 1885): 755–57.

80. Ibid., 756.

81. Ibid., 757.

82. Mead and Bodkin, *Criminal Law Amendment Act,* 15–16.

83. Criminal Law Amendment Act 1885 (48 & 49 Vict., c. 69, s. 4).

84. *Parl. Deb.*, 300 (3 Aug. 1885): 904–5.

85. Ibid., 905–6.

86. Ibid., 908.

87. Ibid.

88. Mead and Bodkin, *Criminal Law Amendment Act,* 18.

89. Richard Ellmann, *Oscar Wilde* (New York: Vintage, 1988), 438.

90. Ibid., 452.

91. Foldy, *Trials,* 31–47.

92. Jackson, "Irish Political Opposition," 200.

93. *Parl. Deb.*, 4th ser., 48 (8 Apr. 1897): 807.

94. Ibid.

95. Ibid., 814.

96. Ibid., 781.

97. The *Times* (London), 26 Apr. 1898, 11.

98. Leader, the *Times* (London), 26 Apr. 1898, 11.

99. Bentley, *English Criminal Justice,* 197.

100. "Lord Justice Lopes on Criminal Law Amendment," the *Times* (London), 7 Jan. 1897, 4.

101. The *Times* (London), 11 Mar. 1898, 6.

102. Letter to the Editor, A. C. Plowden, the *Times* (London), 20 Apr. 1897, 10.

103. The *Times* (London), 11 Mar. 1898, 6.

104. *Parl. Deb.*, 4th ser., 48 (8 Apr. 1897): 790.

105. Ibid.

106. *Parl. Deb.*, 4th ser., 56 (25 Apr. 1898): 989.

107. Ibid., 1010.

108. The *Times* (London), 26 Apr. 1898, 12.

109. Petrow, *Policing Morals,* 14.

110. Public Record Office, Kew (hereafter PRO), HO 45/9784/B2907L.

111. PRO HO 45/9784/B2907L.

112. *Parl. Deb.,* 4th ser., 56 (25 Apr. 1898): 1004.

113. Letter from "An Old Cross-Examiner," the *Times* (London), 20 Apr. 1897, 10.

114. Letter to the Editor, A. C. Plowden, the *Times* (London), 14 Apr. 1898, 10.

115. Letter from Morton Smith, Recorder of Gravesend, to the Home Secretary, 11 Apr. 1891, in PRO HO 45/9784/B2907E.

116. Letter from G. Pitt Lewis to the Home Secretary, 6 July 1893, in PRO HO 45/9784/B2907E.

117. Harry Bodkin Poland, Letter to the Editor, the *Times* (London), 29 June 1897, 4; Evelyn S. Hopkinson, Letter to the Editor, "The Disturbances at Oxford," in the *Times* (London), 18 May 1897, 5.

118. Herbert Stephen, Letter to the Editor, "The Future Prisoner on His Oath," in the *Times* (London), 24 Apr. 1897, 13.

119. Letter from K. Muir Mackenzie, 15 Feb. 1898, in PRO HO 45/9784/B2907M.

120. PRO HO 45/9784/B2907M.

121. Memo, 1 Mar. 1898, PRO HO 45/9784/B2907M.

122. PRO HO 45/9784/B2907M.

123. PRO HO 45/9784/B2907L.

124. Memo, 20 Apr. 1897, PRO HO 45/9784/B2907L.

125. Memo, 21 Feb. 1898, PRO HO 45/9784/B2907M.

126. Henry Arthur Jones, *The Liars* (New York: Macmillan, 1901), vi.

127. Ibid., 73–75.

128. Memo, 20 Apr. 1897, PRO HO 45/9784/B2907L.

129. Bentley, *English Criminal Justice,* 195.

130. "Law of Evidence (Criminal Cases) Bill," in *Law Journal* 32 (3 July 1897): 362.

131. "Evidence in Criminal Cases Bill," in *Law Journal* 31 (14 Mar. 1896): 189.

132. *Parl. Deb.,* 4th ser., 48 (8 Apr. 1897): 784.

133. Ibid., 810.

134. Bentley, *English Criminal Justice,* 202.

135. The *Times* (London), 12 Mar. 1898, 11.

Index